HTTP Essentials

Protocols for Secure, Scaleable Web Sites

HTTP Essentials

Protocols for Secure, Scaleable Web Sites

Stephen A. Thomas

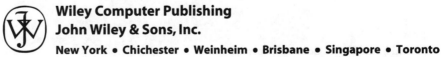

Wiley Computer Publishing

John Wiley & Sons, Inc.

New York • Chichester • Weinheim • Brisbane • Singapore • Toronto

Publisher: Robert Ipsen
Editor: Margaret Eldridge
Managing Editor: Micheline Frederick
Text Design & Composition: Stephen Thomas

Designations used by companies to distinguish their products are often claimed as trademarks. In all instances where John Wiley & Sons, Inc., is aware of a claim, the product names appear in initial capital or ALL CAPITAL LETTERS. Readers, however, should contact the appropriate companies for more complete information regarding trademarks and registration.

This book is printed on acid-free paper. ♾

Published by John Wiley & Sons, Inc.

Published simultaneously in Canada.

This publication is designed to provide accurate and authoritative information in regard to the subject matter covered. It is sold with the understanding that the publisher is not engaged in professional services. If professional advice or other expert assistance is required, the services of a competent professional person should be sought.

ISBN 0471-39823-3 (pbk./cd-rom : alk. paper)

Printed in the United States of America.

10 9 8 7 6 5 4 3 2 1

For the West Avenue Gang

CONTENTS

CHAPTER 1

Introduction — HTTP, the Internet, and the Web

Today's *Wall Street Journal* includes 197 ads, and 159 of them—over 80 percent—feature a World Wide Web address. Even more remarkably, only 121 (61 percent) list a telephone number. If advertisements are a reflection of society, then here in the United States, at least, the Web has become an indispensable part of our lives.

This book is about what makes the Web tick. It explains the protocol that defines how Web browsers communicate with Web servers, the mechanisms that keep that communication secure from counterfeits and eavesdroppers, and the technologies that accelerate our Web experience. In this first chapter we'll get a quick introduction to a few important concepts, including the relationship between the Hypertext Transfer Protocol (HTTP) and the Web, the notion of protocol layers, and the Web's idea of an address. The final section outlines the rest of the text.

By the end of the book we'll have covered all aspects of the Hypertext Transfer Protocol: its operation, message formats, security mechanisms, and acceleration techniques. We will also see how HTTP has evolved, and how newer implementations maintain backward compatibility with old systems. And finally, we will take what we've learned and apply it to building scalable, highly available, and secure Web site architectures.

1.1 HTTP and the World Wide Web

The Internet can trace its roots to research projects begun in the 1960s by the United States Department of Defense. A British physicist working in Switzerland, however, has arguably influenced today's Internet more than any other person. It was in March 1989 that Tim Berners-Lee first outlined the advantages of a hypertext-based, linked information system. And by the end of 1990, Berners-Lee, along with Robert Cailliau, created the first Web browsers and servers. Those browsers needed a protocol to regulate their communications; for that Berners-Lee and Cailliau designed the first version of HTTP.

Since then, Web traffic has grown to dominate the Internet. By 1998, HTTP accounted for over 75 percent of the traffic on Internet backbones[1] dwarfing other protocols such as email, file transfer, and remote login. Today, at least in the common vernacular, the World Wide Web *is* the Internet. And the Web continues to grow. In the fall of 2000, as this book is nearing completion, the Censorware Project reports that the Web has roughly:

- 2 700 000 000 pages
- 50 700 000 000 000 bytes of text
- 608 000 000 images
- 10 100 000 000 000 bytes of image data

---

[1] K. Claffy, Greg Miller, and Kevin Thompson. "The Nature of the Beast: Recent Traffic Measurements from an Internet Backbone." Presented at the INET '98 Conference, April 1998.

During the 24 hours previous, the Web added:

- 5 490 000 new pages
- 103 000 000 000 new bytes of text
- 1 240 000 new images
- 20 600 000 000 new bytes of image data

The Hypertext Transfer Protocol has grown along with the Web. The original specification for HTTP fits comfortably on a single page and, at 656 words long, can be read and understood in just a few minutes. In contrast, the specification for HTTP version 1.1 spans several documents. The core document alone packs nearly 60 000 words on 176 pages.

The 176 pages of the core HTTP specification, along with other documents that make up the HTTP standard, define the rules by which Web browsers, Web servers, proxies, and other Web systems establish and maintain communications with each other. The HTTP standards do not dictate what information the systems exchange once they establish communication. Indeed, one of HTTP's greatest strengths is its ability to accommodate almost any kind of information exchange. Web pages, for example, are often created according to the rules for the Hypertext Markup Language, or HTML (also invented by Berners-Lee). But HTTP is equally adept at transferring remote printing instructions, program files, and multimedia objects. With the ubiquity of Web browsers, the pervasiveness of the Internet, and the power and flexibility of HTTP, the protocol Berners-Lee and Cailliau developed may ultimately become the foundation for all network-based computing.

1.2 Protocol Layers

To understand HTTP, it helps to know a little about the architecture of the Internet. We can look at the Internet's architecture from two perspectives. From one view, the Internet is a loosely connected collection of networks of all sizes and types that cooperate to exchange information. Instead of considering physical systems, however, we'll focus on the software that controls those systems. From that perspective, the Internet is a collection of different communication protocols; these protocols cooperate to provide services.

Providing services over the Internet is actually a very complex undertaking. To make the challenge more manageable, the Internet designers divided the work into different components and assigned those components to several different communications protocols. The designers further organized those protocols into layers.

Figure 1.1 shows the four protocol layers within a computer system. The lowest layer protocol controls the specific network technology, whether it's an Ethernet LAN, a dial-up modem, a fiber optic link, or any other technology. One of the Internet's greatest strengths is its ability to adapt to all types of network technology. Isolating the protocol for that technology within its own layer is one of the reasons for this flexibility; supporting a new network technology is simply a matter of implementing an appropriate low layer protocol.

Communication System

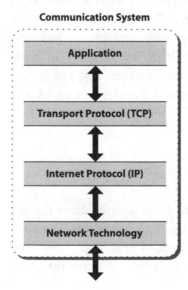

Figure 1.1 ▶
Systems that communicate over the Internet use several protocols. Each protocol operates at its own layer in a protocol stack, fulfilling specific responsibilities. This figure shows the four protocol layers used in an HTTP exchange. HTTP itself is the application.

The protocol layer immediately above the network technology is the Internet Protocol, or IP. And even though IP may not be as famous as other protocols on the Internet, it can easily justify its name as *the* Internet Protocol. Not every system on the Internet uses the same network technology, and different systems rely on different transport and application protocols. Every system on the Internet, however, uses IP. The Internet Protocol's main responsibility is taking individual packets of information and forwarding them to their destination. Most communications between systems require the exchange of many packets, and IP takes responsibility for every one.

The next protocol is the transport protocol. The Internet in general uses three different transport protocols, but Web communications in particular uses one: the Transmission Control Protocol (TCP). While IP has responsibility for moving packets from one system to another, TCP makes that information transfer reliable. It ensures that the packets arrive in the right order, that none get lost in transit, and that no errors appear.

The final protocol layer is the application. This protocol actually does something meaningful with the information that's exchanged, including organizing the exchange into conversations. The application protocol that most interests us here is, of course, HTTP, but there are many other application protocols on the Internet. There are application protocols for exchanging electronic mail, for setting up telephone calls, for authorizing dialup sessions, and so on. Of course, as we noted earlier, HTTP traffic is the bulk of traffic on today's Internet.

The internal protocol organization of a single system isn't what's important for communications. After all, it takes more than one system to have meaningful communications. Figure 1.2 expands the earlier figure by bringing a second system into the diagram. Now we can start to see the way communication actually takes place. The figure shows black

---

The 7 Layer Stack?

Many theoretical descriptions of network communications rely on the Open Systems Interconnection Reference Model. That model, developed by the International Standards Organization as a framework for protocol standards, defines seven protocol layers. The Internet's developers, however, have never been a slave to abstract theory; instead, they've focused on making practical networks operate. In most cases, the four protocol layers of figure 1.1 are sufficient and appropriate.

Figure 1.2 ▶
When two systems communicate,
their protocols interface directly with
other protocols within each individual
system. Effectively, however,
protocols at each layer communicate
with their peers in the other system.

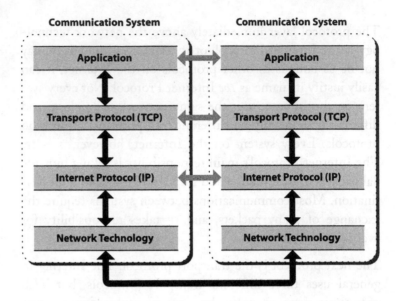

Figure 1.2 ▶
When two systems communicate,
their protocols interface directly with
other protocols within each individual
system. Effectively, however,
protocols at each layer communicate
with their peers in the other system.

arrows between the different protocol layers within a system. Those arrows represent direct interaction. The application protocol in one system interacts directly with the transport protocol. That protocol, in turn, interacts directly with IP, and IP interacts with the protocol controlling the network technology. The different systems can directly interact with each other only through the network technology.

Figure 1.2 shows another form of interaction as well, however. The gray arrows represent a logical interaction, and, as the figure indicates, each protocol layer logically interacts with its peer in the distant system. So even though the application in one system directly interacts only with TCP, the result of that interaction is a logical communication with the application in another system. In the case of HTTP, the HTTP implementation in one system (for example, a Web browser) is effectively communicating with the HTTP implementation in another (a Web server, perhaps).

To see this process in more detail, let's look at how an HTTP message makes its way from your Web browser to a Web server on the Internet. Figure 1.3 shows the first four steps in

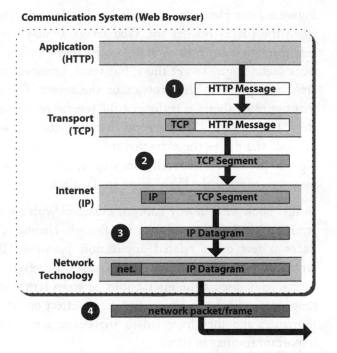

Communication System (Web Browser)

◀ **Figure 1.3**
When the HTTP application has a message to send, it hands that message to a lower layer protocol. The message continues down through the entire protocol stack until it leaves the system. As this figure shows, each protocol has its own name for the unit of data it sends and receives. TCP calls its units segments; IP calls them datagrams, and the network technology sends and receives packets or frames.

the process. First the HTTP process constructs the message it wants to send; then, in step 1, it hands that message to a TCP process. The TCP process adds TCP-specific information to the message, creating a TCP segment. This addition acts a lot like envelopes do for regular letters. Letters themselves carry the real information, but we enclose them in envelopes for the benefit of the postal service. The postal service uses the addressing information on envelopes to deliver mail, without caring about the letters' contents. In step 2, the TCP process passes the segment to the IP process. The IP process builds on this segment by adding more information, in effect adding another envelope. The result is an IP datagram that, in step 3, reaches the protocol implementation controlling the system's network technology. Only in step 4, after still more information is added to the original message, does the information actually leave the computer system. It leaves in the form of a packet or frame.

Figure 1.4 completes the example by showing what happens when the packet reaches the Web server. It may have traveled through many other systems and across a variety of network technologies to get there, but those intermediate steps aren't important to the browser or the server. The process that figure 1.4 shows is really just the reverse of the first four steps. Each protocol layer accepts the message, processes it as needed, and passes the extracted information up to the next highest protocol. Eventually, in step 8, the original HTTP message arrives at the Web server application.

In this book we'll mostly concern ourselves with application layer protocols—primarily HTTP, though chapter 5 introduces a few other related application protocols. Because HTTP relies on TCP to carry its messages, however, we will occasionally discuss the interactions between HTTP and TCP; those interactions can have a significant effect on HTTP performance, and they have led to the development of many important features in HTTP.

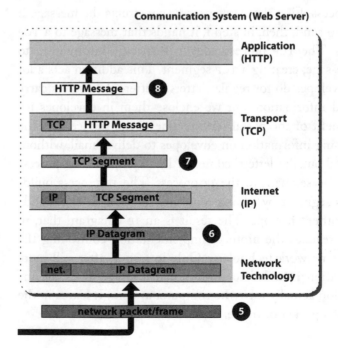

Figure 1.4 ▶
HTTP messages that arrive in a system pass up through the protocol stack until they reach the application layer. Each protocol layer removes its own specific information, as network packets become IP datagrams and then TCP segments. Ultimately, the HTTP message arrives at the HTTP application process.

1.3 Uniform Resource Identifiers

Most likely, you're already familiar with Uniform Resource Locators, or URLs. They are the addresses we use to name Web sites; http://www.waterscreek.com is an example. You might be a little surprised, though, when you see that HTTP continually refers to Uniform Resource Identifiers, or URIs. Actually, there isn't really much difference between the two concepts. Technically, a URL is just one type of a URI. After all, one way to identify an object is to describe its location. As a practical matter, though, the two terms are equivalent. This book generally uses URI because that's the term in the HTTP specifications. If, whenever you see "URI," you mentally translate it as "URL," you won't suffer any ill effects.

In any case, a URI can actually contain quite a lot of information, and a thorough understanding of the URI structure is helpful in appreciating some aspects of HTTP. Figure 1.5 shows a sample URI with nearly all the possible elements. (Entering this URI in a Web browser actually worked when this book was written; of course, there's no guarantee that will still be the case after publication.) Table 1.1 lists the URI's components, along with a description of each one's use.

▼ **Figure 1.5**
A Uniform Resource Identifier (URI) includes many individual components.

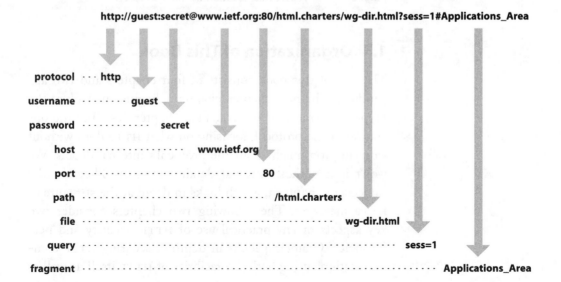

http://guest:secret@www.ietf.org:80/html.charters/wg-dir.html?sess=1#Applications_Area

protocol ···· http
username ········ guest
password ············ secret
host ················ www.ietf.org
port ···························· 80
path ······························ /html.charters
file ······························ wg-dir.html
query ···························· sess=1
fragment ························ Applications_Area

Table 1.1 Components of a Uniform Resource Identifier

Component	Use
protocol	Identifies the application protocol needed to access the resource, in this case HTTP.
username	If the protocol supports the concept of user names, this provides a user name that has access to the resource; the example has a user name "guest."
password	The password associated with the user name, "secret" in the example.
host	The communication system that has the resource; for HTTP this is the Web server, www.ietf.org in the example.
port	The TCP port that the application protocols should use to access the resource; many protocols have an implied TCP port (for HTTP that port is 80), but it can be overridden here if necessary.
path	The path through a hierarchical organization under which the resource is located, often a file system's directory structure or equivalent.
file	The resource itself.
query	Additional information about the resource or the client.
fragment	A particular location within a resource.

1.4 Organization of This Book

The rest of this book consists of four chapters and two appendices. The next chapter, chapter 2, begins our look at the Hypertext Transfer Protocol. That chapter describes the operation of the protocol, focusing on what HTTP does without worrying too much about the protocol's internal details. We won't ignore those internal details, however. They are the subjects of chapter 3, which looks in detail at the structure of HTTP messages. The following two chapters consider two key aspects of any practical use of HTTP, security and performance. Chapter 4 looks in depth at securing HTTP communications using both the facilities of HTTP itself as well as various additional protocols. Chapter 5 provides an overview of the many additional protocols and technologies that can improve HTTP performance, particularly load balancing and caching. This book focuses on the latest version of HTTP, version 1.1. In appendix A, however, we look at the relationship between version 1.1 and earlier HTTP versions; we'll also consider how well common implementations support HTTP version 1.1. The final appendix ties together many of the aspects of HTTP covered throughout the book. Instead of describing and explaining the technology, however, it looks at how to apply the technology to an important and practical problem, building bullet-proof Web sites. The book closes with an annotated list of references, a glossary, and an index.

CHAPTER 2

HTTP Operation — How Clients & Servers Use HTTP

This chapter explores what HTTP allows communicating systems to do, and how those systems go about doing it. The first section of this chapter introduces a concept fundamental to HTTP's operation—the distinction between clients and servers. The following three sections divide HTTP's functions into three types, based on how Web systems use them: Actions that users initiate, functions that clients like Web browsers invoke that are often transparent to users, and operations that take place deep in the network. The chapter concludes with an explanation of an important and often controversial HTTP feature, state management through cookies.

2.1 Clients and Servers

Like many communication protocols, HTTP makes a key distinction between the two communicating parties. In any HTTP exchange, one system assumes the role of a *client* while the other is a *server*. This difference is very important, as

HTTP requires clients and servers to follow very different rules and procedures. In a simple Web session, the Web browsing PC is an HTTP client, while the system hosting the Web site acts as an HTTP server. Even though these two systems both communicate using HTTP, they obviously have vastly different responsibilities in that communication. As we'll see in this section, the client, who always initiates HTTP communications, controls several important characteristics of the session, including the underlying TCP connection, persistence, and pipelining.

2.1.1 Initiating Communication

The most obvious difference between HTTP clients and servers is responsibility for initiating communication. Only a client can do that. A server may have a lot of information it can provide and many functions it can perform, but it does something only when asked to do so by a client. An HTTP client acts, and an HTTP server reacts.

Figure 2.1 illustrates a typical exchange. The Web browser, in its role of client, sends a request to a Web server. The server then returns a response to that client. A client may take further action based on the server's response, but HTTP considers that action to be an entirely new exchange. The new exchange, like every HTTP exchange, begins with a client's request.

Figure 2.1 ▶
The client begins a communications exchange by sending a request to a server. The server simply responds to client requests. It does not initiate communications on its own.

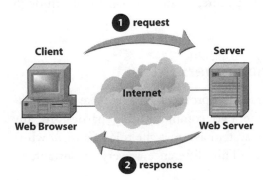

2.1.2 Connections

Like any application protocol that uses TCP, HTTP requires a TCP connection. Because the HTTP client is responsible for initiating HTTP communications, the client is also responsible for initiating the process that creates the TCP connection. As figure 2.2 shows, this process requires the exchange of three TCP messages. The TCP messages are shown in gray text.

After the initial TCP exchange, the client can send its HTTP request. That request and the server's response are in black text. The figure also shows the messages required to close a TCP connection. The server initiates this exchange because it knows when it has fulfilled the client's request.

2.1.3 Persistence

The first versions of HTTP required clients to establish a separate TCP connection with each request. For simple Web pages, this requirement did not present much of a problem. As Web sites grew more complex and graphic, however, TCP connection establishment began to have a noticeable effect

TCP Connections

Figure 2.2 highlights key characteristics of TCP messages. The first message that the client sends has a SYN, for "synchronize," flag. The SYN indicates that the client wishes to establish a connection. The server responds by setting the SYN and ACK (for "acknowledge") flags, indicating its willingness to accept the connection. The client completes the connection establishment by sending a TCP message with only the ACK flag. These three messages are usually called the "three-way handshake." Closing the connection requires only two messages. The first has the FIN (for "finished") flag, and the second has both the FIN and ACK flags set.

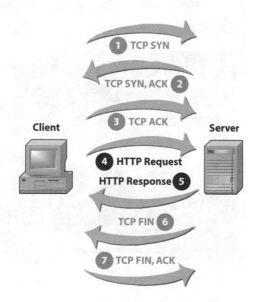

◀ **Figure 2.2**
Before systems can exchange HTTP messages, they must establish a TCP connection. Steps 1, 2, and 3 in this example show the connection establishment. Once the TCP connection is available, the client sends the server an HTTP request. The final two steps, 6 and 7, show the closing of the TCP connection.

on Web performance. That's because complex Web pages consist of many separate objects, and the client must issue a separate HTTP request to retrieve each of those objects. The Web page of figure 2.3, for example, contains over 20 objects (the page itself, plus the individual graphic elements). With early versions of HTTP, Web browsers would have to establish more than 20 separate connections before they could display the page.

Version 1.1 of the HTTP protocol eliminates the problem of multiple TCP connections with a feature known as *persistence*. (Although persistence was introduced in HTTP version 1.0 not all systems could support it; with version 1.1 it is the default behavior.) Persistence allows a client to continue to use an existing TCP connection after its initial request has been fulfilled. The client simply issues a new request on the same connection. Figure 2.4 shows this behavior in operation.

Figure 2.3 ▶
Complex Web pages such as this one contain many objects, each of which requires its own HTTP message exchange to retrieve. In this example, the main page is one object, and each individual graphic element is a separate object. Altogether, a client must issue 20 separate HTTP requests before it can display the page.

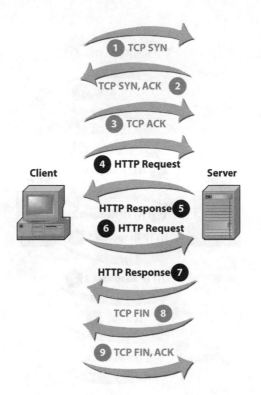

◀ Figure 2.4

With persistent connections, a client can issue many HTTP requests over a single TCP connection. The first request is in step 4, which the server answers in step 5. In step 6 the client continues by sending the server another request on the same TCP connection. The server responds to this request in step 7 and then closes the TCP connection.

Persistence requires cooperation from both the client and the server. The client, obviously, must make the decision to use a connection persistently. It can do so, however, only if the server allows it. The server must not close the TCP connection after fulfilling the client's initial request.

2.1.4 Pipelining

Persistence allows another HTTP feature that improves performance—*pipelining*. With pipelining, a client does not have to wait for a response to one request before issuing a new request on the connection. It can follow the first request immediately with a second request. Figure 2.5 shows how a client can use pipelining to send requests without waiting for responses.

Figure 2.5 ▶
Pipelining lets an HTTP client issue new requests without waiting for responses from its previous messages. In the figure, the client sends its first request in step 4. It immediately follows that with a second request in step 5. The client does not wait for the server's response, which arrives in step 6.

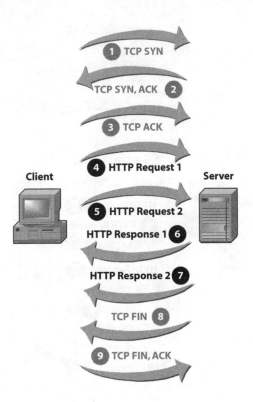

The graph in figure 2.6 compares the performance of pipelining, persistence, and single, serial connections. The figure shows the time it takes to display a Web page consisting of a

Display Time (seconds)

Figure 2.6 ▶
Both persistence and pipelining can offer significant improvements in HTTP performance, especially for complex Web pages with many objects. As the graph shows, a Web page with 20 objects (not atypical) can take about 4 seconds when the client uses serial connections. Persistence and pipelining together can reduce this time to less than 1 second.

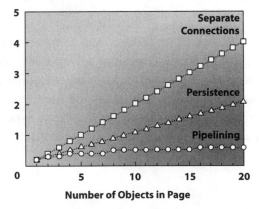

number of objects. The graph assumes that a 50 ms delay separates the browser and server, and that the browser connects using a 56 Kbit/s dial-up modem. As the figure indicates, the enhancements HTTP 1.1 introduces can make a significant difference in performance.

2.2 User Operations

The HTTP protocol defines four basic operations—GET, POST, PUT, and DELETE. We consider these to be user operations because, at least in the context of Web browsing, they are each the direct result of user actions. As we'll see in later sections, user actions may cause other HTTP exchanges, and it doesn't take an end user to initiate one of these. Still, the four operations of this section remain the most basic HTTP operations.

2.2.1 Web Page Retrieval – GET

The simplest HTTP operation of all is GET. It is how a client retrieves an object from the server. On the Web, browsers request a page from a Web server with a GET. For example, clicking on the link in the middle of figure 2.7 will force the browser to issue a GET request to the server asking for the new Web page to display.

As figure 2.8 shows, GET is a simple two-message exchange. The client initiates it by sending a GET message to the server. The message identifies the object the client is requesting with a Uniform Resource Identifier (URI).

If the server can return the requested object, it does so in its response. As the figure shows, the server indicates success with an appropriate status; 200 OK is the status code for a successful response. Along with the status code, the server includes the object itself in its response. If the server cannot return the requested object (or chooses not to), then it can

Figure 2.7 ▶

Following a simple link on a Web page causes the browser to send a GET request for the new page to the server. In this example, clicking on the "… Computers" link will cause the browser to issue a GET request for the new page.

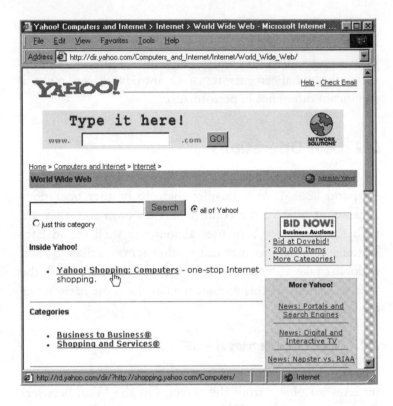

return any number of other status codes. Section 3.3 details all of the status codes HTTP defines.

2.2.2 Web Forms – POST

Although Web browsing began mostly as a way to view pages of information, it soon grew to encompass two-way interaction. While GET lets a server send information to a

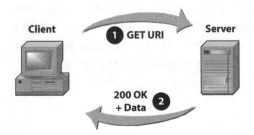

Figure 2.8 ▶

A server responds to a GET request by returning the requested resource, often a new Web page. The new page is the data in the response.

Submitting a Web form often has the browser send a POST request to the server. The POST message includes the form's data. In this example the POST data will include the search term ("HTTP"), the scope (All Fields), the results per page (25), and the link method (FTP).

client, the POST operation provides a way for clients to send information to servers. Web browsers most commonly use POST operations to send forms to Web servers. Figure 2.9 shows an example of such a form. It is a Web page that allows users to search for Internet standards. When a user clicks on the "Search Database" button, the browser sends a POST request to the server; the request includes the information the user has provided in the form.

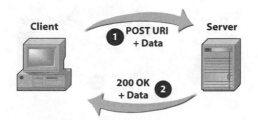

◀ **Figure 2.10**
A server responds to a POST request by returning new information such as search results. This information is carried as data in the response.

As figure 2.10 shows, the POST operation is nearly as simple as GET. The client sends a POST message and includes the information it wishes to send to the server. Like the GET message, part of the POST message is a Uniform Resource Identifier (URI). In this case, the URI identifies the object on the server that can process the included information. On Web servers, this URI is frequently a program or a script.

Also as with the GET operation, a server can return information itself as part of the response. For Web browsing, this information is typically a new Web page to display, often a page acknowledging the user's input; in the case of a search form, the new Web page often shows the search results.

2.2.3 File Upload – PUT

The PUT operation also provides a way for clients to send information to servers. It is significantly different from the POST operation, even though, as figure 2.11 shows, the two look very similar. As with a POST, the client sends a method, a URI, and data. The server returns a status code and, optionally, data.

The difference between POST and PUT is in how the server interprets the Uniform Resource Identifier. With a POST, the URI identifies an object on the server that can process the included data. With a PUT, on the other hand, the URI identifies an object in which the server should place the data. While a POST URI generally indicates a program or script, the PUT URI is usually the path and name for a file. Figure 2.12 shows an example of the PUT operation in action. On this

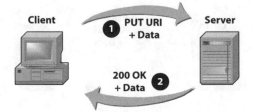

Figure 2.11 ▶
Clients can use the PUT request to send a new object to a server. The URI that's part of the request tells the server where to put the object.

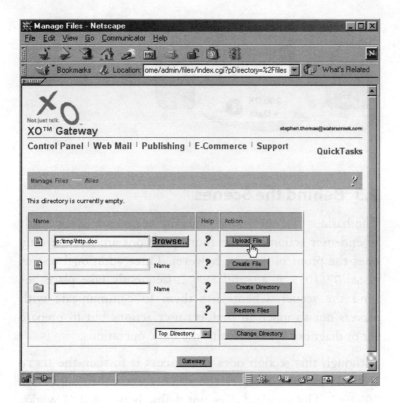

◀ **Figure 2.12**
The PUT request may be used to
upload a file to a server. In this
example the user wants to store the
indicated file on the server.

page the user has identified a local file. By clicking on the
Upload button, the user asks the browser to send a PUT request to the server.

2.2.4 File Deletion – DELETE

With GET and PUT operations, HTTP becomes a serviceable
protocol for simple file transfers. The DELETE operation
completes this function by giving clients a way to delete objects from servers. The message exchange contains no surprises. As figure 2.13 shows, the client sends a DELETE
message along with the URI of the object the server should
remove. The server responds with a status code and, optionally, more data for the client.

Figure 2.13 ▶
The DELETE operation lets a client
remove an object from a server. The
URI identifies the object to delete.

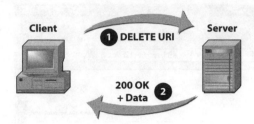

2.3 Behind the Scenes

The basic HTTP operations generally occur as a direct result of end-user actions. Those four operations are not the only ones the protocol defines, however. Three additional operations, OPTIONS, HEAD, and TRACE, frequently take place behind the scenes. Clients use them to communicate with servers not so much to perform user actions but to prepare for or diagnose problems with the basic operations.

Although this section does not discuss it further, the HTTP specification also reserves the name for another operation, CONNECT. The standard does not define how CONNECT works, except to indicate that it is intended to support tunneling. (See section 2.4.3.) Future extensions to HTTP may define CONNECT in more detail.

2.3.1 Capabilities – OPTIONS

Clients can use an OPTIONS message to discover what capabilities a server supports. The exchange is the standard request and response, as figure 2.14 illustrates. If the client includes a URI, the server responds with the options relevant to that object. If the client sends an asterisk (∗) as the URI, the server returns the general options that apply to all objects it maintains.

A client might use the OPTIONS message to determine the version of HTTP that the server supports or, in the case of a specific URI, which encoding methods the server can provide for the object. Such information would let the client adjust

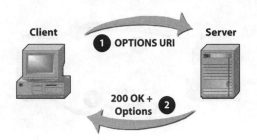

◀ **Figure 2.14**
Clients can use an OPTIONS request to ask about a particular object or about the server itself. The server returns the options data in its response.

how it interacts with the server or how it actually requests a specific object.

2.3.2 Status – HEAD

The HEAD operation is just like a GET operation, except that the server does not return the actual object requested. As figure 2.15 shows, the server returns a status code but no data. (HEAD is short for "header," as the server returns only message headers in response.) Clients can use a HEAD message when they want to verify that an object exists, but they don't need to actually retrieve the object. Programs that verify links in Web pages, for example, can use the HEAD message to ensure that a link refers to a valid object without consuming the network bandwidth and server resources that a full retrieval would require. Cache servers can also use the HEAD operation; it gives them a way to see if an object has changed without actually retrieving the full object.

2.3.3 Path – TRACE

The TRACE message gives clients a way to check the network path to a server. When a server receives a TRACE, it responds

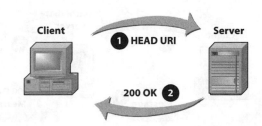

◀ **Figure 2.15**
The HEAD request mimics a GET operation, except that the server does not actually return the requested object, only HTTP headers.

Figure 2.16 ▶
Servers respond to TRACE requests by
echoing the request in their reply.

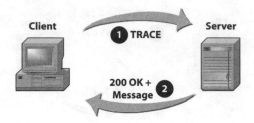

simply by copying the TRACE message itself into the data for the response. Figure 2.16 shows the simplest case.

TRACE messages are more useful when multiple servers are involved in responding to a request. An intermediate server, for example, may accept requests from clients but turn around and forward those requests onto additional servers. (Proxies and cache servers, described in the next section, are examples of such intermediate servers.) When an intermediate server is involved, TRACE works as in figure 2.17. The intermediate server modifies the request by inserting a Via option in the message. This Via option is part of the message that arrives at the destination server, and it is copied into the data of the server's response. When the client receives the response, it can see the Via option in the data and identify any intermediate servers in the path. Section 3.2.34 describes this process in more detail.

2.4 Cooperating Servers

With the exception of the TRACE message, this chapter has so far focused on the communication between a single client

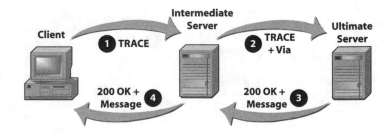

Figure 2.17 ▶
The TRACE request lets clients
discover the path their messages
follow through a network of
intermediate servers.

and a single server. The HTTP protocol defines more complex interactions, however, that frequently involve multiple servers cooperating on a client's behalf. In this section, we'll look at the different ways that multiple servers may be involved in a communication exchange.

2.4.1 Virtual Hosts

Of all the enhancements that HTTP version 1.1 adds to version 1.0, one of the smallest is direct support for virtual hosts. But although the protocol change is small, this feature is a major benefit for the World Wide Web. Virtual host support addresses a key element of the Web's architecture that the designers of version 1.0 did not anticipate—Web hosting providers.

The popularity of the Internet has created a tremendous demand for Web sites, as organizations ranging from corporations to individuals (and even pets!) establish a presence on the Web. In many cases, though, it is impractical or inefficient for the organization itself to own and operate the servers and network infrastructure a Web site requires. To meet this demand, traditional Internet Service Providers, telecommunications carriers, and specialized service providers can host Web sites on behalf of other organizations. A significant majority of sites on the Internet are modest and require little resources from the systems on which they run. Because they don't require a dedicated server, for example, most Web hosting providers actually run many separate Web sites on a single server, as figure 2.18 illustrates.

The problem facing a Web server hosting multiple Web sites is simply stated: When a client requests a Web page, how does the server know which site the client is attempting to access? Consider a client request for the Web page corresponding to http://www.company1.com/news.html. The client first resolves the host part, www.company1.com, to an IP address. Then, as figure 2.19 shows, it establishes a TCP connection and sends the HTTP command GET news.html to

Figure 2.18 ▶
Virtual hosting lets many Web addresses share the same Web server. This configuration is typical in ISPs that provide Web hosting for small businesses and individuals.

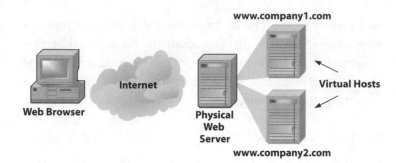

that address. Note, though, that the Web server does not participate in the DNS resolution, so it doesn't know which host the client intends to contact. The Web server has no way of knowing whether "news.html" refers to company1.com or company2.com.

Prior to HTTP 1.1, Web hosting providers had only two ways to solve this problem. They could require the Web sites to use unique URIs for all their pages. So if company1.com had a page named "news.html" on its site, company2.com could not use that same name within its pages. In practice, Web hosting providers implemented this solution by requiring a site identifier in all path names. For example, instead of the straightforward URI "http://www.company1.com/news.html," the company1.com Web site might use the more complicated

Figure 2.19 ▶
Virtual hosts can make it difficult for the Web server to determine which Web site the client is trying to access. In this case the physical Web server has no idea which Web address the client requested because it did not participate in the DNS exchange that mapped the host name to its IP address.

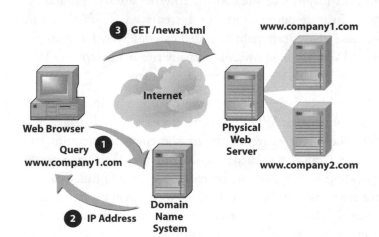

"http://www.company1.com/company1.com/news.html." As an alternative, Web hosting providers could assign separate IP addresses to each site on their servers. The servers then determine which site a client has requested by examining the IP address to which the client connects. Servers end up with multiple IP addresses, and IP addresses are scarce resources.

With version 1.1, HTTP addresses the problem of virtual hosts with a simple addition to the client's request. That addition is the `Host` header, in which the client must place the host name of the site it is requesting. As figure 2.20 shows, the server can easily determine the site to which a request applies, and it can return the appropriate resource.

2.4.2 Redirection

While virtual host support allows a single server to support multiple Web sites easily, redirection offers a way to support a single site to use multiple servers. Redirection lets a server redirect a client to another URI for an object. Figure 2.21 shows the process. First the client requests an object from the first Web server. Instead of returning the requested object, however, the server replies with a `301 Moved` status code. The response also indicates a new URI for the object. The client recognizes this URI and, in step 3, reissues the request. This time the `GET` succeeds, and the second server returns the actual object.

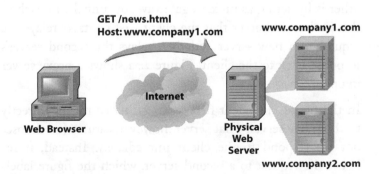

GET /news.html
Host: www.company1.com
www.company1.com

Internet

Web Browser

Physical Web Server

www.company2.com

◀ **Figure 2.20**
The Host feature in HTTP version 1.1 lets clients explicitly identify the Web site they are accessing, so the virtual hosting Web server can return the right content.

Figure 2.21 ▶

A server redirects a client to tell the client that the object it requested is located elsewhere. When, in step 2, the client receives a 301 Moved response, it looks for a new URI in the response message and issues a new GET request for that URI.

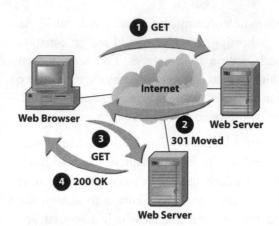

Redirection is essential to the very dynamic Web environment. It provides a convenient way to support revisions within a Web site, relocation of content, and even the change of a corporate identity.

Note that the redirection does not have to specify a different host. Frequently, in fact, redirection is used to inform the client of a new path for the resource on the same host. Note also that there are other techniques for accomplishing the same effect. The server can, for example, answer the original request by providing a JavaScript object that automatically directs the client to a new location.

2.4.3 Proxies, Gateways, and Tunnels

Another way that HTTP servers can cooperate with each other is by acting as proxies, gateways, or tunnels. In each of these roles, the server that the client first contacts relays the request to a new server and then relays the second server's response back to the client. Figure 2.22 shows a proxy server in operation.

In the figure, the client first sends its HTTP request directly to the proxy server. That server, however, cannot (or chooses not to) respond to the client immediately. Instead, it re-issues the request to a second server, which the figure labels

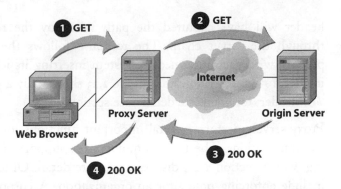

◀ **Figure 2.22**
A proxy server positions itself in between clients and servers. It forwards requests on behalf of clients and relays responses from the servers.

the "origin server" (so called because it is the origin of the requested object). In the most basic case, the second GET has a URI identical to that of the first; it's simply sent to a new server. That server treats the second GET as if it had come from a client and responds with the requested object. The proxy server then has the information the client originally requested, and it returns that object to the client in step 4.

Although figure 2.22 shows a single proxy server, HTTP allows multiple proxies to participate in satisfying a request. The proxies form a chain as in figure 2.23, handing off the request from one to the other until the requested object can be found. The proxies then pass that object back to the client in the reverse direction. As each server processes a request, it adds its own identity to the Via header in the request. By the time the request arrives at the ultimate final server, the Via

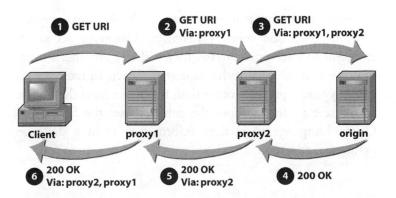

◀ **Figure 2.23**
Proxy servers create or update the Via option as they relay requests or responses. This option may make it easier to diagnose network problems.

header will have captured the path taken by the request through the server chain. The response follows the same process, with each intermediate system inserting its identity in the Via header. (Note that figure 2.23 shows only a partial Via header; for complete details, see section 3.2.50.)

Proxy servers perform several important functions for HTTP communications. The most common is in support of caching, which section 2.4.4 discusses in more detail. Other uses include enforcing policy for an organization. A corporation can direct all its internal clients to use a proxy server to access the public Internet, allowing the proxy server to filter that Internet access appropriately. Frequently this type of operation is part of a firewall. Proxy servers have also been used to provide anonymity to Web browsers, preventing servers from discovering identifying information about actual clients.

If, as is common, a proxy serves multiple origin servers, then the client must usually include the absolute URI in its requests. Without the full URI, the proxy may not be able to tell which server the client wishes to contact. Because this behavior is unusual for many clients, and because clients must know to send their requests to proxy servers rather than the ultimate destination, they must often be explicitly configured to use a proxy server. Chapter 5 describes some of the mechanisms that system administrators can use to automatically configure proxy servers for their users.

Gateways and tunnels operate very much like proxy servers; however, there are subtle differences. Gateways act as an endpoint to a server chain, but they still rely on other servers to provide all or part of the requested object. In many cases, gateways use a protocol other than HTTP to access the object. In figure 2.24, for example, the gateway uses the Structured Query Language to retrieve information from a database management system.

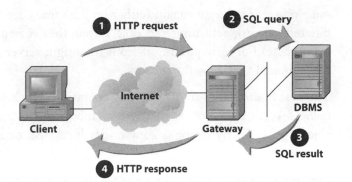

◀ **Figure 2.24**
A gateway accepts HTTP requests and translates them to a different format such as SQL. The gateway also ensures that any reply is a proper HTTP response.

While gateways act as a definite endpoint to a server chain, tunnels are exactly the opposite. As figure 2.25 indicates, they are relatively transparent to the original client; the client may not even be aware that a tunnel exists. Tunnels do provide some service, however. In the example of figure 2.25, the tunnel establishes a secure connection to the actual server, adding security to the communication between client and server. Note that although HTTP 1.1 defines the operation of tunnels in general terms, as of this writing few practical implementations are available.

2.4.4 Cache Servers

Cache servers are a specialized type of proxy servers whose main function is to improve Web performance. They do that by remembering the objects requested by clients and, if the

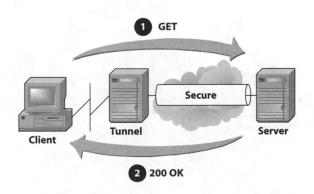

◀ **Figure 2.25**
A tunnel allows a client to communicate directly with a distant server. In this example the tunnel creates a secure path for the client's request and the server's response.

same object is requested again (either by the same client or a different client), returning the object that they've remembered instead of re-requesting it from the origin server. Figures 2.26 and 2.27 show the process.

The first figure shows standard proxy operation. The key to a cache server's operation is that it remembers the requested object, generally by saving a copy on its local disk or in its memory.

Figure 2.27 shows the payoff for the cache server. In this figure, a new client requests the same object as in figure 2.26. This time, however, the cache server does not need to contact the origin server. It simply returns the saved object from its local disk or memory.

Cache servers improve Web performance at both the client and the origin server. For the client, they shorten the distance to the object the client needs. As figures 2.26 and 2.27 illustrate, a cache server may be located on the same local area network as its clients. Local networks typically have higher bandwidth than wide area Internet connections, and the transmission delay across a local network is generally much less.

Cache servers also improve performance by reducing the load on the origin server. When a cache server returns an object to a client, that's one less request to bother the origin

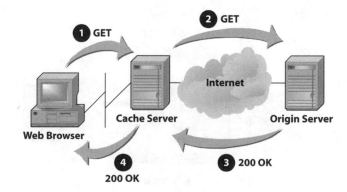

Figure 2.26 ▶
Cache servers are proxy servers that relay requests and responses. In addition, they keep a local copy of any responses they receive.

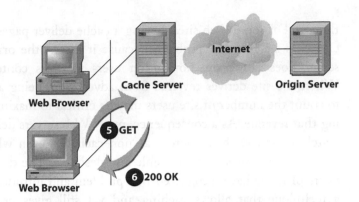

◀ **Figure 2.27**
When a new client asks for the same object, the cache server returns its local copy instead of sending another request all the way to the origin server. This speeds up the response, and it saves bandwidth for the Internet connection.

server. Fewer requests mean less processing and memory resources that the origin server requires, as well as less bandwidth it needs for its connection to the Internet.

One of the more complicated issues facing a cache server is knowing how long the objects it has stored in its cache remain valid. Given the dynamic nature of the Web, an object that an origin server returns at one moment may be superceded by a new object in the next moment. When that happens, the cache server must not return the object from its cache, but, rather, it must re-query the origin server to retrieve the new object.

As we'll see in section 3.2, HTTP 1.1 includes several headers just to support cache servers. Those headers tell cache servers whether an object can be cached and, if so, how long it can be safely stored. Section 5.2 examines cache server operation in more detail, focusing on those aspects outside the scope of the HTTP specification itself.

2.4.5 Counting and Limiting Page Views

Whenever an intermediate cache server processes client requests, the origin server can lose some control over its interactions with clients. In many ways that is a benefit, as cache servers reduce the load on origin servers and can significantly improve their performance. There are some disadvantages, though. For some Web sites, having a cache deliver pages to clients is a significant problem because it means the origin server does not know how often users view its content. When the site derives revenue from advertising, being able to count the number of site users may be critical to maximizing that revenue. As a consequence, many Web servers deliberately designate their content as non-cachable, even when caching is otherwise both possible and desirable. The developers of HTTP have recognized this problem and introduced a technique that allows caching and yet still gives origin servers a way to count and, if desired, limit page views by the cache server clients. This technique is an extension to the base HTTP specification; it is documented in RFC 2777.

The process begins when a proxy inserts a Meter header into a request message as it forwards the message on. (See section 3.2.35 for details of this header.) Steps 2 and 3 of figure 2.28 show this process. By inserting the header here, the proxy

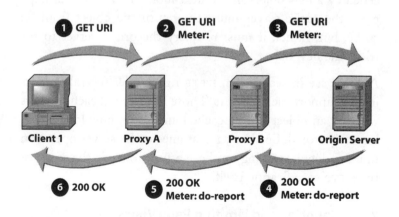

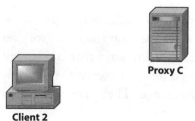

Figure 2.28 ▶
Proxies that support metering insert the Meter header in requests passing through them. Servers ask for metering on a particular object by including the Meter header in their replies.

indicates its willingness to report on and limit the number of times it returns the resulting response from its cache.

The origin server responds to this invitation by including a `Meter` header in its response. This header tells the proxies how to handle the object with respect to reporting and usage limitations.

Later, when another client requests the same object, the proxies that have a cached copy will need to validate that copy with the origin server. When they do, as figure 2.29 shows, they update the `Meter` header in their requests. This meter information is a report of the number of times the cached entry has been provided to clients.

2.5 Cookies and State Maintenance

The HTTP protocol normally operates as if each client request is independent of all others. The server responds to any request strictly on the merits of that request, without

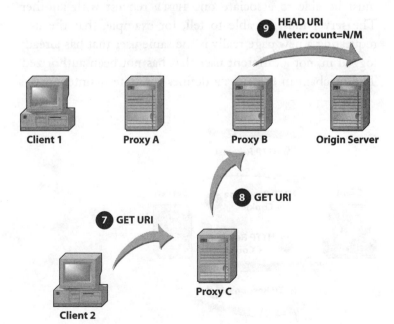

◀ Figure 2.29
Proxies that are metering an object report their results when they send the origin server a new request relating to the object. In this example proxy B issues a HEAD request to make sure its cached copy is still valid. It includes a Meter header in the request.

reference to other requests from the client (or, for that matter, any other client). This type of operation is known as *stateless* because the server does not have to keep track of the state of its clients.

Because maintaining state requires server resources (memory, processing power, etc.), stateless operation is usually desirable. In some applications, however, the server needs to keep some state information about each of its clients. Users that successfully log in to a Web site, for example, shouldn't have to log in again every time they view a different page on that site. A server can avoid this inconvenience by tracking the state of the client. The first time the client requests a page from the site, the server requires the user to log in. As the user continues to browse the site and make additional HTTP requests, however, the server remembers the previously successful login and refrains from requesting additional logins.

2.5.1 Cookies

State maintenance requires one critical capability: Servers must be able to associate one HTTP request with another. The server must be able to tell, for example, that the user requesting a new page really is the same user that has already logged in, not a different user that has not been authorized. The mechanism that HTTP defines for state maintenance is

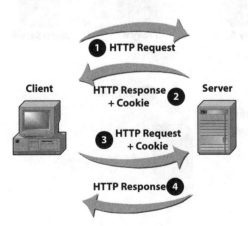

Figure 2.30 ▶
Servers can return state management cookies in their responses. Clients, if they wish, include those cookies in subsequent requests to the same server.

known as a *cookie*. A server creates cookies when it wants to track the state of a client, and it returns those cookies to the client in its response. Once the client receives a cookie, it can include the cookie in subsequent requests to the same server, as figure 2.30 indicates. The client can continue to include the cookie in its requests until either (a) the cookie expires or (b) the server directs the client to discontinue using the cookie.

Not all Web users like the fact that HTTP supports cookies. Many users view state maintenance as an invasion of their privacy. State maintenance, by its very definition, does allow Web sites to track the browsing behavior of its users. Used appropriately, however, state maintenance would not likely raise privacy concerns with most users. Users that click on the "checkout" button of an online shopping cart, for example, probably appreciate that the Web site can remember the items they've added to that shopping cart. In fact, most users would expect a Web site to keep track of their order; a function that cookies make much easier. Problems arise when Web sites use cookies to track users in ways that they do not expect. For example, an online advertising agency may track a user as she travels from an online stock broker, to a sporting goods site, and then to an online community, steadily building a profile of her in order to present her more tightly targeted advertisements. Without cookies, this type of tracking would not be practical.

At first, it might seem that HTTP's rules governing the use of cookies would protect users from this type of tracking. After all, an HTTP client can return a cookie only to the server that originally issued it. If the online broker sends the browser a cookie, how can the sporting goods site, which is on a different server, retrieve that cookie from the user? The trick, in this case, is that cookie doesn't belong to either server. Rather, it is owned by a third party ad server that has arrangements with both the broker and sporting goods sites. Figure 2.31 shows the first step in the process, when the user

Figure 2.31 ▶

A Web page may include objects from multiple servers, and each server may provide its own cookies when returning its objects. In this example the main page is from Web site 1, but the page includes an object from the ad server. The client will request this object, and the ad server may include cookies in its response.

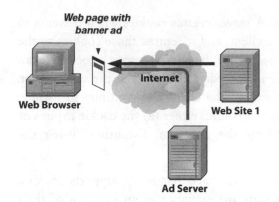

visits the online broker's site. The Web page from the first site contains multiple objects. One of those objects is a banner ad that resides on an ad server operated by the ad agency. The user's Web browser dutifully requests all the objects that make up the page, including the banner. The fact that the ad resides on a different HTTP server is not a problem. The client simply sends its GET request to the server indicated in the Web page. It is in the response to this GET request that the server inserts its cookie.

Later, the user browses to the sporting goods site. As figure 2.32 illustrates, the Web page for this site also includes a banner ad, and that ad also resides on the ad agency's server.

Figure 2.32 ▶

A new Web site may also include objects from an external server; the external server can retrieve its cookies when the client requests those objects. In the figure Web site 2 also includes an object from the ad server. The client will request this object, and, because it's communicating with the same server as before, it may return the server's cookies in that request.

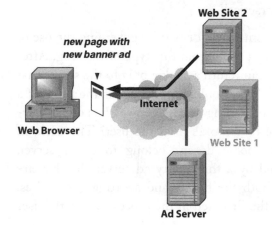

The Web browser dutifully sends a GET request to that server, and, because it is the same server that originally provided the cookie, it includes the cookie in that request. The ad agency now knows which sites the user has visited. Note, however, that the ad agency can track information only for sites with which it has a relationship. If the user visits another Web site that does not have an agreement with the ad agency, that Web site will have no banner ad pointing to the ad agency's server. Without a banner ad and associated cookie exchange, the agency will remain unaware of the user's visit to the site.

2.5.2 Cookie Attributes

Cookies consist of the series of attributes listed in table 2.1. The server chooses values for the required attributes and, if it desires, for the optional attributes as well.

Table 2.1 Cookie Attributes

Attribute	Status	Notes
NAME	Required	An arbitrary name for the cookie, assigned by the server.
Comment	Optional	A comment that the server can add to the cookie; it is intended that clients will be able to inspect the comments for cookies they have received, in which case the comment can be used to explain how the server uses the cookie, possibly reassuring users that may have privacy concerns.
CommentURL	Optional	A URL that the server can provide with a cookie; the URL may elaborate on how the server uses the cookie.
Discard	Optional	Instructs the client to discard the cookie once the user finishes; in effect, this tells Web browsers not to store the cookie on the user's disk drive.

continues...

Table 2.1 Cookie Attributes (continued)

Attribute	Status	Notes
Domain	Optional	The domain (from the Domain Name System) for which the cookie is valid; a server may not specify a domain other than one to which itself belongs, but it may specify a domain more general than a single server.
Max-Age	Optional	The lifetime of the cookie, in seconds.
Path	Optional	The URLs on the server to which the cookie applies.
Port	Optional	A list of TCP ports for which the cookie applies.
Secure	Optional	Instructs the client to only return the cookie in subsequent requests if those requests are secure; it may be used for cookies that should not be exposed to eavesdroppers. Note, however, that HTTP does not specify what "secure" means in this context.
Version	Required	The version of HTTP state maintenance to which the cookie conforms; the current version is 1.

2.5.3 Accepting Cookies

When a client receives a cookie, it saves the attributes that make up the cookie. In addition, if the server has omitted any of the optional attributes, the client supplies default values. Table 2.2 lists the default values that clients apply to missing attributes.

Table 2.2 Default Values for Cookie Attributes

Attribute	Default Value if Missing
Discard	Defer to the Max-Age attribute value for default.
Domain	The domain name of the server that supplied the cookie originally.

Table 2.2 continued

Attribute	Default Value if Missing
Max-Age	Keep the cookie only as long as the current user session is active (e.g., do not store the cookie on the user's hard disk).
Path	The URL for which the cookie was originally returned, up to, but not including, the file specified by that URL.
Port	The cookie applies to any ports. (Note that if the `Port` attribute is present in the cookie but has no value, then the client sets the value of the attribute to the port of its original request.)
Secure	The cookie may be returned with insecure requests.

Note that a client is never required to accept a cookie. Users, for example, may configure their Web browsers to accept cookies or not, as figure 2.33 shows. An HTTP server, therefore, cannot count on a cookie being accepted, even if the cookie is appropriately formatted.

Even if a user is willing to accept cookies, the HTTP specification requires that the client reject cookies under certain

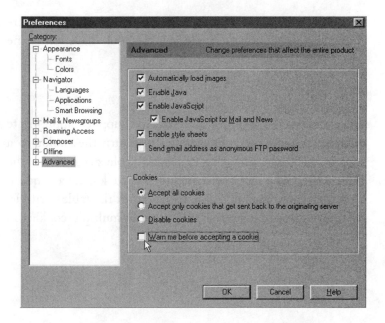

◀ **Figure 2.33**
Most browsers give users some control over cookies and state management. This dialog box shows several options that determine whether the browser will accept a cookie. Other browsers distinguish between persistent cookies (which are stored on the PC's disk drive) and temporary cookies that the browser deletes as soon as the user exits the application.

circumstances. Rejected cookies are simply ignored by the client and, therefore, are never included in subsequent requests. Table 2.3 lists the conditions under which a client must reject a server's cookie. Note that the client considers these conditions after it has applied any default attribute values as outlined in table 2.2.

Table 2.3 Rules for Rejecting Cookies

Conditions Under Which a Client Rejects a Cookie

- The value of the `Path` attribute is not a prefix of the URL in the client's request.

- The value for the `Domain` attribute does not have any dots within it (not just at the beginning), unless the value is ".local".

- The server that returned the cookie does not belong to the domain specified by the `Domain` attribute.

- The host part of the `Domain` attribute, if present, contains a dot within it.

- The port of the client's request is not included in the `Port` attribute (unless the `Port` attribute is absent).

Finally, when a client accepts a cookie, the new cookie supercedes any previously accepted cookies that have the same `NAME`, `Domain`, and `Path` attribute values.

2.5.4 Returning Cookies

Once a client has accepted a cookie and supplied appropriate default values, it determines when to return the cookie to a server in subsequent HTTP requests. Table 2.4 outlines the rules under which a client includes a cookie in a request. Note that more than one cookie may meet the table's criteria, in which case the client should include multiple cookies in its request.

Table 2.4 Rules for Returning Cookies

Conditions Under Which a Client Returns a Cookie

- The domain name for the new request must belong to the domain specified by the cookie's `Domain` attribute.

- The port for the new request must be included in the list of ports of the cookie's `Port` attribute, unless the `Port` attribute was absent from the cookie (indicating all ports).

- The path for the new request must match the cookie's `Path` attribute, or represent a child of the `Path` attribute.

- The cookie must not have expired, as per its `Max-Age` attribute.

When the client returns a cookie to a server, it includes the `Domain`, `Path`, and `Port` attributes if those attributes were present in the original cookie. It does not include those attributes if they were absent from the original cookie.

CHAPTER 3

HTTP Messages — Syntax of HTTP Communications

Now that we've seen how the Hypertext Transfer Protocol operates, it's time to look at its messages in detail. Unlike many other communication protocols, HTTP messages consist of (mostly) English text. Instead of worrying about bits and bytes in this chapter, we consider the words that the HTTP specifications define and the rules for putting those words together. (Those readers whose native language is not English may take some small consolation in the fact that the words HTTP defines are not likely to appear in many English dictionaries.)

This chapter first looks at the overall structure of HTTP messages. As we'll see, an HTTP message begins with either a request line or a status line, which may be followed by various headers and a message body. After describing this overall structure in more detail, the chapter examines every HTTP header field and every defined status code from all of the current HTTP specifications.

3.1 The Structure of HTTP Messages

As we saw in the previous chapter, HTTP is a client/server protocol; clients issues requests, and servers respond to those requests. The HTTP message structure mirrors that division. There is one format for HTTP requests and another, slightly different, format for responses. The next two subsections consider each in turn.

3.1.1 HTTP Requests

Figure 3.1 shows the basic structure of HTTP requests. Each request begins with a Request-Line. This line of text indicates the method that the client is requesting, the resource to which the method applies, and the version of HTTP that the client can support. The Request-Line may be followed by one or more message headers and a message body. A blank line follows the Request-Line and any message headers that are present.

To make the figure more concrete, the text that follows shows the actual HTTP message that Microsoft's Internet Explorer sends when a user accesses the home page of the Financial Times (www.ft.com). The first line is the Request-Line, and message headers make up the rest of the text.

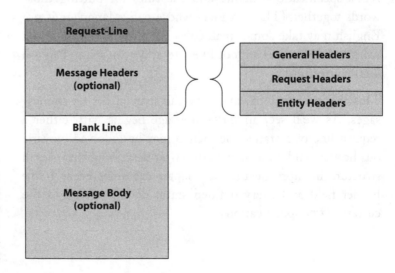

Figure 3.1 ▶
An HTTP request begins with a Request-Line and may include headers and a message body. The headers can describe general communications, the specific request, or the included message body.

```
GET / HTTP/1.1
Accept: */*
Accept-Language: en-us
Accept-Encoding: gzip, deflate
User-Agent: Mozilla/4.0
    (compatible; MSIE 5.5; Windows NT 5.0)
Host: www.ft.com
Connection: Keep-Alive
```

The HTTP Request-Line contains, as figure 3.2 highlights, three separate items. They are a method, a URI, and an HTTP version, each separated by one or more blank spaces.

The blank line here marks the end of the message; there's no message body.

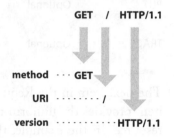

◀ **Figure 3.2**
An HTTP Request-Line has a method, a uniform resource identifier (URI), and an HTTP version indicator.

The specific method appears first in the Request-Line. In the preceding example the method is a GET, but as table 3.1 indicates, HTTP defines a total of eight different methods (each described in chapter 2). As the table also indicates, HTTP servers are required to support only the GET and HEAD methods; if they support other HTTP methods, however, that support must adhere to the rules of the HTTP specifications. The HTTP specifications also leave open the possibility that other methods may be added in the future.

Table 3.1 HTTP Methods

Method	Server Support	Use
CONNECT	Optional	Asks server (usually a proxy) to establish a tunnel.
DELETE	Optional	Asks server to delete the indicated resource.
GET	Required	Asks server to return requested resource.

continues…

Table 3.1 HTTP Methods (continued)

Method	Server Support	Use
HEAD	Required	Asks server to reply as if it were going to return the requested resource, but not to include the resource itself in the response.
OPTIONS	Optional	Asks server to indicate the options it supports for the indicated resource.
POST	Optional	Asks server to pass the message body to the indicated resource.
PUT	Optional	Asks server to accept the message body as the indicated resource.
TRACE	Optional	Asks server simply to respond to the request.

The next item in the Request-Line is the Request-URI. This item provides the uniform resource identifier for the affected resource. In the example, the Request-URI is /, indicating a request for the root resource. For requests that don't apply to any specific resource (such as the TRACE request or, in some cases, the OPTIONS request), the client may use an asterisk as the Request-URI.

The final item of the Request-Line is the HTTP version. As the example shows, HTTP version 1.1 includes the text HTTP/1.1 for this item. The first 1 is the major version number, while the second 1 is the minor version number. The minor version changes when the HTTP specification changes significantly enough to affect communications behavior, but not so much that an older system cannot parse the messages. The major version number changes whenever the specification changes so drastically that an older system will not be able to parse the new messages. In other words, an HTTP version 1.1 server will be able to interpret an HTTP 1.2 message, but it won't necessarily be able to respond; the same server, on the other hand, may not even be able to interpret an HTTP 2.0 message. Note that the client includes the HTTP version in its request to indicate the version it is capable of supporting. It does not use the version to indicate which features are actually employed in a given request. For example, a client that supports HTTP 1.1 would use that version number on all its requests, even for requests that include only HTTP 1.0 features.

After the Request-Line, an HTTP request may include one or more lines of message headers. As figure 3.1 indicates, message headers may be general headers, request headers, or entity headers. The general headers apply to the HTTP communications in general; the request headers apply to the specific request, and entity headers apply to the message body included in the request. The next section looks at each of these headers in more detail.

An HTTP request always includes a blank line after the Request-Line and any included headers. If the request includes a message body, that body follows the blank line. The blank line is important because it lets the server identify the end of the request, or, if a message body is present, the end of the headers for the request. Without the blank line, a server receiving a message could never be sure that additional message headers weren't still in transit. If a message body is present, the server can't rely on a blank line to indicate the end of the message. Instead, however, it counts on the client to explicitly indicate the size of the message body with entity headers. By knowing the size of the message body, the server can find the overall end of the request.

3.1.2 HTTP Responses

As figure 3.3 indicates, HTTP responses look a lot like HTTP requests. The only significant difference is that responses begin with a status line rather than a Request-Line.

The text below shows an actual HTTP response, including the beginning Status-Line. Much like the Request-Line, a Status-Line contains three items separated by blank spaces,

Figure 3.3 ▶
An HTTP response begins with a
Status-Line and may include headers
and a message body. The headers can
describe the general communications,
the specific response, or the included
message body.

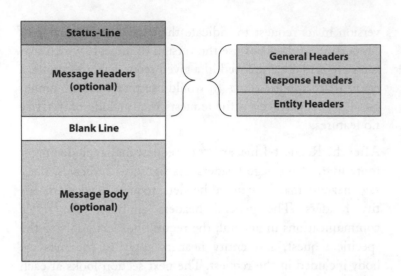

which figure 3.4 also highlights. The line begins with the
highest HTTP version that the server supports. As with the
client, this does not indicate that the response necessarily
includes options defined by that version. An HTTP 1.1 server
that receives a request from an HTTP 1.0 client, for example,
may still indicate HTTP/1.1 in its Status-Line. That server,
however, must be careful to include only HTTP 1.0 options in
its response. Otherwise it may be sending the client information that the client cannot understand.

```
HTTP/1.1 200 OK
Date: Sun, 08 Oct 2000 18:46:12 GMT
Server: Apache/1.3.6 (Unix)
Keep-Alive: timeout=5, max=120
Connection: Keep-Alive
Content-Type: text/html

<html>...
```

The blank line here marks the end of
message headers; the message body
follows. ☞

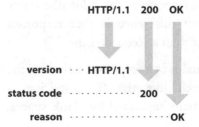

Figure 3.4 ▶
An HTTP Status-Line begins with an
HTTP version indicator and includes a
numerical status code and a textual
description of the response.

The remaining two items on the Status-Line are the Status-Code and the Reason-Phrase. The Status-Code is a three-digit number that indicates the result of the request. The most common Status-Code is the 200 of the example. That value indicates that the client's request succeeded. The first digit in the Status-Code identifies the type of result and gives a high-level indication of whether the request succeeded; additional digits provide more details. Table 3.2 lists the main categories of status code values, while section 3.3 discusses all the HTTP status codes in detail.

Table 3.2 HTTP Status Code Categories

Status Code	Meaning
100-199	Informational; the server received the request but a final result is not yet available.
200-299	Success; the server was able to act on the request successfully.
300-399	Redirection; the client should redirect the request to a different server or resource.
400-499	Client error; the request contained an error that prevented the server from acting on it successfully.
500-599	Server error; the server failed to act on a request even though the request appears to be valid.

The Reason-Phrase that follows the Status-Code merely helps humans interpret the Status-Code value. Servers include it as a convenience to humans, but clients pay no attention to its contents (other than, if appropriate, displaying it to a human user).

3.2 Header Fields

As we saw previously, HTTP requests and responses may both include one or more message headers. Message headers begin with a field name and a colon (":"). In some cases, the field name alone is sufficient for the header. Most of the time, though, the header includes additional information. If present, this information follows the colon.

A message header generally ends when the line ends, but if a client needs to continue a header beyond a single line; it can do so by beginning the continuation lines with one or more spaces or horizontal tabs (ASCII character 8). The request example from the previous section includes a continuation line for the User-Agent header; you can see it again highlighted in the following.

Continuation of the
User-Agent Header ☞

```
GET / HTTP/1.1
Accept: */*
Accept-Language: en-us
Accept-Encoding: gzip, deflate
User-Agent: Mozilla/4.0
    (compatible; MSIE 5.5; Windows NT 5.0)
Host: www.ft.com
Connection: Keep-Alive
```

If a message header can contain of a series of field values, each separated by a comma, for example, then it is acceptable to include the same message header multiple times in the same message. Such a message is treated identically to a message that only includes the field once but with all field values. The following text is an alternate, but completely equivalent, version of the example request. Note that in this case the Accept-Encoding header appears twice.

```
GET / HTTP/1.1
Accept: */*
Accept-Language: en-us
Accept-Encoding: gzip
Accept-Encoding: deflate
User-Agent: Mozilla/4.0
    (compatible; MSIE 5.5; Windows NT 5.0)
Host: www.ft.com
Connection: Keep-Alive
```

Before diving into the individual header fields, table 3.3 provides a summary list of all message headers that the HTTP specifications have so far defined. The table emphasizes that headers can apply to HTTP in general, to a specific request or response, or to the message body (entity) included in the request or response. Although the specifications don't strictly require it, HTTP suggests that implementations include message fields in that order: general headers, then request or response headers, and finally entity headers.

Table 3.3 HTTP Header Fields

Header	General	Request	Response	Entity
Accept		●		
Accept-Charset		●		
Accept-Encoding		●		
Accept-Language		●		
Accept-Ranges			●	
Age			●	
Allow				●
Authentication-Info			●	
Authorization		●		
Cache-Control	●			
Connection	●			
Content-Encoding				●
Content-Language				●
Content-Length				●
Content-Location				●
Content-MD5				●
Content-Range				●
Content-Type				●
Cookie		●		
Cookie2		●		
Date	●			
ETag			●	

continues…

Table 3.3 HTTP Header Fields (continued)

Header	General	Request	Response	Entity
Expect		●		
Expires				●
From		●		
Host		●		
If-Match		●		
If-Modified-Since		●		
If-None-Match		●		
If-Range		●		
If-Unmodified-Since		●		
Last-Modified				●
Location			●	
Max-Forwards		●		
Meter		●	●	
Pragma	●			
Proxy-Authenticate			●	
Proxy-Authorization		●		
Range		●		
Referer		●		
Retry-After			●	
Server			●	
Set-Cookie2			●	
TE		●		
Trailer	●			
Transfer-Encoding	●			
Upgrade	●			
User-Agent	●			
Vary			●	
Warning	●			
WWW-Authenticate			●	

Also, the specification notes that new entity headers may be added to the protocol. Implementations that receive a message header that they do not recognize should treat it as an entity header.

3.2.1 Accept

The Accept header, which is a request header, lets a client explicitly indicate what types of content it can accept in the message body of the server's response, as well as its relative preference for each content type. Here is an example of an Accept header that a client might include in its request.

```
Accept: text/plain; q=0.5, text/html,
        text/x-dvi; q=0.8, text/x-c
```

As you can see from the example, the Accept header can include a list of multiple content types. Commas separate individual types, and each type may include an optional quality factor. The quality factor is a parameter of a type, and a semi-colon separates it from the type. The previous example indicates that the client can accept any of the following four content types:

- text/plain; q=0.5
- text/html
- text/x-dvi; q=0.8
- text/x-c

Each individual content type consists of a type and a subtype, with a slash (/) separating the two. All of the content types have the main type text, but they differ in the subtypes. Clients can use the asterisk as a wildcard for a subtype value or for both type and subtype. The content type text/*, for example, would indicate that the client could accept any text content, and the content type */* indicates that the client can accept any content whatsoever.

Defining Content Types

The content types that HTTP specifies in the Accept header are defined by the Internet Assigned Numbers Authority, or IANA (www.iana.org), although responsibility will eventually shift to The Internet Corporation for Assigned Names and Numbers (www.icann.org). As of this writing, IANA has registered over 350 different media types (their term for content type) in a two-level hierarchy. The top level indicates the general format of the content while the second level designates the specific format. The top-level types include text, multipart, message, application, image, audio, video, and model.

The quality factor is a number between zero and one. (The HTTP specification limits it to three digits after the decimal point.) If a content type doesn't have an explicit quality factor, it is assumed to be one. The text/html and text/x-c content types of the example, therefore, have an implied quality factor of 1.0. If a server is capable of returning multiple content types for a given request, it should pick the one with the highest quality factor. Here's the full interpretation of our example: The client prefers the response to contain a message body of type text/html or text/x-c. If the server cannot comply with that preference, the client is willing to accept a content type of text/x-dvi. And if that content type isn't available either, the client will accept, as a last resort, text/plain content.

3.2.2 Accept-Charset

Clients can include an Accept-Charset header in their requests to tell the server which character encodings they prefer for the message body returned in the response. The Accept-Charset header acts much like the basic Accept header (as well as other headers in the Accept- family). Clients may include a list of different character sets, and they can indicate a relative preference for different character sets by including a quality factor. If the quality factor is absent, the server assumes a value of 1.0.

The HTTP protocol does treat the ISO 8859-1 differently than other character sets. Unless the client explicitly lists that character set and explicitly assigns it a quality factor other than 1.0, the server assumes that the client can accept ISO 8859-1 and would prefer that with a quality factor of 1.0. This behavior nearly ensures that ISO 8859-1 is the default character set for responses, as the client has to take extra steps to suggest otherwise.

The message fragment that follows shows how a client may choose to request a special character set. With such a header, the client indicates that it prefers the Unicode character set, but that it will accept any other (including ISO 8859-1) with a relative preference of 0.8.

```
Accept-Charset: unicode, *; q=0.8
```

The Internet Assigned Numbers Authority currently maintains the list of defined character sets. At the time of this writing, that list included 235 different character sets.

As a final point, note that this header (and all the Accept- headers) applies to the message body of the response. It does not influence either the Status-Line or the HTTP headers of the response, all of which are always constructed from the ISO 8859-1 character set.

3.2.3 Accept-Encoding

The Accept-Encoding header gives clients another way to express their preferences for the message body of the server's response. In addition to content type (the Accept header) and character set (the Accept-Charset header), this header lets clients suggest content encodings for the response. (The TE header, described in section 3.2.44, lets clients express preferences for transfer encodings.) The format of the header is the same as the other Accept headers, a list of acceptable encodings, each with an optional quality factor.

```
Accept-Encoding: compress, gzip; q=0.9,
                 identity; q=0.8
```

With the preceding fragment, the client requests that the response be encoded with the UNIX compress format, the GNU gzip format if that is unavailable, and, if all else fails, the identity encoding.

3.2.4 Accept-Language

The Accept-Language header is the last of the Accept- series that gives clients ways to express their preferences for the response. (The Accept-Ranges field acts quite differently.)

This header lets the client express a preference for the language of the returned message.

To designate particular languages, clients can use a multi-level hierarchy, with each level separated by dashes. In its most common form, the first level is a two-letter ISO 639 language abbreviation, and the second level, if present, is a two-letter ISO 3166 country code. For example, the code en represents English, and the code en-us represents American English. The Accept-Language header supports the same quality factors as the other Accept- headers, so a client can express preferences from among many languages. The following text asks for UK English first and any other English form if the first choice isn't available.

```
Accept-Language: en-gb, en; q=0.8
```

Note that HTTP servers do not automatically fall back to higher levels in a language hierarchy. The following header, for example, would be satisfied by only a US English response. The server would not return a version in UK English, even if one were available.

```
Accept-Language: en-us, *; q=0.0
```

3.2.5 Accept-Ranges

Unlike the other Accept- headers, the Accept-Ranges header is a response header; as such it appears in servers' responses rather than clients' requests. The current HTTP specifications limit this header to two forms. The first form, shown in the example header below, lets a server indicate that it can accept range requests for the resource.

```
Accept-Ranges: bytes
```

As we'll see in section 3.2.39, clients can issue requests for a range of bytes of a resource rather than the entire resource. This feature is particularly useful for downloading large files. If a download fails before completion, the client can use a range request to ask for only the missing bytes; it doesn't have to receive the entire file all over again.

If the server cannot accept range requests for a resource, it may indicate that with the following header.

```
Accept-Ranges: none
```

Note that servers are not required to include an Accept-Ranges header, regardless of whether they can accept range requests. Clients are also free to issue range requests even if they haven't received an Accept-Ranges header. If the client happens to send a range request to a server that cannot support it, the server simply returns the entire resource.

3.2.6 Age

The Age header is a response header that estimates the age of the associated resource. Cache servers use this value to judge whether a cached resource is still valid or whether it has expired and must be refreshed from the origin server. The Age header's value is the number of seconds that the sender estimates have elapsed since the origin server generated or re-validated the response.

The best way to understand how the Age header works is with an example. Consider, therefore, the scenario that begins with figure 3.5. That figure shows the initial request for a resource, and in it the request traverses two intermediate cache servers before reaching the origin server.

As the figure shows, the origin server includes two important headers in its response. Those headers are the Date header, which is the time that it generates the response, and a Cache-Control header, which specifies the maximum age. In the example the server indicates that the response can be considered fresh (and, thus, cachable) for up to 600 seconds.

The scenario continues in figure 3.6, which takes place about 10 minutes later. In that figure, a client makes a request for the same resource. The first cache server no longer has a

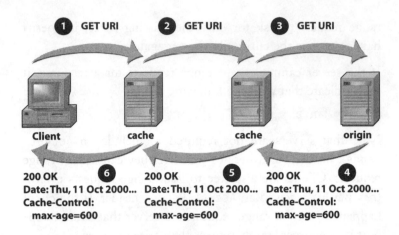

Figure 3.5 ▶
An origin server may identify the
maximum age for cached copies of an
object it returns. In this example the
server limits caching to 10 minutes
(600 seconds).

copy in its cache, so it passes the request to the second cache. That server returns the object with the message headers that the figure includes in step 9.

At this point the first cache server has an important decision to make: Is the object that the second cache returned still valid? To answer that question, the first cache server calculates several values based on the parameters in table 3.4.

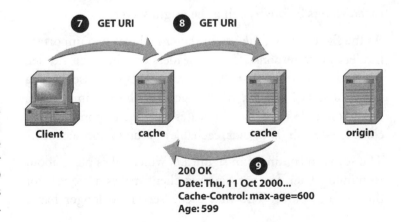

Figure 3.6 ▶
Cache servers can indicate how old
they believe an object to be with the
Age header. This cache server
estimates the object to be 599
seconds old, one less that its
maximum life.

Table 3.4 Parameters for Cache Freshness Calculations

Parameter	Interpretation
age_value	The value in the Age header of the response (step 9); 599 in the example.
date_value	The date assigned to the resource by the origin server (step 4); 11 October 2000 … in the example.
now	Current time at the first cache server.
request_time	The time that the cache made the request (step 8).
response_time	The time that the response (step 9) arrived.

Table 3.5 shows the steps in the calculation. Note that the server actually bases its estimate of the resource's age on two independent sources. It looks at the Age header explicitly, and it calculates the elapsed time from the resource's original Date header. (An accurate elapsed time calculation assumes that the cache server and origin server have reasonable synchronized time-of-day clocks.) The steps in table 3.5 ensure that the cache server picks the most conservative of these two values in its estimate, thus minimizing the chance that it inappropriately returns a stale resource.

Table 3.5 Calculating the Freshness of a Cached Object

Step	Procedure
1	Calculate the apparent age as the difference between response_time and date_value.
2	Estimate the age of the resource as the maximum of the apparent age from step 1 and the Age header in the response.
3	Add the difference between response_time and request_time to the estimated age of step 2 (to conservatively account for network transit delays).
4	Add the difference between now and response time (to account for any delays within the cache server).

The cache server uses this result as the actual age of the resource. If the actual age exceeds the origin server's max-age value, then the cache server should not use the cached object for the response. Instead, it should reissue the request to the origin server.

To continue the example, suppose that one second has elapsed between the time that the first cache issued the request at step 8 and received the response of step 9. And further suppose that an additional one second of delay occurred after the response arrived but before the cache server could process it. In such a case, the server will calculate the age of the object as 601 seconds. That value exceeds the origin server's limit of 600 seconds, so the cache server should reject the response. As a result, it may begin the process of figure 3.7, in which it reissues the request. (In the figure the first cache server adds its own Cache-Control header to the request of step 10; by setting the max-age directive to 0 in a response, the first cache server forces the second cache server to revalidate its own cache entry with the origin server.)

The HTTP specifications limit the Age header's value to 2 147 483 648 (or 2^{31}) seconds. Whenever an age value exceeds that limit in a server's calculations, the server uses that maximum value instead.

Figure 3.7 ▶
When the Age of a cached object exceeds its limit, cache servers must consult the origin server for a new copy or for revalidation of their existing copy. This example, which is a continuation of figure 3.6, has the cache server request a new copy.

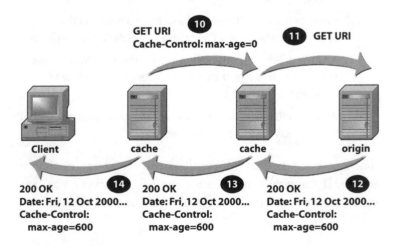

3.2.7 Allow

The Allow header identifies which HTTP methods a particular resource supports. The header simply lists those methods as its value. The text below, for example, indicates that a resource supports the GET, HEAD, and PUT methods.

```
Allow: GET, HEAD, PUT
```

This header is particular useful (indeed, it is mandatory) when the server must return a 405 Method Not Allowed status. Clients may also use the header when they send a resource to a server with the PUT method. In that case, the client recommends to the server which methods it should allow for the resource. The server, however, is not compelled to honor that recommendation.

3.2.8 Authentication-Info

The Authentication-Info completes a three-message user authentication exchange. It is a response header that servers can include in a successful response, and it gives the client additional information about the authentication exchange. For details, see section 4.1.

3.2.9 Authorization

Clients use the Authorization header to identify and authenticate themselves—or their users—to a server. The process of securing HTTP sessions is important enough (and complicated enough) to merit its own chapter, so you'll find a thorough description of authorization in the next chapter. Section 4.1, in particular, documents this specific header.

3.2.10 Cache-Control

The Cache-Control header is a master header for several different directives that specify caching behavior. These directives, some of which have parameters associated with them and some of which do not, are separated from each other by commas. The following fragment, for example, specifies three cache control directives.

```
Cache-Control: max-age=3600, no-transform,
    no-cache="Accept-Ranges"
```

Like headers, individual directives may be used in requests and responses. Table 3.6 lists HTTP's cache-control directives.

Table 3.6 Cache-Control Directives

Directive	Parameters	Request	Response
max-age	Required	●	●
max-stale	Optional	●	
min-fresh	Required	●	
must-revalidate	None		●
no-cache	Optional[1]	●	●
no-store	None	●	●
no-transform	None	●	●
only-if-cached	None	●	
Private	Optional		●
proxy-revalidate	None		●
Public	None		●
s-maxage	Required		●

[1]Optional in responses; no parameters in requests

The rest of this subsection considers each directive in turn.

```
Cache-Control: max-age=3600
```

The max-age directive serves two major purposes. First, when used by a server, it indicates the maximum time (in seconds) that a cache should retain the resource in its cache without revalidating it. In this role max-age is similar to the Expires header. If both a max-age directive and an Expires header are present in the same response, cache servers should ignore the Expires header, even if it is more restrictive than the max-age value. This rule allows origin servers to specify different behaviors for HTTP 1.0 caches than for HTTP 1.1

caches, because the 1.0 cache servers will not understand (and will, consequently, ignore) any max-age directive.

The max-age directive serves its second major purpose when clients use it. When a client includes the directive in its request, the client indicates that it is willing to accept a cached object no older than the indicated value. If a cache server has an entry that's older than the client's requested age, it should not return the cached entry, even if the origin server's original response indicates the entry is still valid. In an extreme case, the client may specify a max-age of zero, in which case cache servers should always pass the request to the origin server for revalidation of locally cached entries.

Cache-Control: max-stale

With the max-stale directive, a client indicates that it is willing to accept a response that includes a cached object, even if the object has apparently expired. The client can optionally limit how long past the apparent expiration time it is prepared to accept responses. A directive of max-stale=600, for example, indicates that the client is willing to accept responses up to 10 minutes (600 seconds) past their apparent expiration time.

Cache-Control: min-fresh=60

When a client includes the min-fresh directive in its request, it tells cache servers to return a cached entry only if the entry will remain fresh for at least the specified number of seconds. If, for example, a cache contained an object that would not expire for another 45 seconds, the cache server could not return the local copy in response to the request header example above. The example above requires that any local copy has at least 60 seconds of life remaining, and 45 seconds doesn't qualify.

Cache-Control: must-revalidate

The must-revalidate directive lets servers counteract the use of max-stale by their clients. When a server includes must-revalidate in its response, cache servers should ignore the max-stale directive in any future client requests.

Cache-Control: no-cache

The no-cache directive may appear in either requests or responses. In a request, this directive indicates that the client is not willing to accept cached responses; any intermediate cache servers must pass the request on to the origin server. Note that this request differs slightly from a request that includes a max-age=0 directive. In the case of no-cache requests, cache servers must always retrieve the response from the origin server. With max-age=0, however, cache servers need only revalidate their local cache with the origin server. If the origin server indicates the cached entry is still valid, the cache server may use it as a response.

When the origin server includes a no-cache directive in its response, it tells cache servers not to use the response for subsequent requests without revalidating it. This rule doesn't exactly prohibit cache servers from caching the response (despite the directive's name); it merely forces them to revalidate a locally cached copy with each request.

If an origin server wants to restrict caching of only certain header fields rather than the entire response, it can do that by naming those headers in this directive. By including no-cache="Accept-Ranges" in its response, for example, the origin server tells cache servers that they can cache the response, but they should not include the response's Accept-Ranges header when they answer subsequent requests with the cached copy.

Cache-Control: no-store

The no-store directive identifies sensitive information, either in a request (and its subsequent response) or in a response alone. This directive tells cache servers not to store the messages in any local storage, particularly if its contents may be retained (e.g., on backup tapes) after the exchange.

`Cache-Control: no-transform`

The `no-transform` directive, which can appear in either a request or a response, tells cache servers not to modify the format of the response's message body. Some cache servers might otherwise do so, for example, to save cache space by converting a high-resolution image to a lower resolution.

`Cache-Control: only-if-cached`

With the `only-if-cached` directive, a client asks cache servers to respond successfully only if they have the object in their local cache. In particular, the client asks the cache not to reload the response or revalidate it with the origin server. This behavior may be useful in the environments with especially poor network connectivity where the client feels the delay in reaching the origin server is unacceptable. If a cache server cannot answer the request from its local cache, it should return a `504 Gateway Timeout` status.

`Cache-Control: private`

The `private` directive in a response indicates that the response is intended strictly for a specific user. Cache servers may retain a copy for responses to subsequent requests from the same user, but they should not return that cached copy to other users, even if those users issue the same request.

`Cache-Control: proxy-revalidate`

The `proxy-revalidate` directive tells any intermediate cache servers that they should not return the response to subsequent requests without revalidating it. Unlike the `must-revalidate` directive, however, this directive does permit clients themselves to cache the response and reuse the cached entry without revalidation.

`Cache-Control: public`

The `public` directive is the opposite of the `private` directive. With it, a server explicitly indicates that its response may be cached and returned to other users, even if the response would otherwise be restricted to the original user or even non-cachable at all. If a client provides user authentication information, for example, cache servers should normally treat any response as private to that user. But if the server is merely responding with a `301 Moved Permanently` status, for example, it can use the `public` cache control directive to tell cache servers to override their normal behavior and cache the response.

```
Cache-Control: s-maxage=1800
```

The `s-maxage` directive acts much like the `max-age` directive in responses, except that it applies only to caches serving multiple users. For such cache servers, the `s-maxage` directive overrides both the `max-age` directive and the `Expires` header. Cache servers responding to the same user multiple times, however, can ignore this directive.

3.2.11 Connection

According to the HTTP specifications, the `Connection` header allows the message sender (the client in the case of requests, the server for responses) to indicate to proxies any other headers in the message that should not be forwarded further. Consider the example of figure 3.8. In the figure, the client issues a request that includes two message headers: `Upgrade` and `Connection`. The proxy server, when it sees the `Connection` header, removes the indicated `Upgrade` header from the request before forwarding it. The `Connection` header, therefore, identifies other HTTP headers that should be delivered only to the next hop.

Figure 3.8 ▶
The Connection header identifies other HTTP headers that proxy servers should remove from messages that they relay. In this example the proxy does not include the Upgrade header when it forwards the GET request.

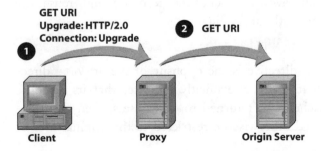

Most hop-by-hop headers are explicitly identified as such in the specifications. The Upgrade header of the figure, for example, is defined to have significance only to the next hop. Strictly speaking, therefore, the Connection header is not necessary. As long as all the systems follow the same HTTP standards, they'll already know which headers are hop-by-hop. The Connection header's real benefit, however, comes into play if the HTTP standards are ever extended. It allows HTTP to define new hop-by-hop headers, safe in the knowledge that existing systems will treat them as hop-by-hop so long as the Connection header identifies them.

The Connection header also has another use, and that is to manage persistent connections. In fact, the Connection header actually has two important uses related to persistent connections. The first is rather simple; it provides a way for either party to gracefully signal that they're about to close a connection. The second use supports persistence in a way that is backwards compatible with HTTP version 1.0.

As section 2.1.3 notes, with HTTP version 1.1, persistent connections are the default behavior. When a client opens a connection for a request, it expects the connection to remain open for additional requests to the same server. But what if the server doesn't want to keep the connection open? It could, of course, just close the connection after it sends its response. That behavior is legal, and the client will eventually recognize what has happened and act appropriately. The problem, though, is that the client doesn't receive any warning. It may be preparing to send a new request just when the server effectively yanks the rug out from underneath it. When that happens, it may take the client several seconds (possibly much longer) to recognize what has happened and recover. A more polite server will include the following header in its initial response.

```
Connection: close
```

This header tells the client that the server is planning to close the connection after completing its response. The client should prepare accordingly. Clients can also include a `Connection: close` header in their requests. In such a case the client is letting the server know that it does not plan to use a persistent connection and will, instead, close the current connection as soon as it receives its response. Note that `Connection: close` is not restricted to the first request or response in a connection. Either party can use it even after a connection has been established and used for previous exchanges. Once this header appears, though, future exchanges on the connection will not take place.

The second major use of the `Connection` header is supporting older systems. Because persistence was not the default behavior before HTTP 1.1, earlier implementations used explicit headers to request persistence connections. Those headers include a `Connection: Keep-Alive` and, optionally, the `Keep-Alive` header itself. (Because it is no longer needed, HTTP 1.1 does not define a `Keep-Alive` header.)

```
GET / HTTP/1.1
Keep-Alive: timeout=5
Connection: Keep-Alive
```

The server agrees to use persistent connections by responding with its own `Connection` and `Keep-Alive` headers.

```
HTTP/1.1 200 OK
Keep-Alive: timeout=5, max=120
Connection: Keep-Alive
Content-Type: text/html

<html>...
```

As a practical matter, the presence of the `Connection: Keep-Alive` header indicates HTTP persistence, not the `Keep-Alive` header itself.

3.2.12 Content-Encoding

The Content-Encoding header identifies any special encodings that are an inherent part of the resource contained in the message body. Together with the Content-Type header, this header specifies the format of the resource. If, for example, a client requested the file manual.ps.gz, it might receive the file in a response with the following message headers. The Content-Type header identifies the ultimate object as a PostScript file, but the Content-Encoding header notes that the file has been compressed with the gzip program.

```
HTTP/1.1 200 OK
Content-Type: application/postscript
Content-Encoding: gzip
```

The HTTP specifications recognize four different content encodings, all of which are listed in table 3.7.

Table 3.7 HTTP Content-Encodings

Identifier	Meaning
compress	The encoding format produced by the UNIX program compress. (Older implementations may use x-compress.)
deflate	The zlib encoding format defined in RFC 1950.
gzip	The encoding format produced by the gzip program, as described in RFC 1952. (Older implementations may use x-gzip.)
identity	The absence of any special encoding format.

Note that Content-Encoding is similar to, but slightly different from, Transfer-Encoding. Content-Encoding is an intrinsic characteristic of the resource, while Transfer-Encoding is applied externally by the HTTP server just for the purpose of transferring the resource. As a practical matter, though, receiving systems treat both encodings the same; they both must be reversed to uncover the actual resource. The trick is ensuring that the reverse transformations occur in the correct order. In the following fragment, for example, the resource was first compressed using gzip; the result was then further encoded using compress, and, finally, the "chunked" transfer encoding was applied. (The example is, admittedly, rather artificial.) The receiving system should undo those encodings in the reverse order: first `chunked`, then `compress`, and finally `gzip`.

```
Content-Encoding: gzip, compress
Transfer-Encoding: chunked
```

3.2.13 Content-Language

The `Content-Language` header identifies the natural language of the included resource. The format is the same as in the `Accept-Language` header described in section 3.2.4. Note that the HTTP specification intends this field specifically for human languages such as English. It should not be used to indicate computer languages like C or Java.

3.2.14 Content-Length

The `Content-Length` header gives the size of the message body in bytes or, in the case of a response to a `HEAD` method, the size of the message body if it were to be included. The `Content-Length` header is actually one of several different ways that the recipient may determine the size of a message. A recipient may also determine message length from the transfer encoding or content type format, and it can infer the end of a message when the underlying TCP connection closes.

Table 3.8 lists the rules that a recipient uses to determine the end of an HTTP message, in order of priority. As the rules indicate, a sender should not include the `Content-Length` header if the message is a response that does not permit message bodies, or if the message body is encoded using the chunked format.

Table 3.8 Rules for Determining the End of an HTTP Message

Priority	Rule
1	If the response has a status code that does not permit message bodies (e.g., $1xx$, 204, and 304 status codes) then the message ends at the first empty line after the header fields. Any further message content is ignored.
2	If the Transfer-Encoding for the message is chunked, then the message length is determined by the chunked format. (See section 3.2.46.)
3	If the Content-Length header is present, then it provides the length of the message.
4	If the message has a Content-Type of multipart/byteranges, then the media type format defines the end of the message.
5	If the server closes the connection, the last byte sent is the end of the message.

3.2.15 Content-Location

The Content-Location header provides the Uniform Resource Identifier corresponding to the message body. A server may choose to use this header if the resource it returns depends on more than the request's URI. For example, a server may have different language translations of a resource available, and it may decide to return one particular translation based on the Accept-Language header in the request. In such a case, the Content-Location header may identify the translated object instead of the original requested object.

In practice, the Content-Location header is rarely used. It should not be confused with the Location header (see section 3.2.33.), which does appear quite frequently in Web transactions. While the Content-Location header specifies the URI of the resource being returned in the message body, the Location header identifies an alternate URI for the requested resource; the resource itself is not part of the message body when the Location header appears.

The MD5 Algorithm

RFC 1321 documents the MD5 algorithm in full. It includes a complete implementation of the algorithm in C-Language source code.

3.2.16 Content-MD5

The `Content-MD5` header provides assurance that a message body reaches its destination without modification. The value of this header is the result of running the Message Digest 5 (MD5) algorithm with the message body (before any transfer encoding) as input. The MD5 algorithm, which chapter 4 discusses in more depth, resembles a checksum, but it uses cryptographic principles to make the result relatively immune to undetectable errors.

Here's how a system calculates the value for this header beginning with the following HTML page as the message body.

```
<HTML>
    <BODY>
        <P>Hello World!</P>
    </BODY>
</HTML>
```

Running the MD5 algorithm on the HTML page results in the following 128-bit binary value. The fragment shows the result as 16 bytes, each represented in hexadecimal notation.

```
B2 B3 59 59 1E 96 1C 6B 0F 46 8F E5 36 BC D9 20
```

Because the MD5 algorithm creates a binary value, and HTTP headers must be text, the `Content-MD5` header uses the base64 algorithm to convert binary to ASCII. The result of the base64 encoding is as follows.

```
Content-MD5: srNZWR6WHGsPRo/1NrzZIA==
```

To see the full context for the `Content-MD5` header, here is a full response from the server, including both the HTTP headers and the message body.

```
HTTP/1.1 200 OK
Date: Sun, 08 Oct 2000 18:46:12 GMT
Server: Apache/1.3.6 (Unix)
Content-Type: text/html
Content-Length: 66
Content-MD5: srNZWR6WHGsPRo/1NrzZIA==

<HTML>
```

Base64 Encoding

Base64 encoding was originally developed as a way to send binary objects using email. It is defined in RFC 2045, one of the series of specifications for Multipurpose Internet Mail Extensions (MIME).

```
    <BODY>
        <P>Hello World!</P>
    </BODY>
</HTML>
```

The `Content-MD5` header provides end-to-end protection of the content so that recipients can detect problems introduced by the network or by intervening proxy servers. To ensure this behavior the HTTP specification expressly prohibits intermediate servers from creating or modifying the `Content-MD5` header. Only the origin server (for responses) or the client (for requests) can create this header.

As one final note, the Content-MD5 header can identify accidental changes to the message content, but it cannot detect malicious attacks. An attacker that modifies HTTP content merely needs to adjust the Content-MD5 header value to match. Chapter 4 discusses more secure ways to protect HTTP content.

3.2.17 Content-Range

When a server includes only part of a resource in its message body, the `Content-Range` header specifies which part. This feature is particularly useful for resuming a file download after that download aborted. To see this process in action, consider figure 3.9. In that figure, the scenario begins when

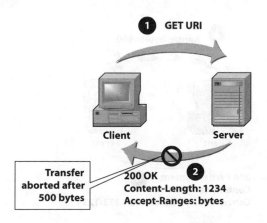

◀ Figure 3.9
When problems occur, a client may not receive all of a requested object. In this example the client requests an object that consists of 1234 total bytes, but the transfer aborts after only 500 bytes actually reach the client.

the client requests an object. As the figure shows, the server begins returning the resource, which consists of 1234 bytes of information. The transfer aborts, however, after only 500 bytes of the object successfully make it to the client.

In its original response, however, the server indicates that it can accept range requests for the object. The Accept-Ranges header conveys that information. Consequently, when the client realizes that the transfer has aborted, it does not have to request the entire object again. Instead, as figure 3.10 shows, it includes a Range header in its re-issued request.

With the request of step 3, the client asks only for bytes 500 through the end of the resource. The server obliges in step 4. Here is where the Content-Range header appears. The first part of the header's value identifies the unit. Currently HTTP supports only bytes. The next part lists the range of bytes included. In this example, the server's response begins with byte 500 of the object and ends with byte 1233. The last part of the header provides the total size of the object, 1234 bytes in the example. As these examples indicate, HTTP numbers bytes beginning at 0; the first byte of a resource is byte 0.

3.2.18 Content-Type

The Content-Type header identifies the type of object the message body contains. (In a response to the HEAD method,

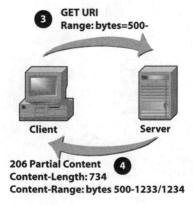

Figure 3.10 ▶
With the Range header, a client can ask for only part of an object. This example, which continues figure 3.9, shows how the client asks for the rest of the object.

3 **GET URI**
Range: bytes=500-

Client   **Server**

206 Partial Content **4**
Content-Length: 734
Content-Range: bytes 500-1233/1234

the Content-Type identifies the type of object that would be in the message body, if one were present.) Values for the Content-Type header follow the same type/subtype format we first saw with the Accept header. In addition, many of the defined content types allow for additional parameters that provide further information. For example, the fragment below indicates that the resource is a text file and that it uses the iso 8859-4 character set.

```
Content-Type: text/plain; Charset=ISO-8859-4
```

3.2.19 Cookie

If a client wishes to support HTTP state management (see section 2.5), it provides any cookies it has received from a server in subsequent requests to that server. Those cookies are carried in a Cookie header, much like the following. This example shows only a single cookie, but a client may conceivably have multiple cookies from the server, in which case it may combine all of them in one header or use separate headers.

```
Cookie: $Version="1"; NAME="VALUE";
        $Path="/shopping"; $Domain="www.shop.com";
        $Port="80"
```

Each cookie begins by identifying the version of HTTP state management the client is using; the current version is 1, as in the example. The version is always followed by the name of the cookie and its value. These are set by the server in its Set-Cookie or Set-Cookie2 header, but note that the server cannot use a cookie name of $Version. Otherwise it would be impossible to recognize the cookie in a header. The HTTP specification, in fact, prohibits cookie names from starting with the $ character.

The additional fields that follow the cookie name and value are optional. If present, they identify the path, domain, and port of the cookie.

3.2.20 Cookie2

Despite the similarity in names, the relationship between the Cookie2 and Cookie headers is not at all like that between the Set-Cookie2 and Set-Cookie headers. While Set-Cookie2 is just a slightly modified version of Set-Cookie, Cookie2 and Cookie are different headers with completely different uses.

The Cookie2 header merely indicates which version of the state management specification the client supports. The current version is 1, so the header will look like the following.

```
Cookie2: 1
```

A client should include this header whenever it sends a Cookie header. That will let the server know it can use Set-Cookie2 headers as well as Set-Cookie headers in subsequent responses. Clients that don't fully support Set-Cookie2 will omit the Cookie2 header, even though they might include a Cookie header. Servers will know not to send those clients Set-Cookie2 responses.

3.2.21 Date

The Date header indicates the time that the system sending a message originally generated that message. Note that Date values apply to the message, not necessarily to the resource identified or contained in the message. The Last-Modified header (see section 3.2.32) provides the time of the resource.

With version 1.1 of HTTP, systems are required to use the following format for date values that they generate. This format is defined in RFC 1123.

```
Date: Sun, 06 Nov 1994 08:49:37 GMT
```

To remain compatible with earlier implementations, HTTP 1.1 systems should accept dates in two other formats. The first format, shown in the fragment below, is defined in RFC 850. Note that it provides only for two-digit years, and the day of the week is of variable length.

```
Date: Sunday, 06-Nov-94 08:49:37 GMT
```

Another common format in earlier HTTP implementations is the following. This is the output of the function asctime(), part of the standard C-Language library.

```
Date: Sun Nov  6 08:49:47 1994
```

The HTTP specifications require origin servers to include a Date header in their responses, unless one of three conditions applies. If the response status is a 100 Continue or 101 Switching Protocols, the server may omit the Date header. Also, if the response status indicates a server error (e.g., 500 Internal Server Error) and the server cannot conveniently generate a valid date, it can omit the Date header. And finally, servers without a reasonably accurate clock should not include a Date header. This last condition doesn't often apply to traditional Web servers running on standard computing platforms, but it may be the case for special-purpose devices that include embedded Web server functionality.

3.2.22 ETag

The ETag header gives servers a more reliable way to identify resources, especially to improve caching performance. Without the ETag header, it can be difficult for caches (whether in proxy servers or in the client) to unambiguously identify requested resources. Consider, for example, the URL http://www.yahoo.com/. The actual resource returned may vary based not just on time, but also on geographic location. Users in the United Kingdom may see a different home page than users in France, as figures 3.11 and 3.12 demonstrate.

This problem can seriously complicate the life of Web caches, especially if all they have to identify a resource is its URL. The ETag header solves the problem by providing a simple and unambiguous way to identify resources. Origin servers can assign an ETag, which is short for "entity tag," value to resources as they return them.

Figure 3.11 ▶
Figure 3.11 ▶
Web servers can tailor the contents of
a Web page to suit specific users. In
this example the user is located in the
United Kingdom, so the server returns
content especially for that location.

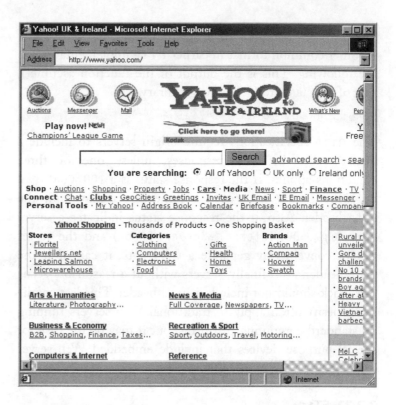

An `ETag` value can contain arbitrary characters within double
quotation marks; the actual value is completely up to the origin server. The following fragment is how a server might
assign an `ETag` value in its response.

```
ETag: "xyzzy"
```

`ETag` values also come in two varieties: strong and weak. Resources with the same strong `ETag` value are identical, byte
for byte. Resources with the same weak `ETag` value, however,
are merely equivalent. Weak `ETag` values begin with the w/
prefix, as the text below illustrates.

```
ETag: w/"xyzzy"
```

Caches normally use `ETag` values with `If-Match` and `If-
None-Match` headers. Sections 3.2.27 and 3.2.29 document
their operation.

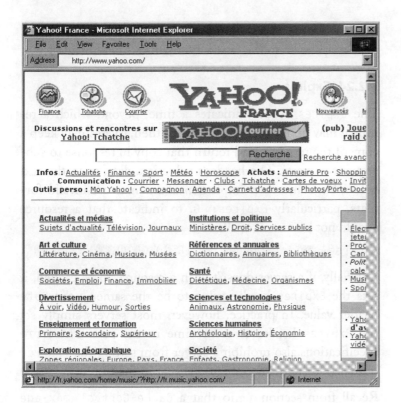

◀ **Figure 3.12**
A user in France who requests the same URI may get entirely different content, making it difficult for cache servers to tell if a locally cached copy is appropriate for a given request.

3.2.23 Expect

With the `Expect` header, a client tells a server that it expects a particular behavior. The HTTP specifications define `Expect` as an extensible header, but the only currently defined use for it is if a client expects a server to send a `100 Continue` status. In that case the client includes the following header. (For more details on the `100 Continue` status, see section 3.3.1.)

```
Expect: 100-continue
```

If a server receives an `Expect` header with which it cannot comply, it responds with a `417 Expectation Failed` status.

When the client is communicating through a series of proxy servers, each proxy in the chain is expected to respond to the

`Expect`. In addition, the proxy should pass the `Expect` header upstream to the next server without modification.

3.2.24 Expires

The `Expires` header indicates a time, beyond which a resource may no longer be valid. Until then, caches may keep a copy of the response and return that copy in response to subsequent requests. The header's value is a date, as in the text below, but some older implementations may use invalid formats, particularly `Expires: 0`, to indicate that a resource should not be cached at all.

```
Expires: Thu, 01 Dec 1994 16:00:00 GMT
```

Officially, if a server doesn't wish a resource to be cached, it sets the `Expires` header value to be the same as the `Date` header value. In practice, however, most servers simply set the `Expires` header to some time in the past. The HTTP specifications also prohibit a server from setting the `Expires` header value to be more than one year in the future.

Recall from section 3.2.10 that a `Cache-Control max-age` directive overrides the `Expires` header. Because HTTP introduced `Cache-Control` with version 1.1, and many earlier implementations supported `Expires`, the combination of both headers lets servers specify different expiration times for version 1.1 and pre-version 1.1 caches. A server might do that if there are additional 1.1 features that allow it to safely extend the age of the resource.

3.2.25 From

Clients can use the `From` header to identify the human user for a request. The value of this header, as the example below shows, is an email address. Because unsolicited email has made many users very wary of revealing their email addresses, most HTTP clients no longer include this field in their requests.

```
From: stephen.thomas@waterscreek.com
```

3.2.26 Host

With version 1.1, HTTP introduced the Host header specifically to help Web hosting providers. Without the Host header, such providers are often forced use their hosting resources inefficiently. The problem, as we saw in section 2.4.1, is that providers like to run multiple companies' Web sites on the same physical server system. But if, for example, a single physical server supports both www.companyA.com and www.companyB.com, how does that server respond to the following request? Is the client asking for the home page of company A or company B?

```
GET / HTTP/1.1
Accept: */*
User-Agent: Mozilla/4.0
    (compatible; MSIE 5.5; Windows NT 5.0)
```

Without the Host header, providers are forced to dedicate different IP addresses for each client. (All standard Web servers allow the host system to have multiple, simultaneous IP addresses.) The server can then determine the response based on the IP address to which the client sent the request. Unfortunately, IP addresses are a scarce commodity, and providers would rather not use them unnecessarily. The Host header comes to their rescue by allowing clients to explicitly indicate the DNS name for the resource they're requesting. With a Host header, the preceding request might instead look like the following. This time the client specifically identifies the host as company A.

```
GET / HTTP/1.1
Accept: */*
User-Agent: Mozilla/4.0
    (compatible; MSIE 5.5; Windows NT 5.0)
Host: www.companyA.com
```

Although it's rarely used in practice, HTTP 1.1 does allow a client to specify a full URI in its request. In such cases the server should ignore the value of the Host header if one is present. For example, a server would treat the following request as a request for Company B's home page, even though the Host header indicates something else.

```
GET http://www.companyB.com/ HTTP/1.1
Accept: */*
User-Agent: Mozilla/4.0
    (compatible; MSIE 5.5; Windows NT 5.0)
Host: www.companyA.com
```

3.2.27 If-Match

The If-Match header makes a client's request conditional; the server accepts the request only if certain conditions are true. Specifically, the If-Match header lists one or more entity tags, and the server should process the request only if the identified resource matches one of the entity tags. The server must not use weak ETag values (see section 3.2.22.) for its comparison.

The If-Match header can be a significant help when clients are editing resources stored on a server. In that type of environment, If-Match can prevent conflicts that may occur when multiple users edit the same resource. For example, look at the scenario that starts with figure 3.13. In that figure

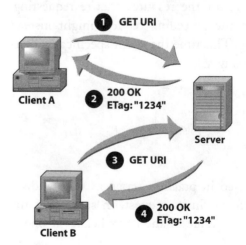

Figure 3.13 ▶
Two different clients request the same object. Since the object is identical in both responses, the server assigns it the same ETag value.

two different clients request a resource. In both cases the server returns the resource with an `ETag` header of 1234.

The example continues with figure 3.14. There the first client finishes editing the resource and returns the modified object to the server with a `PUT` method. The `If-Match` header tells the server to process the request only if the resource's entity tag is still 1234. As far as the server knows, the resource hasn't changed, so the server accepts the request. At this point, however, the resource has changed. It takes the new value supplied by the first client. Because of this change, the server must assign the resource a new entity tag.

Sometime later, the second client finishes its modifications and attempts to return the new object to the server. That request is step 8 and, as the figure shows, it also includes an `If-Match` header. In this case, though, the 1234 doesn't match the resource's new entity tag. The server rejects the request with a `412 Precondition Failed` status.

Clients can also use an `If-Match` header with an asterisk for the entity tag, as in the example that follows. In this case the client asks the server to carry out the request only if the resource already exists, regardless of its current entity tag. A

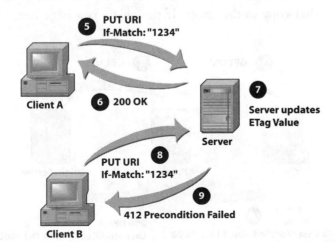

◀ **Figure 3.14**
Client A returns a modified version of the object in step 5. Because the object has now changed, the server gives it a new ETag value. Later, when client B tries to update the original object (with the old ETag value), the server recognizes the conflict and refuses the request.

client might use this option if it wanted to prevent its PUT request from creating a brand new resource.

```
If-Match: *
```

3.2.28 If-Modified-Since

The If-Modified-Since header lets clients and proxy servers make more efficient use of their caches. It asks a server to respond to a request only if the resource has changed since the specified date. Figure 3.15 shows how HTTP systems can use this header. The figure shows a standard GET request that passes through a proxy server. A key element of the server's response is the Last-Modified header, with which the server identifies the last time the requested resource changed.

The example continues in figure 3.16. Some time later the client issues another request for the same resource. The proxy has a copy of the earlier response in its local cache, so it inserts the If-Modified-Since header into the request before passing it to the origin server. The value of that header is the same as the server's original Last-Modified time.

In the example, the resource has not changed. Instead of returning the entire object, the origin server responds with a 304 Not Modified status. This status tells the proxy server that its cached copy of the object is still valid, so it returns that copy to the client. If the object is a large one, this step

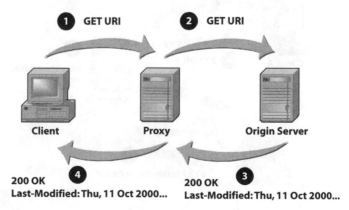

Figure 3.15 ▶
When a server returns an object, it indicates the last time that the object changed by specifying the Last-Modified header value.

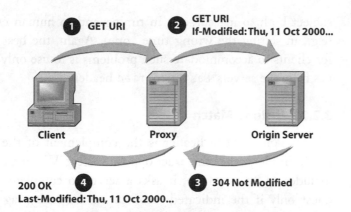

A proxy server can use the If-Modified header to ask for an object only if it has changed. In this example the object has not changed, so the server returns a 304 status.

may have saved considerable network bandwidth and delay because the object doesn't have to travel from the origin server to the proxy a second time.

Clients can use the If-Modified-Since header not only for standard requests, but also for partial requests with the Range header. In such cases, the If-Modified-Since value applies to the object as a whole, not just to the requested part of the object.

Servers receiving requests with If-Modified-Since headers should honor that header only if they would otherwise return a 200 OK status. Also, if the date in an If-Modified-Since header is invalid, either because it is in the wrong format or because it is later than the server's current time, then the server should ignore the header and return the resource.

Clients that use the If-Modified-Since header should take into account two problems with many deployed servers. First, some servers compare the If-Modified-Since value for an exact match with the resource's Last-Modified value. Even if the If-Modified-Since value is later than the Last-Modified value, those servers will return the full entity. Clients that want to accommodate this behavior should use only values from Last-Modified headers. The second issue is one of clock synchronization. Clients should be aware that server clocks may not always be correct; they are subject both to inaccuracies in timing and to human errors (e.g., in setting the wrong time zone). Again, the best way for clients to accommodate such problems is to use only values from the servers' Last-Modified headers.

3.2.29 If-None-Match

The If-None-Match header is the complement of the If-Match header; it has the exact opposite effect. When a client includes If-None-Match, it asks a server to complete a request only if the indicated resource has an entity tag that differs from that in the header. Servers can consider strong ETag values (see section 3.2.22.) for all requests and weak ETag values only with GET or HEAD methods.

For GET and HEAD requests, the If-None-Match header works like the If-Modified-Since. If the server finds that the entity tag for the resource is the same as one listed in the If-None-Match header, the server returns a 304 Not Modified status. If the client includes both an If-None-Match and an If-Modified-Since header in its request, the If-Modified-Since header takes precedence. If the server believes the resource is more recent than the If-Modified-Since time, it returns the complete resource regardless of the value of the If-None-Match header.

In all cases, if the request would result in any status other than 2xx or 304 were the If-None-Match header not present, the server should return that status and ignore the If-None-Match.

Just as with the If-Match header, If-None-Match lets a client use the asterisk to represent any entity tag value. This use, which the example below illustrates, asks the server to accept the request only if the resource does not currently exist. A client might use this header value on a PUT request if it wanted to be sure and not overwrite an existing object.

```
If-None-Match: *
```

3.2.30 If-Range

The If-Range header improves performance for clients or proxies that have part of an object in their local cache. Without If-Range, the client may require two separate exchanges to get a new copy of the object once that object has been modified. Figure 3.17 shows the message exchanges when If-Range isn't used.

In step 1, the client asks for bytes 500 through 1000 of the resource, but only if the entity tag for that resource is still "1234". When the server recognizes that the resource has changed, it responds with a 412 Precondition Failed status. The client then has to issue the request again, this time asking for the new object.

The If-Range header lets a client combine both of these requests into one, as figure 3.18 illustrates. In its request, the client includes an If-Range header and a Range header. Together, those two tell the server to return only the requested range if the resource's entity tag is still "1234"; otherwise, the server should return the entire object. In the example, the object has changed, so the server returns the full object with a 200 OK response.

For those servers that don't use entity tags, the If-Range header has an alternative format. Instead of an entity tag for

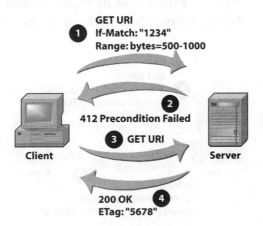

GET URI
If-Match: "1234"
Range: bytes=500-1000

412 Precondition Failed

GET URI

200 OK
ETag: "5678"

Client   **Server**

◀ **Figure 3.17**
Without the If-Range header, a client may have to make two requests when it has part of an object but the part is no longer valid. The first request tells the client that its copy is invalid, and the second request actually retrieves the entire new object.

Figure 3.18 ▶
The If-Range header lets a client ask
for either part of an object or, if the
part is no longer valid, the entire
object, all in a single request.

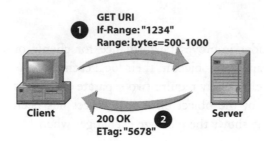

the If-Range value, the client may use a date. In those cases the client asks the server to return the partial range if the resource has not been modified since the specified date. Otherwise the server returns the full object. Figure 3.19 shows how a client might use this option. In this figure, unlike the previous two, the resource hasn't changed, so the server returns only the requested range.

The If-Range header doesn't use any special formatting to distinguish If-Range entity tags for If-Range dates. It is the server's responsibility to interpret the header correctly. Because entity tags are enclosed in double quotation marks and dates are not, servers can easily make that determination.

3.2.31 If-Unmodified-Since

As you might expect, the If-Unmodified-Since header is the opposite of If-Modified-Since. If a client includes If-Unmodified-Since in its request, it asks the server to accept the request only if the referenced resource has not changed

Figure 3.19 ▶
A client can indicate a date as well as
an ETag value with the If-Range
header. In both cases the server
returns a partial object only if the
client's existing part is still valid.

since the indicated date. A client might use this header in PUT requests if it wanted to ensure that no other party had modified a resource while the client was editing it.

As with the other If- headers, servers should consider the If-Unmodified-Since header only if the request would otherwise return a 200 OK status. When that is the case, but the If-Unmodified-Since condition does not hold, a server returns a 412 Precondition Failed status.

3.2.32 Last-Modified

The Last-Modified header provides the date the origin server believes the indicated resource was last modified. This header, an example of which appears below, is primarily of benefit to proxies and clients that cache objects, as it allows them to date an object in their local cache. When the system needs to get a new copy of an object, it can use this date, along with the If-Modified-Since header, to prevent the server from resending the entire resource if it has not changed. Figures 3.15 and 3.16 show this operation.

```
Last-Modified: Tue, 15 Nov 1994 12:45:26 GMT
```

3.2.33 Location

Servers use the Location header to redirect clients to a new URI for a resource. The most common use of Location is in responses with 3xx status codes, but a server might also use Location in a 201 Created response. In that case, the header would tell a client where it could retrieve a copy of a resource that it just sent to the server using a PUT method.

Figure 3.20 shows the typical operation of a Location header. In step 1, the client sends a standard GET request to server A. That server doesn't have the resource, but it does know where the resource may be found. In its reply, therefore, server A returns a status code of 302 Found, and it includes a Location header. The value of the Location header is a full URI for the resource. The client uses this information

Figure 3.20 ▶
The Location header gives the client a
new Uniform Resource Identifier for
an object. If appropriate, the client
may request the object from that
location. In this example server A tells
the client to retrieve the object from
server B.

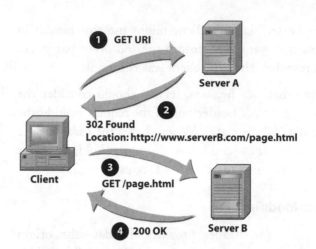

to reissue the request to the indicated server, which, in step 4, finally returns the resource.

The Location header is quite different from the Content-Location header, despite the similarity in their names. When a server includes a Content-Location header, it tells the client where a resource came from; a Location header, in contrast, tells the client where a resource is now located.

3.2.34 Max-Forwards

The Max-Forwards header, along with the OPTIONS and TRACE methods, helps clients fix problems that prevent them from getting any response from a server. There are two classes of problems that can be particularly difficult to diagnose without the Max-Forwards header—failed intermediaries and request looping.

Figure 3.21 shows the situation when an intermediary fails. In the figure, proxy server B receives the request in step 2, but it fails to forward the request on to the origin server. The situation is particularly vexing for the client. The client is communicating directly with proxy A and can probably verify that proxy A is working fine. The client may even be able to verify that the origin server is working correctly (by calling

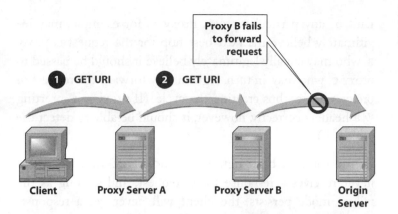

the server's technical support, for example). Somehow the request doesn't make it all the way to the origin server, though.

Request looping also prevents the client from receiving any response, but it's even more harmful to the network as a whole. When looping occurs, requests circulate among proxy servers indefinitely, tying up network and server resources. Figure 3.22 illustrates this problem. Instead of reaching the origin server, the client's request continuously passes among the three proxy servers. This condition is not necessarily the

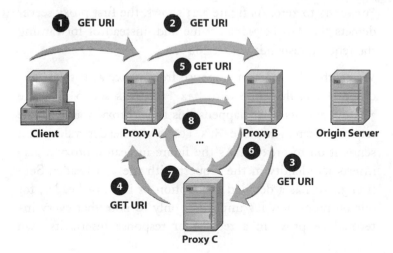

◄ **Figure 3.22**
Loops can develop when proxies circulate a request among themselves without ever delivering it to the origin server. This is another error that prevents a client from receiving any response.

fault of any particular proxy. Proxy A, for example, may legitimately believe the next best hop for the request is proxy B, who may equally legitimately believe it should be passed to proxy C, who may, in turn, legitimately forward the request to proxy A again, thus creating the cycle. (If proxy A is inserting Via headers correctly, however, it should be able to detect the problem.)

In the cases of both figure 3.21 and figure 3.22, the client never receives a response to its request, and as long as the failure mode persists, the client will never get a response, even by repeating the request. When that happens, a client can call on the TRACE method, along with the Max-Forwards and Via headers.

The Max-Forwards header limits the number of intermediate systems through which a request may pass. The client (or even an intermediate proxy server) sets it to an initial value, and subsequent proxy servers that receive the request decrement it before passing it on. If an intermediate server receives a request with Max-Forwards set to zero, it must not forward the request any further. Instead, it responds as if it were the origin server.

Here's how the client could detect the request loop of figure 3.22. It starts by sending a TRACE method with Max-Forwards to zero. As figure 3.23 shows, the first proxy server detects the Max-Forwards value and, instead of forwarding the request, responds with a 200 OK.

When the client gets a response from proxy A, it sends another TRACE, this time with Max-Forwards set to 1. Figure 3.24 documents what happens this time. Proxy A accepts the request, decrements the Max-Forwards header value, and sends it on to proxy B. As the figure indicates, proxy A also inserts its identity in the request with the Via header. Section 3.2.50 has a detailed description of the Via header; for our purposes now it's important only to note that every intermediate proxy in a request or response inserts its own

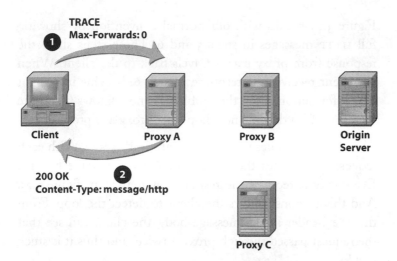

identity in each message. When, in step 4, the message reaches proxy B, the `Max-Forwards` header prevents proxy B from sending it any further. Instead, proxy B returns its own response to the client.

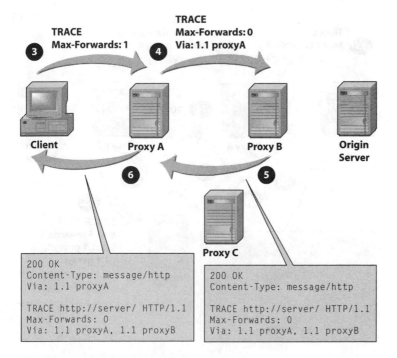

Figure 3.24 breaks with our normal convention by showing full HTTP messages in steps 5 and 6. These steps show the response from proxy B as it travels back to the client. When the client receives the response in step 6, it gains important new information about the problem. It now knows (from the message body) that the next hop after proxy A is proxy B.

The client continues probing the path in this way. With each request it increases the initial Max-Forwards value by one. Eventually it receives the response of step 20 in figure 3.25. And this response allows the client to detect the loop. From the Via header in the message body, the client can see that the request passed through proxy A twice, and thus it is stuck in a loop.

Clients can use a similar process to detect intermediate server failures. They start with a Max-Forwards value of zero and increment it each time they get a response to the TRACE request. When no response arrives, the client knows where the request fails.

Figure 3.25 ▶
The Max-Forwards header can limit the looping of a request. Each proxy decrements the header's value as it passes through, until the value reaches zero. In this example Max-Forwards is zero when the request reaches proxy A the second time (at step 16). At that point proxy A responds to the request rather than relaying it further.

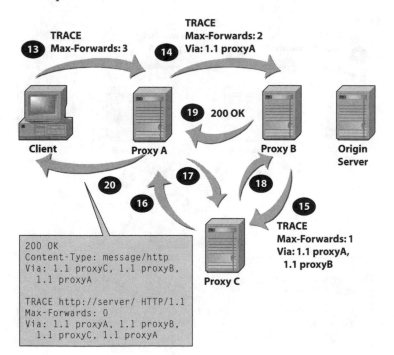

3.2.35 Meter

Like the Cache-Control header we saw before, the Meter header supports several different options known as directives. Caching proxy servers and origin servers use these directives to report the cached page views and to limit the caching of resources, as section 2.4.5 explains. This metering process occurs in three phases. First, the proxy advertises its willingness to support metering in the initial request. Second, the origin server asks for specific metering services in its response. And finally, the proxy actually reports usage in later requests for the same object. Table 3.9 lists the individual Meter directives, as well as the phase in which each is employed. As the table indicates, each directive has both a regular and a short form.

Table 3.9 Meter Header Directives

Directive	Short	Used In	Use
count=n/m	c=n/m	Later request	Proxy server reports usage.
do-report	d	Response	Origin server asks proxy to provide reports.
dont-report	e	Response	Origin server tells proxy not to provide reports.
max-reuses=n	r=n	Response	Origin server specifies a limit for non-unique page views.
max-uses=n	u=n	Response	Origin server specifies a limit for unique page views.
timeout=n	t=n	Response	Origin server specifies the maximum time between reports.
will-report-and-limit	w	Initial request	Proxy can support metering.
wont-ask	n	Response	Origin server indicates it will not ask for metering of any objects.

continues...

Table 3.9 Meter Header Directives (continued)

Directive	Short	Used In	Use
wont-limit	y	Initial request	Proxy understands metering, but won't limit usage.
wont-report	x	Initial request	Proxy understands metering, but won't report usage.

The metering process begins when a request passes through a proxy server. If the proxy server is willing to support metering, it adds a `Meter` header to the request. In the header, the proxy can identify the type of support it is offering with the `will-report-and-limit`, `wont-limit`, or `wont-report directive`. Without any specific directive, the default is to both report and limit. The proxy must also add a `Connection: Meter` header to the request, as the `Meter` header must be limited to the immediate connection. In fact, if the proxy is content with the default case (supporting both reporting and limiting), it need include only the `Connection` header, as `Connection: Meter` implies the presence of the `Meter` header.

```
GET / HTTP/1.1
Via: proxy
Connection: Meter
```

When the server responds to this request, it provides guidance to the proxy with a `Meter` header in the response. That header may include a series of directives. It can tell the proxy whether the server wants to receive reports (`do-report` or `dont-report`); it can specify the maximum number of times the proxy should return the response from its cache (`max-uses` and `max-reuses`), and it can specify a time limit before which the proxy should send a new report (`timeout=n`). Note that, unlike many HTTP header values, the `Meter: timeout=n` specifies minutes, not seconds. In the example below, the origin server asks the proxy to provide reports at least as often as every hour. The response also specifies no limits. If the server wants to tell the proxy not to send it any more `Meter` headers, it can use the `wont-ask` directive in its own `Meter` header.

```
HTTP/1.1 200 OK
Date: Sun, 08 Oct 2000 18:46:12 GMT
Meter: do-report, timeout=60
Connection: Meter

...
```

When the proxy sees the server's response and caches the message body, it begins counting the number of times it returns the object from its cache. It should count both the number of unique page views (requests from new users) and the number of non-unique page views (re-requests from the same user). Proxies consider any response in which they actually return the object (with a `200 OK` status, in other words) as a unique page view and any response that simply confirms the client's previously stored copy (a `304 Not Modified` status) as a non-unique page view. Whenever either of these counts reaches the maximum specified by the origin server, the proxy revalidates the object with the origin server before returning it to a client.

As the proxy server continues to receive requests for the cached object, it must determine when to send a usage report to the origin. The proxy sends this report whenever it must send or forward a conditional `GET` or `HEAD` to the origin server, whenever the origin server's time limit expires, or whenever the proxy removes the object from its cache. The report consists of a `Meter` header with a `count` directive. The two `count` values are the number of uses and the number of reuses. The example below reports 934 uses and 201 reuses.

```
GET / HTTP/1.1
Via: proxy
Meter: count=934/201
Connection: Meter
```

3.2.36 Pragma

The Pragma header is a holdover from earlier versions of HTTP. With HTTP version 1.1, there is only one format for this header; it is illustrated in the following fragment.

```
Pragma: no-cache
```

Officially, this header is intended as a way for clients to indicate that they do not want any intermediate servers to reply to the request with a cached response. Instead, they're asking proxies to forward the request all the way to the origin server. In practice, many servers include Pragma: no-cache in their responses as a way to tell intermediate servers not to save the response in their caches. This behavior is so common that many cache servers honor it, even though it has never been standardized. Servers are cautioned, however, not to assume that all intermediate servers will accept the header. A safer alternative for origin servers that don't want their response cached is to include an Expires header with a date in the past.

At some point in the future all intermediate systems will be compliant with HTTP version 1.1. At that time, servers and clients can both use the Cache-Control: no-cache header, which is HTTP 1.1's preferred method of controlling caching.

3.2.37 Proxy-Authenticate

The Proxy-Authenticate header lets intermediate proxy servers authenticate a client. By including this header in a response, the proxy asks the client to reissue the request but to include its authorization credentials. Proxy servers must always include Proxy-Authenticate in any response with a 407 Proxy Authentication Required status. In operation, Proxy-Authenticate is similar to WWW-Authenticate, except that it is generated by proxy servers rather than origin servers. Both proxy and origin server authentication techniques are discussed in more detail in section 4.1.

3.2.38 Proxy-Authorization

A client responds to a proxy server's demand for authentication by including a `Proxy-Authorization` when it reissues its request. Section 4.1 describes the approach in detail.

3.2.39 Range

The `Range` header lets a client request part of a resource instead of the entire object. As we first saw in section 3.2.5, the header takes the following form. In a request, this header asks for the second 500 bytes (byte number 500 through byte number 999, inclusive) and for the last 2 bytes of the resource. Note that HTTP 1.1 numbers bytes starting with 0.

```
Range: bytes 500-999, -2
```

If a server is able to honor the client's request, it returns a status code of `206 Partial Content`. The server also includes the `Content-Range` header in its response. If the server cannot return the requested range but it can respond with the entire object, the server does so with a status of `200 OK`. Because of this rule, and because some servers may not understand the `Range` header, clients that use it should be prepared to receive the entire object in a response.

3.2.40 Referer

The `Referer` header (yes, it is misspelled) appears in client requests so the server can identify where the client obtained the URI in its request. As an example, look at the Web page of figure 3.26. That is the home page of the Internet Engineering Task Force, found at http://www.ietf.org.

Notice that the page includes a link to the Web site for the Internet Assigned Numbers Authority (IANA). The link appears at the bottom of figure 3.26, toward the right, and the HTML fragment for the link is the following.

```
<A href="http://www.iana.org">IANA</A>
```

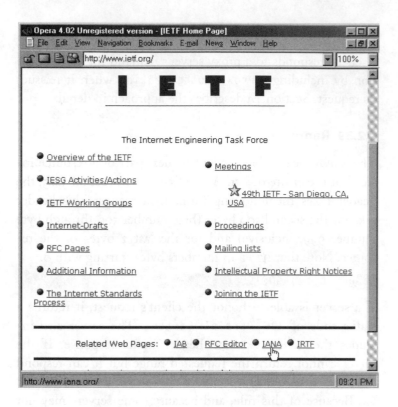

If the user clicks on the link, the browser issues an HTTP GET request to www.iana.org. Because the link appears on the www.ietf.org page, the request will list the IETF's page in the Referer header. Here is the actual HTTP GET request.

```
GET / HTTP/1.1
Referer: http://www.ietf.org/
Accept-Language: en-us
Accept-Encoding: gzip, deflate
User-Agent: Mozilla/4.0 (compatible;
            MSIE 5.5; Windows NT 5.0)
Host: www.iana.org
Connection: Keep-Alive
```

3.2.41 Retry-After

Servers use the `Retry-After` header to tell a client when it should retry its request. The header can specify a date, so that the following header asks a client to wait until 1 January 2001 to reissue its request.

```
Retry-After: Sun, 31 Dec 2000 23:59:59 GMT
```

The header can also simply indicate a number of seconds. The example below tells the client to wait 2 minutes (120 seconds) before retrying.

```
Retry-After: 120
```

Servers can use this header with `503 Service Unavailable` or with any of the `3xx` status code responses. In the latter case, the client should delay its redirected request by the indicated amount; there is no suggestion as to how long the client should wait before reissuing its request to the original server.

3.2.42 Server

With the `Server` header, an HTTP server identifies the software that it uses to implement HTTP. This header is the server's version of the `User-Agent` header. (See section 3.2.48.) The following examples show some of the `Server` header values that can be found on the Web today.

```
Server: Apache/1.3.6 (Unix)  (Red Hat/Linux)
```

```
Server: IBM-Planetwide/10.45
        Domino-Go-Webserver/4.6
```

```
Server: Microsoft-IIS/5.0
```

```
Server: NaviServer/2.0 AOLserver/2.3.3
```

```
Server: Netscape-Enterprise/3.6 SP3
```

```
Server: Xitami
```

3.2.43 Set-Cookie2

The Set-Cookie2 header is a slightly updated form of the Set-Cookie header from HTTP version 1.0. Both headers are used by servers to initiate HTTP state management with a client. (See section 2.5.) By including a Set-Cookie2 header in its response, a server provides a state management cookie to the client, and it implicitly asks the client to return that cookie in subsequent requests to the server.

The header begins by giving the cookie a name and a value, and then it may provide any of the attributes listed in table 2.1. An example header with all possible attributes follows.

```
Set-Cookie2: NAME="VALUE";
    Comment="Shopping Cart";
    CommentURL="http://merchant.com/cookies.html";
    Discard; Max-Age="300"; Path="/shopping";
    Port="443"; Secure; Version="1"
```

Section 2.5 describes the state management process, including the interpretation of the various attributes and the rules clients and servers must follow when using cookies.

3.2.44 TE

The TE header tells a server which transfer encodings the client can accept in a response, and it can indicate the client's relative preferences for those transfer encodings. This header is very similar to the Accept-Encoding header, except that it applies to transfer encodings rather than content encodings.

The format for the TE header is very similar to that for the Accept-Encoding header. The header value is a comma-separated list of transfer encoding names, each with an optional quality factor. For example, the following header indicates that the client can accept gzip and deflate transfer encodings, but it prefers gzip because that has a higher quality factor. (As with other headers, if the client doesn't explicitly indicate a quality factor for a particular option, the server assumes a value of 1.0.)

```
TE: gzip, deflate;q=0.9
```

In addition to the standard transfer encodings, the TE header defines a special value to identify the chunked transfer encoding with trailer fields. That value is simply trailers, as in the following example. Note that there is no need for a client to list the chunked transfer encoding itself in a TE header, as all HTTP 1.1 clients must be prepared to accept the chunked transfer encoding. The use of trailer fields with chunked encoding, however, is optional; this header value lets a client advertise that it understands that format.

```
TE: trailers
```

3.2.45 Trailer

Clients and servers may include the Trailer header when they use the chunked transfer encoding for the message body. This header lists any other HTTP headers that appear after the message body, rather than in the normal position before the body. It tells the recipient which HTTP headers it can expect in the chunked transfer encoding's trailer. There are three HTTP header fields that cannot appear in a chunked trailer: Transfer-Encoding, Content-Length, and Trailer. These fields, therefore, cannot appear in the Trailer header.

The following example shows a sample response with the Trailer header. The response uses the chunked transfer encoding, and the Trailer header lists Expires. As expected, the Expires "header" then appears after the message body.

```
HTTP/1.1 200 OK
Date: Fri, 31 Dec 1999 23:59:59 GMT
Content-Type: text/plain
Transfer-Encoding: chunked
Trailer: Expires

1a
ABCDEFGHIJKLMNOPQRSTUVWXYZ
0
Expires: Sat, 01 Jan 2000 23:59:50 GMT
```

3.2.46 Transfer-Encoding

The `Transfer-Encoding` header identifies the transfer encoding format of a message body. Although the HTTP 1.1 specifications define this header in a general way, current implementations use it almost exclusively to identity the chunked transfer encoding.

`Transfer-Encoding: chunked`

The developers of HTTP 1.1 created the chunked transfer encoding to improve the performance of HTTP servers. With this feature, servers can begin sending a response while they're composing it; without chunked encoding, on the other hand, they're forced to delay responding until the entire message is complete.

The issue arises because HTTP 1.1 servers must indicate the size of their response messages. That wasn't the case with earlier versions of HTTP. Before HTTP 1.1, servers could just send their response and then close the TCP connection. A client could tell that it had received the full response when the connection closed. With HTTP 1.1, though, persistent connections are the default behavior, and closing the connection after every response makes persistent connections impossible. Clients still need some way to know when they've received all of a message, however. The `Content-Length` header is the simplest solution to this problem. When the server includes a `Content-Length` header in a response, the client merely needs to count bytes to know when it has the complete response.

Although simple and easy to use, the `Content-Length` header introduces its own problem. As an HTTP header, `Content-Length` is one of the first parts of a response. In particular, it precedes the message body. But before a server can calculate the value for `Content-Length`, it must know the full size of the message body. This restriction means that before a server can begin sending a response, it must compose the full message body and calculate its size. When the message body is large, and when the server constructs the message dynamically, the resulting delay can significantly degrade the server's performance.

A more efficient approach would allow the server to begin sending its response as soon as it began composing the message body. As the server creates additional parts of the response message, it immediately sends them to the client. This approach is exactly what chunked transfer enables.

With chunked transfer encoding, the server divides the message body into one or more *chunks*. In its response, the server sends each of these chunks, one after the other. Each chunk is preceded by a line that indicates the chunk size in hexadecimal. The last chunk has a size of zero bytes. Here is an example of a response message with three chunks. (The third chunk has a size of 0, so only the first two chunks contain any content.) The total size of the message body is 36 bytes. (The first chunk is $1A_{16}$, or 26 bytes; the second adds $0A_{16}$, or 10, more.)

```
HTTP/1.1 200 OK
Date: Fri, 31 Dec 1999 23:59:59 GMT
Content-Type: text/plain
Transfer-Encoding: chunked

1a
ABCDEFGHIJKLMNOPQRSTUVWXYZ
0a
0123456789
0
```

For comparison, here is how the same message body could be conveyed without chunked transfer encoding.

```
HTTP/1.1 200 OK
Date: Fri, 31 Dec 1999 23:59:59 GMT
Content-Type: text/plain
Content-Length: 36

ABCDEFGHIJKLMNOPQRSTUVWXYZ0123456789
```

3.2.47 Upgrade

The Upgrade header lets a client and server gracefully negotiate an upgrade to a different communications protocol. The
new protocol may be a newer version of HTTP or a completely different protocol such as Transport Layer Security.
(Section 4.3.3 describes how TLS can use Upgrade.) The client proposes the protocol upgrade by including an Upgrade
header in its request.

```
GET http://www.bank.com/acct.html?749394889300
HTTP/1.1
Host: www.bank.com
Upgrade: TLS/1.0
Connection: Upgrade
```

The server can respond to this request with a 101 Switching Protocols status, and it includes its own Upgrade
header.

```
HTTP/1.1 101 Switching Protocols
Upgrade: TLS/1.0, HTTP/1.1
Connection: Upgrade
```

Notice that both the request and response also include the
Connection: Upgrade header. This header must always appear when Upgrade is used because any upgrade applies only
to the immediate connection between the client and the first
server. If a client wants to upgrade its communications with
an origin server, it can use the CONNECT method to establish a
virtual connection with that server and then upgrade that
virtual connection.

The example also shows that the 101 Switching
Protocols response lists a series of protocols in the Upgrade
header. In that response, the server indicates that it is up-
grading to HTTP 1.1 over TLS 1.0.

3.2.48 User-Agent

The User-Agent header is the client's version of the Server
header. With User-Agent, a client identifies the specific

HTTP implementation it is using. For example, the following is how Netscape Navigator on an Apple Macintosh identifies itself.

```
User-Agent: Mozilla/4.x (Macintosh)
```

The Web site http://browserwatch.internet.com keeps track of the different client implementations accessing its pages. Recently, it had detected 213 variations of Microsoft's Internet Explorer, 65 variations of Netscape's Navigator, and 510 other HTTP clients.

3.2.49 Vary

With the Vary header origin servers give proxy servers extra guidance in the management of their local caches. The Vary header lists other HTTP headers that, in addition to the URI, determine which resource the server returns in its response. For example, some origin servers may return different resources depending on the User-Agent value in the client's request. (They may have one page optimized for Microsoft's Internet Explorer and a different page for Netscape Navigator.) In such cases the server should include a Vary header in its response.

```
HTTP/1.1 200 OK
Date: Fri, 31 Dec 1999 23:59:59 GMT
Content-Type: text/html
Vary: User-Agent


...
```

A proxy server will then know that it can return a cached copy of this response to subsequent requests, but only if those requests have the same User-Agent value as the original request. A different User-Agent value forces the cache to query the origin server again.

An asterisk as the value for the Vary header indicates that parameters other than HTTP headers also influenced the content of the response, effectively marking the response as not cachable.

3.2.50 Via

The Via header traces the path of a message as it travels through proxy servers. The HTTP specifications require that every intermediate server that handles a request or response identify itself with a Via header before forwarding the message. A proxy can add its own Via header or simply build on an existing one. Figure 3.27 shows how the Via header grows as a request travels from client to origin server.

The first proxy server creates a Via header and adds its own identity as the value. (Although the figure shows this identity as proxyA, the server would normally use a full domain name.) The 1.1 that precedes the server name is the HTTP version that was in force when the server received the request. When the request passes through proxy B, that proxy doesn't add a completely new Via header (though it could do so if desired). Instead, it simply appends its own name to the existing Via header. Proxy B also includes an HTTP version immediately before its name.

It is important that proxy servers create or adjust the Via header before they perform any other processing of the message. For example, a proxy may receive a TRACE request with Max-Forwards of 0, indicating that the proxy cannot forward the request any further. That is the case for proxy B in figure 3.28. Before proxy B responds to the TRACE request, however, it must insert its identity in the Via header. After doing so, it generates the response of step 3. Only by adjusting the Via

Figure 3.27 ▶
The Via header records the path of an HTTP message as it travels through a network of proxy servers. The servers also indicate the HTTP version under which they accepted the message.

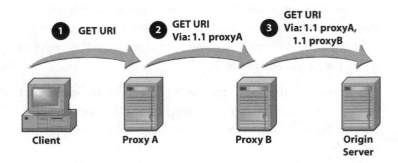

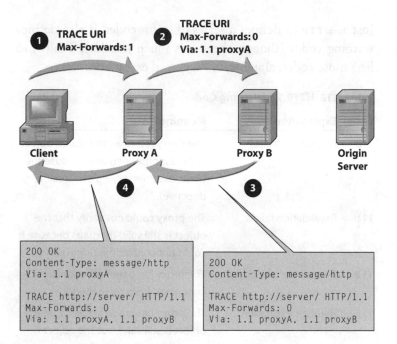

◀ **Figure 3.28**
A client can discover the path its messages are taking looking for Via headers in a TRACE response message. Note that proxy B updates the Via header, by inserting its own identity, before it responds to the request.

header before processing the request is proxy B able to ensure that its identity appears in the TRACE response.

3.2.51 Warning

The Warning header carries additional information about a response, usually intended to alert the user to potential cache problems. Its format is as follows, though the date is optional. A Warning header may include many individual warnings, each separated by a comma.

```
Warning: 110 proxy.com "Response is stale"
         Fri, 31 Dec 1999 23:59:59 GMT
```

The first field is a warning code, and the next field identifies the server that created the warning. The quoted string is a natural language explanation of the warning, appropriate for human users. The optional final field carries the time of the warning.

Just as HTTP 1.1 defines a series of status codes, it also defines warning codes (though the list is much smaller). Table 3.10 lists those codes, along with suggested explanation text.

Table 3.10 HTTP 1.1 Warning Codes

Code	Explanation	Meaning
110	Response is stale	The proxy returned an expired object in its response (perhaps because the client used the `max-stale` cache directive).
111	Revalidation failed	The proxy could not verify that the object is still valid (perhaps because it could not contact the origin server).
112	Disconnection operation	The proxy has been intentionally disconnected from the network.
113	Heuristic expiration	The proxy has made a guess that the object is still valid, but the object is more than 24 hours old.
199	Miscellaneous warning	An arbitrary warning.
214	Transformation applied	The proxy has modified the object in some way (perhaps by changing its image format to save cache space).
299	Miscellaneous persistent warning	An arbitrary warning that may continue to recur.

When a proxy receives a `Warning` header with a date that differs from the `Date` header in the response, the proxy deletes that particular warning from the header. If that leaves the `Warning` header with no warnings, the proxy also removes the `Warning` header. This behavior ensures that warnings are not propagated inappropriately through a network of cache servers. Without it, an object might get "stuck" with an inappropriate warning.

3.2.52 WWW-Authenticate

The `WWW-Authenticate` header lets origin servers authenticate a client. By including this header in a response (usually one with a `401 Unauthorized` status), the server asks the client to reissue the request but to include its authorization credentials. The subject of HTTP authentication is worthy of its own chapter, and indeed, it is the topic of section 4.1, which examines `WWW-Authenticate` in detail.

3.3 Status Codes

As we've seen in many examples, an important part of every HTTP response is the status code. That code defines whether a client's request succeeded and can provide additional information about the request's outcome. Every status code value is a three-digit number, and the HTTP specification classifies status codes based on the first digit of these values. Status codes provide information (100-199), indicate success (200-299), redirect a client (300-399), indicate a client error (400-499), or indicate a server problem (500-599). In each class, the x00 status code is the master status for the class. If a client receives a status code value that it does not understand, it can safely treat it the same as it would treat the x00 value in the class. For example, a status code value of `237` should be treated the same as `200`.

Table 3.11 provides a complete list of all status codes that HTTP defines, grouped by their class. We'll look at each code in more detail throughout this section.

Table 3.11 HTTP Status Codes

Class	Code	Description
1xx		Informational
	100	Continue
	101	Switching Protocols
2xx		Successful
	200	OK
	201	Created
	202	Accepted

continues...

Table 3.11 HTTP Status Codes (continued)

Class	Code	Description
	203	Non-Authoritative Information
	204	No Content
	205	Reset Content
	206	Partial Content
3xx		Redirection
	300	Multiple Choices
	301	Moved Permanently
	302	Found
	303	See Other
	304	Not Modified
	305	Use Proxy
	306	(unused)
	307	Temporary Redirect
4xx		Client Error
	400	Bad Request
	401	Unauthorized
	402	Payment Required
	403	Forbidden
	404	Not Found
	405	Method Not Allowed
	406	Not Acceptable
	407	Proxy Authentication Required
	408	Request Timeout
	409	Conflict
	410	Gone
	411	Length Required
	412	Precondition Failed
	413	Request Entity Too Large
	414	Request-URI Too Long
	415	Unsupported Media Type

Table 3.11 continued

Class	Code	Description
	416	Requested Range Not Satisfiable
	417	Expectation Failed
	426	Upgrade Required
5xx		Server Error
	500	Internal Server Error
	501	Not Implemented
	502	Bad Gateway
	503	Service Unavailable
	504	Gateway Timeout
	505	Version Not Supported

3.3.1 Informational (1xx)

Status codes in the range from 100 to 199 are provisional. They give the server a way to provide some feedback to the client, even though the server hasn't yet finished its response.

`100 Continue`

The `100 Continue` status code is part of a process that lets clients "test the waters" with a server. This ability may be important, for example, if the client has a large message body and it wants to make sure the server can accept it before going to the trouble of sending it. There may also be circumstances in which it might be inappropriate to send the message body without knowing the server can receive it.

As an example, suppose a client has a large file that it wants to `PUT` to a server. The client may be able to use the continuation mechanism to avoid wasting network resources. To do that, the client begins its request with normal HTTP message headers. To trigger continuation, it includes the `Expect: 100-continue` header in that message. Importantly, though, the client does not (yet) send the message body. This is step 1 in figure 3.29.

Figure 3.29 ▶

Clients can ask a server to accept a request before they send the entire message body. The Expect header asks the server to signal its acceptance by returning a 100 status. Once the client receives a 100 status, it continues by sending the rest of the request.

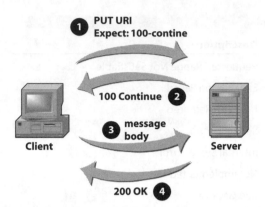

If, after seeing the request's headers, the server decides that it can accept the request, the server responds with a 100 Continue status, as in step 2. This interim response tells the client to proceed with its request, so it sends the message body in step 3. The server completes the exchange with the 200 OK response of step 4.

If, in step 2, the server realizes that it cannot accept the request, it responds with a different status code. A server might require authentication (necessitating a 401 Unauthorized response), or, after seeing the Content-Length value, the server might recognize that it doesn't have sufficient disk space to store the object (413 Request Entity Too Large).

In order to cope with servers that don't fully support the continuation mechanism, any client that sends an Expect: 100-continue header should not wait indefinitely for a 100 Continue response. If the server has not responded at all after some reasonable period of time, the client should proceed with its request anyway.

101 Switching Protocols

Servers use the 101 Switching Protocols response to accept a client's request to upgrade protocols. In figure 3.30, for example, the client requests an upgrade to Transport Layer Security by including the Upgrade: TLS/1.0 header in its

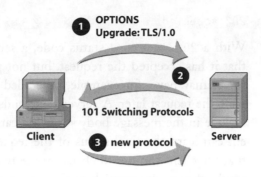

◀ **Figure 3.30**
The 101 status indicates that the sender is going to change protocols. The client should being using the new protocol as soon as it receives the 101 response.

request. The server accepts the upgrade in step 2 with a 101 Switching Protocols interim status, and, in step 3, the exchange continues using the new protocol.

3.3.2 Successful (2xx)

Status codes that begin with a 2 represent success. With these responses, the server tells the client that its request was received, understood, and accepted.

200 OK

The 200 OK status code is the most basic HTTP response. It simply says that the client's request succeeded. Depending on the request method, the response is likely to include additional information. For example, in responding successfully to a GET request, the server includes the requested resource in the message body. With a HEAD request, however, the server returns only the response headers, including any entity headers that would apply to the requested resource; the message body itself, however, is omitted.

201 Created

Servers reply with a 201 Created status when a successful request results in the creation of a new resource. The Location header in the response provides a definitive URI for the new resource, but the server may include other representations of the resource or its location in the response's message body.

202 Accepted

With a `202 Accepted` status code, a server tells the client that it has accepted the request, but not yet fulfilled it. The server may have, for example, scheduled a process to complete the request later. A server that sends this response may include in the message body some indication of how the client can learn the final status of the request. If there's a URI that the client can use to check on the request status, for example, the server may include that URI in the response.

203 Non-Authoritative Information

The `203 Non-Authoritative Information` status code indicates that some of the response's headers may not be definitive. They may have, instead, been created by an intermediate server. The message body itself, however, is completely valid.

204 No Content

The `204 No Content` status indicates that the server accepted the request, but it does not need to return any information to the client in response. This type of response is valuable in many dynamic and interactive Web sessions. Consider figure 3.31, for example, which shows a browser-based user interface for a telecommunications server. The mouse pointer is hovering over a checkbox (in the bottom left of the screen) that lets the user disable automatic updating of the display.

If the user clicks on the checkbox, the browser may need to send an HTTP request to the server, and the most likely candidate is a `GET` or `POST` method. Normally, however, a server would respond to a `GET` or `POST` request by sending the indicated resource, and the browser accepts the resource and displays it for the user. In this case the user should see the same page after clicking the checkbox, only the checkbox state will now be disabled. But that means that the server must send the entire Web page again, including its complex tables and graphic images. That's neither necessary (because the

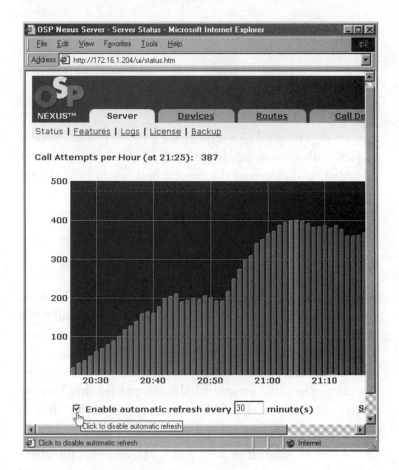

◀ **Figure 3.31**
If a server just needs to acknowledge a client's request without actually sending the client new information, it can return a 204 status. In this example the browser already has all the information it needs to update the display if the user clicks the checkbox; a 204 response avoids having to send the full Web page again.

browser already has all the information it needs to display the page) nor efficient.

A better approach would have the server respond to the request with a `204 No Content` status. That tells the client that its request was successful, but there is no new information available. The browser can continue to display the existing Web page (though with a new checkbox status), saving time, bandwidth, and server resources.

205 Reset Content

The `205 Reset Content` status is similar to the `204 No Content`. In both cases the response does not contain any message body. With a `205 Reset Content`, however, the server directs the client to reset the document view that generated the request. Typically that's equivalent to the user clicking a Reset button on a Web form.

206 Partial Content

Servers that respond to a request for a subset of a resource (a request with a `Range` header) use the `206 Partial Content` status when they accept the request and return only the requested subset. The response also includes a `Content-Range` header to identify which parts of the resource are present in the response's message.

3.3.3 Redirection (3xx)

Status codes from 300 to 399 tell the client that it needs to take further action to fulfill its request. Specifically, the server asks the client to reissue its request, but for a different URI. If there is only one alternative location available, or if the server has a preference for one particular location among the alternatives, the server includes the URI for that location in the `Location` header. Other alternatives may be listed in the message body.

If the client's original request was a `GET` or `HEAD`, the client can safely reissue the request to the indicated URI automatically, without consulting the user. With other requests, however, there may be security implications, and the client should first ask permission from the user.

300 Multiple Choices

The `300 Multiple Choices` status gives the client a list of alternative locations for the request. The server provides these in the response's message body, and it may include one in a `Location` header.

301 Moved Permanently

When a resource's URI has changed permanently, the server may respond with a `301 Moved Permanently` status. The client (and any proxies) should, henceforth, use the indicated URI for all future references to the resource. All of the other 3xx status codes represent temporary conditions.

302 Found

The 302 Found status indicates that the resource has temporarily moved to a new location, and the client should reissue its request to the new URI. In practice, many clients that receive a 302 Found status will send a GET request to the new URI, even if the original request used another method. This behavior actually violates the HTTP specifications, but it is so common that servers should take it into account. With version 1.1, HTTP introduced the 303 See Other and 307 Temporary Redirect status codes to address this problem.

303 See Other

The 303 See Other status is the HTTP specification's way of properly asking clients to do what many already do in reaction to a 302 Found response—send a GET request to the indicated URI. The 303 See Other status is intended primarily as a response to a POST request. After the client issues the POST, this response tells it where to get the next resource to display for the user. Consequently, the location indicated by a 303 See Other status is not a new location for the original resource. It is, rather, a reference to an entirely new resource.

304 Not Modified

If a request includes a condition (such as an If-Match or If-Modified-Since header) and that condition is not met, the server responds with a 304 Not Modified status. Typically this allows the client (or proxy server that forwarded the request) to use a cached copy of the resource.

305 Use Proxy

The 305 Use Proxy status asks the client to reissue the request to a proxy server. Only origin servers should generate this status, and the status applies only to the initial request.

`307 Temporary Redirect`

The `307 Temporary Redirect` status officially means the same as a `302 Found` status: The resource has temporarily moved to a new location, and the client should reissue its request there. In particular, the client should use the same request method. As noted previously, HTTP 1.1 added this status code because so many clients react improperly to the `302 Found` status.

3.3.4 Client Error (4xx)

If a server encounters a problem with a client's request, it can use one of the `4xx` status codes in its response. The specific status code may provide more information about the problem the server detected.

`400 Bad Request`

The standard status code for client errors is `400 Bad Request`. This response indicates that the server did not understand the request, perhaps because there is an error in its formatting. The client should not reissue the same request, as it will be rejected as well.

`401 Unauthorized`

The `401 Unauthorized` status code tells the client that the server requires user authentication before granting access to the resource. The server includes a `WWW-Authenticate` header in its response to give the client guidance on the type of authentication it requires. As section 4.1 explains, clients react to this status by reissuing the request with an appropriate `Authorization` header.

`402 Payment Required`

Although the HTTP specifications define this status code, it is currently just reserved for future use. Of course, its meaning is fairly self-explanatory. It is much less clear, however, how a client should react to receiving it.

403 Forbidden

A client that receives a 403 Forbidden status code has attempted to access a resource that cannot be accessed. Unlike the case for a 401 Unauthorized status code, no Authorization header will grant the client access. Servers should note that by returning a 403 Forbidden response, they imply that the requested resource does, in fact, exist. If revealing this information is not appropriate, the server can use a 404 Not Found status code instead.

404 Not Found

The 404 Not Found status code indicates that the requested resource does not exist. It does not give any information about whether this condition is permanent or temporary. If a server wishes to explicitly indicate a permanent condition, it may use the 410 Gone status instead.

405 Method Not Allowed

The 405 Method Not Allowed status tells the client that the method it used is not permitted with the referenced resource. Servers include an Allow header in their response to tell clients what methods are permitted.

406 Not Acceptable

When a server returns a 406 Not Acceptable status, the client's request can generate only responses that the client has indicated are not acceptable. The message body of the response may indicate the entity characteristics that the request can generate. This status should appear only in response to requests with Accept, Accept-Charset, Accept-Encoding, or Accept-Language headers.

407 Proxy Authentication Required

The 407 Proxy Authentication Required tells a client that it must authenticate itself with a proxy server before its request can proceed. The proxy server that generates this response includes a Proxy-Authenticate header to guide the client in providing an appropriate Proxy-Authorization header in its reissued request.

408 Request Timeout

With the 408 Request Timeout status, a server indicates that it has timed out waiting for a request from the client.

409 Conflict

The 409 Conflict status indicates that the server could not complete the request because of a conflict with the current state of the resource. This conflict could arise, for example, when a PUT request includes changes to a resource that would conflict with changes already accepted by a third party.

410 Gone

The 410 Gone status indicates that a resource is no longer available. This condition should be considered permanent.

411 Length Required

When a server returns a 411 Length Required status, it refuses to accept a request unless the client reissues the request with a valid Content-Length header.

412 Precondition Failed

The 412 Precondition Failed status indicates that one of the conditions the client included in its request (through, for example, an If-Match header) did not apply.

413 Request Entity Too Large

The 413 Request Entity Too Large status indicates that the message body of a request was larger than the server could accept. If the server expects this condition to be temporary, it can include a Retry-After header in its response.

414 Request-URI Too Long

If a client includes a URI in its request that is longer than the server is willing to interpret, the server can respond with a 414 Request-URI Too Large status.

415 Unsupported Media Type

By returning a `415 Unsupported Media Type` status, a server indicates that it cannot understand the media type of the request's message body.

416 Requested Range Not Satisfiable

When a client asks for a range of a resource (with the `Range` header) and the range is not valid, the server responds with a `416 Requested Range Not Satisfiable` status.

417 Expectation Failed

If a server cannot meet a client's expectations as conveyed in a request's `Expect` header, it returns a `417 Expectation Failed` status.

426 Upgrade Required

The `426 Upgrade Required` status lets a server tell a client that it must upgrade the application it's using for the request. A server that wanted to force its client to upgrade to Transport Level Security (TLS), for example, would return this status along with an `Upgrade` header identifying TLS as the required application upgrade.

3.3.5 Server Error (5xx)

In contrast to the `4xx` status codes, which point to a client problem, the `5xx` status codes indicate a problem on the server.

500 Internal Server Error

The `500 Internal Server Error` status is a general indication of a server problem. If the server can provide further details, it may do so in the response's message body.

501 Not Implemented

The `501 Not Implemented` status indicates that the server does not support the request's method for any resource, not just the resource requested.

502 Bad Gateway

If a proxy server receives an invalid response from the server to whom it forwarded a request, it responds to the client with a 502 Bad Gateway status.

503 Service Unavailable

The 503 Service Unavailable status indicates that the server is temporarily unable to satisfy the request, perhaps because the server is currently overloaded or undergoing maintenance. The server may include a Retry-After header in its response if it anticipates that the problem will be corrected by that time.

504 Gateway Timeout

When a proxy server times out waiting for a response from another server, it returns a 504 Gateway Timeout status to the client.

505 Version Not Supported

The 505 Version Not Supported status indicates that the server cannot support the HTTP version identified in the client's request.

CHAPTER 4

Securing HTTP — Adding Authentication & Privacy

If the World Wide Web were nothing more than a linked collection of static information, then securing the Web's protocols would be less important. With the growth of electronic commerce and the extension of HTTP to critical environments outside of the Web, however, adding security to HTTP is critical for many applications. Security allows the communicating parties to verify each other's identity, to ensure the privacy of their communication, and to protect their messages from modification or corruption.

This chapter looks at the various ways to add security to HTTP. The first section, Web Authentication, details the procedures built into HTTP 1.1. The second section introduces the Secure Sockets Layer (SSL) protocol. By far the most common way of providing security on the Web, SSL is a separate protocol that adds security to many applications. It was designed, however, especially for HTTP. The Transport Layer Security (TLS) protocol is the most recent revision of SSL. It is very similar to SSL, but it includes a few additional features tailored for HTTP communications. Finally, the chapter takes a brief look at Secure-HTTP (SHTTP). Originally developed about the same time as SSL, SHTTP defines extensions directly to the HTTP protocol for security. SHTTP has largely been supplanted by SSL in actual operation, but a few implementations still exist.

4.1 Web Authentication

Although some sections of this chapter discusses securing HTTP using additional protocols or extensions, HTTP includes its own security mechanisms. The HTTP security mechanisms are not as formidable as other approaches, but they are sufficiently secure for many applications.

The security mechanisms built into HTTP rely on user passwords for their security. That makes them relatively simple, but it is also the source of their weakness. User passwords are notoriously insecure, as human users often select passwords that are easy for adversaries to guess. Humans can also be rather careless about their passwords, reusing the same password for many systems, leaving passwords on a sticky note attached to their monitor, or revealing those passwords to an adversary posing as an administrator or other employee of a system.

4.1.1 Basic Authentication

The simplest form of HTTP security is basic authentication. It allows a server to request a username and password from a client, and it defines how the client should send that information to the server. Figure 4.1 shows the process. The client first sends its HTTP request as usual. For its reply, however, the server responds with a status code of 401 Unauthorized. This status code tells the client that it must supply a username and password.

The 401 Unauthorized response includes the WWW-Authenticate header, and for basic authentication the

---

Caution:
Basic Authentication

Even though HTTP 1.1 defines the Basic Authentication mechanism, it does so very reluctantly. As we'll see in this section, the security Basic Authentication offers is extremely weak security. Many, in fact, have argued that it is better to use no security at all than to rely on Basic Authentication. We cover it in this text because it is part of the specification, however, and because there are implementations that do use it. When given a choice, however, this author, along with the authors of the HTTP standard, strongly recommends against using Basic Authentication in any application.

◀ **Figure 4.1**
When a server wants a client to authenticate its user, the server returns a 401 status. The client can then reissue the request with appropriate information included in the Authorization header.

header includes the challenge "Basic," as well as a value for the challenge's realm. One possible response from a server is as follows.

```
HTTP/1.1 401 Unauthorized
WWW-Authenticate: Basic
     realm="users@hundredacrewoods.com"
```

The server can choose any value it wants for the realm, but in Web browsing it is typical to use a value that human users can understand. That's because Web browsers typically display the realm for the user when asking for the username and password. Figure 4.2 shows how a browser might query a user.

Once the user supplies a username and password, the client can continue the communication with step 3 of figure 4.1. In

◀ **Figure 4.2**
Web browsers ask their users for authentication with a pop-up window like this. HTTP authorization is never part of a Web page itself, unlike the SSL-secured server authorization of figure 4.3.

that step it reissues the original request. This time, though, the client includes the `Authorization` header in its request. The `Authorization` header contains the username and password the user provides.

To provide the username and password, the client combines the two, separated by a colon (:), and encodes them according to the rules for Base64 encoding. By using the colon to separate usernames from passwords, HTTP prohibits the username from itself containing a password. (Otherwise, the server would not be able to tell where the username ended and the password began.)

Base64 encoding is a way to convert binary data and encode it using only the normal, printable characters. It was originally developed as a way to send email attachments. By encoding the username and password using Base64, HTTP allows passwords to contain any arbitrary characters, not just those that are printable. The HTTP specification does loosen one restriction on standard Base64 encoding. Strict Base64 encoding requires a new line at least every 76 characters. In this case the encoded credentials must fit on a single line of text, no matter its length. Once a client has encoded the user's credentials, it can construct a request such as the following example.

```
GET /secret/honeypot.html HTTP/1.1
Authorization: Basic QwxhZGRpbjpvcGVuIHNlc2FtZQ==
```

When the server sees a valid username and password, it can finally return the requested object. Figure 4.1 shows that in step 4.

After an HTTP client successfully retrieves an object using Basic Authentication, the client may continue to include the `Authorization` header on subsequent requests to the same URI or to child URIs. Doing so avoids the delay of forcing the server to return more `401 Unauthorized` responses to prompt for the authorization information.

One of the more significant problems with Basic Authentication is that the username and password travel completely exposed across the network. Any intermediate party that can intercept or eavesdrop on the communication can recover the username and password. Because many public networks comprise the Internet, this vulnerability is a substantial one, and the HTTP specification recommends that it be used only when the application's security requirements are extremely minimal. The specification further cautions that, even if the information being secured is relatively unimportant, server administrators should consider a broader context when deciding to use Basic Authentication. Many human users, for example, reuse the same username and password for many different systems. An adversary that intercepts a username and password from a relatively insecure Web site may be able to use that same combination for other, more valuable, sites.

To address the lack of real security in HTTP's Basic Authentication, many Web sites create their own login process. Figure 4.3 shows one such Web site. Here users are asked for their name and password via a Web form rather than HTTP authentication. Even though HTTP is used to convey the form to the user and, via a POST method, return the user's response, HTTP itself has no knowledge that an authentication process is active. As far as HTTP is concerned, it is simply performing standard GET and POST actions. Note also the padlock icon in the extreme lower left corner of the browser's window. That icon indicates that the data the user sends to the Web site will be encrypted using the facilities of the Secure Sockets Layer (SSL) or Transport Layer Security (TLS) protocol, both of which we'll meet later in this chapter. With this protection usernames and passwords are immune to interception and eavesdropping.

4.1.2 Original Digest Authentication

Digest Authentication addresses the major weaknesses of Basic Authentication, namely that usernames and passwords

Figure 4.3 ▶

Figure 4.3 ▶
Some Web sites manage usernames
and passwords themselves rather
than relying on HTTP
authentication. As this example
shows, users input their
authentication information to such
sites via a standard Web page
rather than a browser's pop-up
dialog box.

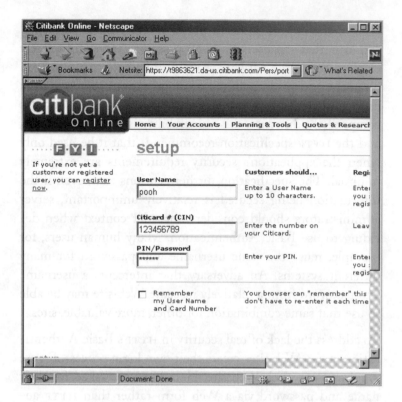

are vulnerable to interception. The Digest Authentication process was initially defined as an extension to HTTP version 1.0. An improved version has been developed as an extension to HTTP version 1.1. Because the Digest Authentication procedures are defined in separate specifications, however, it is possible to use the original version even in HTTP 1.1 implementations. For that reason, it is important to understand both versions. In this subsection we focus on the initial version, what we've called "Original Digest Authentication." Later subsections explore the enhancements available with the latest Digest Authentication procedures. Collectively, we call those procedures "Improved Digest Authentication."

Digest Authentication uses simple cryptographic principles to avoid transmitting passwords across the network. Instead, clients prove to the server that they know their passwords without actually sending them to the server.

To prove knowledge of a password, clients create a *message digest* (also known as *secure hash*) using the password and a value supplied by the server. They then transfer the digest to the server. The server verifies the password by duplicating this calculation. It takes a known value, combines it with the password it expects the client to use, and calculates a message digest. If the server's calculation matches the client's, then the server can believe the client knows the correct password. Figure 4.4 illustrates the process.

For message digests, the server's choice of data to be combined with the password is critical to the overall security. Most importantly, the server must choose a different data value each time. Otherwise an adversary eavesdropping on the communication could simply reuse a digest value and impersonate the client. (If neither the data nor the password change, then the digest value remains the same as well.)

In the case of HTTP, the server begins the Digest Authentication process with a `401 Unauthorized` response, just as with Basic Authentication. The `WWW-Authenticate` header, however, explicitly requests Digest Authentication. The simplest possible case follows.

> **Message Digest Algorithms**
>
> Message digest algorithms are based on mathematical operations known as *one-way functions*. A one-way function is a mathematical transformation that is relatively easy to perform, but extremely difficult to reverse. It is easy for a computer to start with a password and other information and calculate a message digest, but it is mathematically impossible, given just the resulting digest, to figure out the password and information used to create it.
>
> Today there are two common message digest algorithms. One is Message Digest 5 (MD5), created by Ron Rivest. Another common algorithm is the Secure Hash Algorithm (SHA), developed by the U.S. National Institute of Standards and Technology.

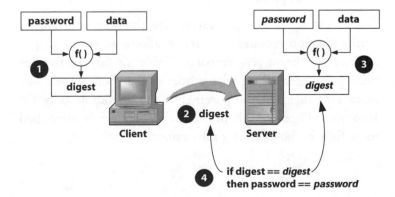

◀ **Figure 4.4**
Both clients and servers compute message digest values. If the two calculations match, then both parties have the same password.

```
HTTP/1.1 401 Unauthorized
WWW-Authenticate: Digest
    realm="users@hundredacrewoods.com",
    nonce="dcd98bc09f81043d3a8cb935ae393db90674"
```

As the example shows, Digest Authentication requires more parameters than Basic Authentication. Digest Authentication also requires the nonce parameter. The value of this parameter is the data that the client combines with its password when creating the digest. Servers are free to use this value any way they see fit, but the HTTP specification suggests one particular strategy. For GET requests, it suggests that the nonce be composed of a timestamp and a message digest of three quantities: the timestamp, the ETag being requested, and a secret value known only to the server. The timestamp lets the server assign the nonce a limited lifetime; the ETag value protects against an adversary replaying a client's request to gain access to an updated value of the requested object, and the secret value ensures that adversaries cannot predict the value of the nonce in advance. This approach lets clients reissue requests without triggering a new 401 Unauthorized response and the resulting recalculation of digest values. Because the server is able to see the timestamp in the nonce, it can tell how old the nonce is and accept any repeated requests within an appropriate time window. For POST and PUT requests, the HTTP specification suggests using one-time nonces that expressly prohibit reissuing the request.

The realm and nonce parameters are the only ones Digest Authentication requires, but HTTP allows a few more parameters in the server's response. Table 4.1 lists all the defined parameters, along with a brief explanation of their use. Note that many of the parameters are applicable only for Improved Digest Authentication. Their use is described more fully in the following subsections.

Caution:
Original Digest Authentication

The digest authentication process described in this section, which we've called "Original Digest Authentication," is a procedure that HTTP 1.1 defines only for compatibility with older versions of the standard. Newer implementations are encouraged to use Improved Digest Authentication procedures.

Table 4.1 WWW-Authenticate Parameters

Parameter	Improved	Required	Use
algorithm	MD5-sess	No	The specific digest algorithm to use; either "MD5" (the default) or "MD5-sess"; if the qop parameter is absent, this parameter must either be absent or "MD5."
domain	No	No	A list of URIs (separated by spaces) that identify the resources for which this authentication applies.
nonce	No	Yes	The data to be combined with the password in generating the digest.
opaque	No	No	An arbitrary value supplied by the server that the client should return, unmodified, with its request; may be used by the server to assist in processing the request.
qop	Yes	No	The quality of protection; either digest authentication ("auth") or digest authentication with integrity protection ("auth-int"); the presence of this parameter triggers advanced digest authentication (see subsection 4.1.3).
realm	No	Yes	A character string to be displayed to human users to help them identify which username and password to supply.
stale	No	No	A flag that, if it has the value "true," indicates that the supplied username and password are apparently valid (as far as the server is concerned) but the authenticated request relied on a nonce that the server no longer considers valid; indicates to the client that it can recalculate the digest using a new nonce without querying the human user for username and password.

Representing Digest Values

The result of a digest calculation is a binary value. (In the case of MD5, that value is 128 bits in size.) Parameters for HTTP messages, however, are conveniently represented as printable ASCII characters. To convert from binary to ASCII, implementations use a hexadecimal expression. Every four bits in the binary value, beginning with the most significant, are expressed as a character from the sets "0" to "9" and "a" to "f."

When the client receives a Digest Authentication response from a server, it computes the message digest to add to its next message. Table 4.2 shows the procedure for Original Digest Authentication, which must be used when the server omits a qop parameter from its response. In such cases the clients are communicating with a server relying on an older version of the HTTP specification. If the qop parameter is present then, regardless of its value, the rules of Improved Digest Authentication apply.

Table 4.2 Client Calculation for Digest Authentication

Step	Action
1	Construct a character string consisting of the username, realm, and the user's password, each item separated by a colon. `pooh:users@hundredacrewoods.com:honey`, for example. (The specification calls this string "A1.")
2	Calculate the MD5 digest for this character string and represent the 128-bit binary result in hexadecimal as 32 ASCII characters from "0" to "9" and "a" to "f." (See box.)
3	Construct a second character string consisting of the method (e.g., `GET`, `POST`, etc.) and the URI, again separated by colons. For example, `GET:/secret/honeypot.html`. (The specification calls this string "A2.")
4	Calculate the MD5 digest for this character string and represent the result as 32 ASCII characters.
5	Construct a character string by combining the result from step 2, the nonce supplied by the server, and the result from step 4, all separated by colons (:).
6	Calculate the MD5 digest for the character string obtained in step 5 and represent the result as 32 ASCII characters. This value is the digest.

With the digest calculation complete, the client is now able to reissue its request with appropriate authorization information. One possible message is shown in the following.

```
GET /secret/honeypot.html HTTP/1.1
Authorization: Digest username="pooh",
   realm="users@hundredacrewoods.com",
   nonce="dcd98bc09f81043d3a8cb935ae393db90674",
   uri="/secret/honeypot.html",
   response="dcd98bc09f81043d3a8cb935ae393db90674"
```

The reissued request repeats the `realm` and `nonce` from the server, and it includes the username, the URI being requested (in case a proxy server has modified the `GET` request's URI in transit), and the digest result, which appears as the value for the `response` parameter. These parameters are the only ones required in the client's response, but HTTP defines several optional parameters. Table 4.3 provides the complete list. As with `WWW-Authenticate`, note that some of the parameters are appropriate only for Improved Digest Authentication.

Table 4.3 Authorization Parameters

Parameter	Improved	Required	Use
algorithm	MD5-sess	No	The specific digest algorithm used; either "MD5" (the default) or "MD5-sess"; if the qop parameter is not included, this parameter must either be absent or "MD5."
cnonce	Yes	No	A nonce value created by the client that triggers mutual authentication (see subsection 4.1.5); note that the client must include this parameter if the server explicitly indicated a qop parameter.
nc	Yes	Yes	The number of times the client has issued a request with the same nonce value; this is expressed in hexadecimal and begins at "00000001"; note that the client must include this parameter if the server explicitly indicated a qop parameter.

continues…

Table 4.3 Authorization Parameters (continued)

Parameter	Improved	Required	Use
nonce	No	Yes	The nonce value from the server's original response.
opaque	No	No	The opaque value originally sent by the server.
qop	Yes	No	The quality of protection used by the client; this can be returned only if the server explicitly specified one or more qop values in its original response, in which case the client's value must be chosen from among those the server listed.
realm	No	Yes	The realm defined by the server.
response	No	Yes	The result of the digest calculation.
uri	No	Yes	The URI for the object the client is requesting; note that the HTTP specification indicates that values for this parameter should not be enclosed in quotation marks, though all examples in the specification (as well as most implementations) do use quotation marks.
username	No	Yes	The username for the client.

When the server verifies the digest of the client's request, the Simple Digest Authentication process is normally complete. There is, however, one more optional step. The server may, if it chooses, add a header to its response. That header is the `Authentication-Info` header. Practically speaking, `Authentication-Info` is practical only with Improved Digest Authentication, so we'll cover it more completely in subsection 4.1.3. One parameter, however, may be used with Original Digest Authentication. That parameter is `nextnonce`, and it is intended to give the server a way to tell the client a new nonce value to use for subsequent requests.

Table 4.4 Authentication-Info Parameters

Parameter	Improved	Required	Use
cnonce	Yes	No	The cnonce value in the client's request; this parameter must be present if a qop value is specified.
nc	Yes	No	The nc value in the client's request; this parameter must be present if a qop value is specified.
nextnonce	No	Yes (but see text)	A nonce value that the server wishes the client to use on its next request.
qop	Yes	No	The quality of protection used by the client.
rspauth	Yes	No	The result of the server's digest calculation; this parameter must be present if a qop value is specified.

As the table indicates, the `Authorization-Info` header requires a `nextnonce` parameter. Unfortunately, although servers could reasonably use `nextnonce` with HTTP 1.0, the performance enhancements of HTTP 1.1 strongly discourage its use. The problem is that `nextnonce` interferes with pipelining. Recall that pipelining allows a client to construct and send one request before it receives a response to a previous request. If, however, when the response finally arrives it contains a new `nextnonce` value, the client's efforts in constructing the new request will have gone to naught, as they would have necessarily used a (now) outdated nonce value. The client will have to redo that work using the new nonce.

The main advantage to `nextnonce` is that it allows servers to change the nonce value frequently, conceivably with every request. Frequent changes to the nonce do improve security, and they can protect against replay attacks. The Improved Digest Authentication procedures, however, define better solutions to both problems, and they should be used instead of `nextnonce` whenever possible. That still leaves the problem of what the server should do with the parameter. The practical approach, and one that avoids violating the Digest Authentication specification, is to always include the `nextnonce` parameter, but not to change its value.

4.1.3 Improved Digest Authentication

The Original Digest Authentication specification was developed for version 1.0 of HTTP. With the release of HTTP 1.1, improvements to the original process have been defined. These enhancements include defense against replay attacks, support for mutual authentication, better security for frequent clients, and integrity protection of the communication between client and server. Some of those features are automatically part of Improved Digest Authentication, while others are made available only with the advanced services. Servers and clients must agree to use the optional services. Table 4.5 lists the additional services available with Improved Digest Authentication, as well as the mechanism that invokes them. We'll discuss each of these advanced services separately in the subsections that follow.

Table 4.5 Digest Authentication Enhancements

Service	Mechanism
Replay Protection	Always a part of Improved Digest Authentication.
Mutual Authentication	Always a part of Improved Digest Authentication.
Repeat Client Security	Used if algorithm is MD5-sess.
Integrity Protection	Used if qop is auth-int.

One factor common to each of these enhanced services, however, is the trigger that tells the client whether or not they are available. That trigger is present in the very first response from the server, the `401 Unauthorized`. To indicate its support for Improved Digest Authentication, the server explicitly includes a quality of protection, or qop, parameter. The value of the parameter isn't important, just its presence in the server's response.

```
HTTP/1.1 401 Unauthorized
WWW-Authenticate: Digest
    realm="users@hundredacrewoods.com",
    qop="auth",
    nonce="dcd98bc09f81043d3a8cb935ae393db90674"
```

Although the qop parameter is explicitly for only one of the advanced services (integrity protection), the Digest Authentication standard introduced all the advanced authentication features at the same time. Any client that receives the qop parameter from a server can assume that the server supports at least that version of the Digest Authentication specification, so it can also assume that the server supports advanced authentication. The qop parameter is, in effect, a convenient indication that the server can support advanced authentication services.

In addition to indicating support for advanced authentication, the qop parameter value can define particular security services. The Improved Digest Authentication specification defines two cases: auth and auth-int. The first case, auth, indicates authentication only, while the auth-int value indicates authentication with integrity protection. Integrity protection is the subject of subsection 4.1.7, so we'll defer discussion until then. Note, though, that a server need not select only a single value for qop. It can, if it wishes, include both auth and auth-int in its response by using the header qop="auth,auth-int" in its message. This tells the client that the server is capable of supporting either, and the client should choose one to use for the connection. Because auth-int, which includes integrity protection as well as authentication, offers stronger security than auth, clients that are capable of supporting auth-int should always do so when given the choice.

4.1.4 Protecting Against Replay Attacks

One of the more important services available with Improved Digest Authentication is protection against replay attacks. A replay attack is a particular type of security attack in which an adversary fools the server into thinking it has a valid password, even when it doesn't. Figure 4.5 shows a simple scenario. In the figure, step 1 is a standard, authenticated request from the client. It includes the `Authorization` header with a valid digest. Because this message is sent across the public Internet, however, its contents are not confidential and the adversary, as the figure indicates, observes the request. In step 2 the adversary simply sends the same request over again to the server. It is, in effect, replaying the request. Without knowing the user's password, the adversary cannot calculate a valid digest. In this case, though, the adversary doesn't need to calculate the digest. The client already did that in the initial request. The attack is complete in step 3. In that step the server verifies the digest in the request, finds it to be valid, and returns the requested object.

Although it may seem as if the server is acting inappropriately here by answering the adversary's request, in fact the server has little choice. Without the replay protection service of Improved Digest Authentication, the server has no way of distinguishing the adversary's request from, for example, an impatient Web user clicking on the browser's "Refresh" or "Reload" button.

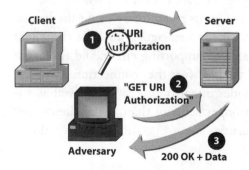

Figure 4.5 ▶

In a replay attack, an adversary copies a victim's message and later resends it to the same server.

To protect against replay attacks, the client adds another parameter to its `Authorization` header when it reissues its request. The parameter is a nonce count, and its name is `nc`. The value for `nc` is an eight-digit hexadecimal number that increments each time the client issues the request with the same `nonce` value.

```
GET /secret/honeypot.html HTTP/1.1
Authorization: Digest username="pooh",
   realm="users@hundredacrewoods.com",
   qop=auth,
   nonce="dcd98bc09f81043d3a8cb935ae393db90674",
   nc=00000001,
   cnonce="32cfe192fd109232aa1b8fe09d18d5efe53",
   uri="/secret/honeypot.html",
   response="dcd98bc09f81043d3a8cb935ae393db90674"
```

For their part in replay protection, servers must keep track of the nc value from each client. Each time they receive a request, they make sure that the nc is greater than the last nc value they received. If a server sees a new request with the same nc value as before, the server should suspect a replay attack and act accordingly.

Note that it is not possible for an adversary to capture a legitimate request and just increment the nc in that request. As we'll see later, with Improved Digest Authentication the nc value is part of the input to the digest. If an adversary alters the nc value without changing the digest, the digest will no longer be correct. And, because the adversary doesn't know the user's password, that adversary cannot correctly adjust the digest for an altered nc value.

4.1.5 Mutual Authentication

The Original Digest Authentication process gives HTTP servers a way to verify the identity of clients, but it doesn't help clients verify the identity of the server. Fortunately, digest authentication in general can support mutual authentication with only a few minor modifications. For that reason,

Improved Digest Authentication automatically includes server authentication in the security process. If a server indicates its support for advanced authentication by including a qop parameter in its initial response, the client must employ the mutual authentication process.

Server authentication is much like client authentication, only backward. Clients send the server their own data. The server combines that data with the user's password, calculates a digest, and returns that digest along with the requested object. The client can then verify the digest before accepting the object. Figure 4.6 shows the steps involved. The key step is in step 4. It is here that the server includes the Authentication-Info parameter that proves its knowledge of the user's password.

The server triggers the mutual authentication process by including a qop parameter in its 401 Unauthorized response. If the client supports Improved Digest Authentication, it must, according to the rules of the Digest Authentication standard, initiate server authentication.

```
HTTP/1.1 401 Unauthorized
WWW-Authenticate: Digest
    realm="users@hundredacrewoods.com",
    qop="auth",
    nonce="dcd98bc09f81043d3a8cb935ae393db90674"
```

Figure 4.6 ▶

With improved digest authentication, a server can prove that it knows the client's password. The Authentication-Info header carries this proof. This service provides greater security than the basic authentication exchange, where only the client actually demonstrates that it knows the password.

To initiate server authentication, the client adds one more parameter to the `Authorization` header in its reissued request. That parameter is `cnonce`, which is short for client nonce. The `cnonce` parameter has the same format as the server's `nonce` parameter.

```
GET /secret/honeypot.html HTTP/1.1
Authorization: Digest username="pooh",
   realm="users@hundredacrewoods.com",
   qop=auth,
   nonce="dcd98bc09f81043d3a8cb935ae393db90674",
   nc=00000001,
   cnonce="32cfe192fd109232aa1b8fe09d18d5efe53",
   uri="/secret/honeypot.html",
   response="dcd98bc09f81043d3a8cb935ae393db90674"
```

Clients using Improved Digest Authentication also calculate the digest slightly differently than for Original Digest Authentication. Unlike with the original service, clients include the value of their `nc`, `cnonce`, and `qop` parameters in the calculation. Table 4.6 outlines the steps. Note that table 4.6 lists the steps when the parties are not using protection for repeat clients (subsection 4.1.6) and when they are not employing integrity protection (subsection 4.1.7).

Table 4.6 Improved Client Calculation

Step	Action
1	Construct a character string containing the username, realm, and password, each item separated by a colon, `pooh:users@hundredacrewoods.com:honey`, for example. (This is string "A1.")
2	Calculate the MD5 digest for this character string and represent the result in hexadecimal as 32 ASCII characters.
3	Construct a second character string consisting of the method (e.g., `GET`, `POST`, etc.) and the URI, again separated by colons. For example, `GET:/secret/honeypot.html`. (This is string "A2.")
4	Calculate the MD5 digest for this character string and represent the result as 32 ASCII characters.

continues…

Table 4.6 Improved Client Calculation (continued)

Step	Action
5	Construct a character string by combining the result from step 2, the `nonce` supplied by the server, the `nc` value, the `cnonce` value, the `qop` value, and the result from step 4, all separated by colons (:).
6	Calculate the MD5 digest for the character string obtained in step 5 and represent the result as 32 ASCII characters. This value is the digest.

Of course, the server side of mutual authentication only begins with the client's request. The server has to confirm that it knows the user's password when it returns its response. To do that, the server uses the `Authentication-Info` header. The header repeats the values for the `qop`, `cnonce`, and `nc` parameters in the client's request, and it includes the `rspauth` parameter, which contains the digest calculated by the server.

```
HTTP/1.1 200 OK
Authentication-Info: qop=auth,
    rspauth="78d98bc09f81ba3d3a8cb935a9993db90674",
    cnonce="32cfe192fd109232aa1b8fe09d18d5efe53",
    nc=00000001
```

The server calculates its digest value using the same procedure as the client, with one small exception: Servers do not include the method in their construction of A2. They omit the method from the character string so that the first character of the A2 string is a colon. Table 4.7 provides the details. Again, note that this table assumes that neither frequent client protection nor integrity protection is in use.

Table 4.7 Improved Server Calculation

Step	Action
1	Construct a character string consisting of the username, realm, and password, each item separated by a colon, `pooh:users@hundredacrewoods.com:honey`, for example. (This is string "A1.")

Table 4.7 continued

Step	Action
2	Calculate the MD5 digest for this character string and represent the result in hexadecimal as 32 ASCII characters.
3	Construct a second character string consisting of a colon followed by the URI of the client's request. As an example, `:/secret/honeypot.html`. (This is string "A2.")
4	Calculate the MD5 digest for this character string and represent the result as 32 ASCII characters.
5	Construct a character string by combining the result from step 2, the `nonce` value, the `nc` value, the `cnonce` value, the `qop` value, and the result from step 4, all separated by colons (:).
6	Calculate the MD5 digest for the character string obtained in step 5 and represent the result as 32 ASCII characters. This value is the digest.

4.1.6 Protection for Frequent Clients

While replay protection and mutual authentication are mandatory features of Improved Digest Authentication, the other advanced services are optional. The optional services are quite valuable, however, and should be used whenever they are available. A case in point is the optional protection for "frequent clients." We use the term "frequent client" for an HTTP client that makes many requests of an HTTP server. Those many requests could be a product of a single, complex session, or they may be due to clients that make the same request many times. The problem facing those clients is that the more they interact with a server, the more vulnerable their password becomes.

The root of this problem is the method clients (and servers) use to convert the password into the value, known in cryptography as a *key*, that actually protects the data. In the examples described previously, that key is A1, and it is the combination of three items—the username, the realm, and the password. What's noteworthy is that those three items do not normally change as the client makes repeated requests of a host. Every request to the host will use the same key to protect its authentication information.

In cryptography, the more information protected with a given key, the less secure that key becomes. Adversaries have more data to analyze, and the more data they have, the easier the analysis becomes. If a client continues to use the same key long enough, eventually an adversary will be able to discover its value.

To protect against this type of analysis, the Improved Digest Authentication approach introduces an option that modifies the way the key is created. This modification results in a key that changes periodically, based on responses from the server. By forcing the client to change keys occasionally, the server prevents adversaries from gathering a substantial amount of data protected by the same key, ultimately giving users greater protection of their passwords.

Clients use the improved approach whenever the `algorithm` parameter specifies `MD5-sess`. The server can propose this algorithm in its original response, as below.

```
HTTP/1.1 401 Unauthorized
WWW-Authenticate: Digest
    realm="users@hundredacrewoods.com",
    qop="auth",
    algorithm=MD5-sess,
    nonce="dcd98bc09f81043d3a8cb935ae393db90674"
WWW-Authenticate: Digest
    realm="users@hundredacrewoods.com",
    qop="auth",
    algorithm=MD5,
    nonce="dcd98bc09f81043d3a8cb935ae393db90674"
```

Note that in this example the server proposes both the MD5 and the MD5-sess algorithms. By proposing both options, the server can support clients that implement only MD5. Those clients will ignore the first WWW-Authenticate but accept the second one. Clients that can support both MD5 and

MD5-sess, however, should always choose to use MD5-sess, as that provides greater security.

Clients accept one of the proposed algorithms when they reissue their request. The following fragment shows a client accepting the MD5-sess algorithm.

```
GET /secret/honeypot.html HTTP/1.1
Authorization: Digest username="pooh",
  realm="users@hundredacrewoods.com",
  qop=auth,
  algorithm=MD5-sess,
  nonce="dcd98bc09f81043d3a8cb935ae393db90674",
  nc=00000001,
  cnonce="32cfe192fd109232aa1b8fe09d18d5efe53",
  uri="/secret/honeypot.html",
  response="dcd98bc09f81043d3a8cb935ae393db90674"
```

When MD5-sess is selected, table 4.8 shows the algorithm that the clients use to calculate their digest. It differs from the original algorithm only in step 1 (which is now, as you can see, really two steps).

Table 4.8 Digest Calculation with MD5-sess Algorithm

Step	Action
1a	Construct a character string consisting of the username, the realm, the user's password, the nonce value, and the cnonce value, each item separated by a colon.
1b	Calculate the MD5 digest for this character string and represent the result in hexadecimal as 32 ASCII characters. (This is string "A1.")
2	Calculate the MD5 digest for this new character string and represent the result in hexadecimal as 32 ASCII characters.
3	Construct a second character string consisting of the method (e.g., GET, POST, etc.) and the URI for the method, again separated by colons. For example, GET:/secret/honeypot.html. (This is string "A2.")
4	Calculate the MD5 digest for this character string and represent the result as 32 ASCII characters.

continues...

Table 4.8 Digest Calculation with MD5-sess Algorithm (continued)

Step	Action
5	Construct a character string by combining the result from step 2, the `nonce` supplied by the server, the `nc` value, the `cnonce` value, the `qop` value, and the result from step 4, all separated by colons (:).
6	Calculate the MD5 digest for the character string obtained in step 5 and represent the result as 32 ASCII characters. This value is the digest.

4.1.7 Integrity Protection

Until this point, we've discussed how Digest Authentication verifies the identities of the communicating parties. That is certainly a valuable security service, but, with just a minor modification, the same mechanisms can provide an additional security as well—integrity protection. Integrity protection gives the communicating systems a way to verify not only each other's identity, but also the authenticity of the information they send.

To understand the value of this service, consider the example of figures 4.7 and 4.8. The first figure shows the client's view of a transaction. The figure illustrates a standard electronic banking transaction, and it begins after the server has sent a WWW-Authenticate response asking the client to identify itself. The client sends its instruction with an HTTP POST message, and it appears to receive the 200 OK response from the server.

Figure 4.7 ▶
A client may think that the server is receiving and responding to its messages, as in this figure. As figure 4.8 shows, however, something more sinister may actually be taking place.

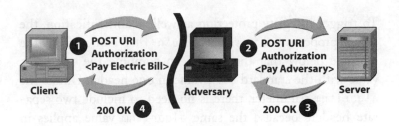

◀ **Figure 4.8**
Without integrity protection, an adversary may be intercepting and modifying the contents of a client's messages.

Figure 4.8 shows what's really happening, however. As that figure shows, an adversary has placed itself between the client and the server, and neither the client nor the server are aware of that fact. The adversary pretends to be the server in its interaction with the client, and it pretends to be a client in its interaction with the server. (Because of the adversary's position, this type of attack is known as a *man-in-the-middle attack* in security circles.)

Notice how the adversary takes advantage of its position. It accepts the client's request and then modifies the message body before passing it on to the server. The user intended to pay an electric bill but has, unwittingly, transferred money to the adversary instead. The insidious part of this attack is that the adversary does not modify the Authorization header in the client's request. When the server calculates the digest to verify the client's identity, it will find that the digest matches perfectly with the response parameter in the request.

This vulnerability is clearly a serious one. Fortunately, it is fairly simple to protect against. The trick is in the calculation of the digest. If the client includes the entire contents of its message in the digest calculation, then the digest process will protect those contents just as it protects the user's password. If an intermediate adversary modifies the data, then the server's calculation of the digest (based on the modified data) will not match the digest in the Authorization header (which the client calculated using the original data). Of course, no adversary can adjust the digest value to account for this because no adversary possesses the user's password.

To trigger integrity protection as well as authentication, the server proposes a `qop` value of `auth-int`. Notice from the example below that the server can combine the `auth-int` value with the standard `auth` value in one header. Unlike the `algorithm` parameter, there is no need to include two separate headers because the same `algorithm` value applies in either case.

```
HTTP/1.1 401 Unauthorized
WWW-Authenticate: Digest
    realm="users@hundredacrewoods.com",
    qop="auth,auth-int",
    algorithm=MD5,
    nonce="dcd98bc09f81043d3a8cb935ae393db90674"
```

When the client wishes to use integrity protection, it includes the entire entity body of its message in the input to the digest function. As table 4.9 shows, that change affects the value of A2, which is calculated in step 3. All the other steps remain the same. (Note that table 4.9 does not include the frequent client protection section 4.1.6 describes.)

Table 4.9 Client Digest Calculation for Integrity Protection

Step	Action
1	Construct a character string consisting of the username, realm, and password, each item separated by a colon, `pooh:users@hundredacrewoods.com:honey.`, for example. (This is string "A1.")
2	Calculate the MD5 digest for this character string and represent the result in hexadecimal as 32 ASCII characters.
3	Construct a second character string consisting of the method (e.g., `GET`, `POST`, etc.), the URI for the method, and the entire entity body, prior to any transfer encoding, again separated by colons.
4	Calculate the MD5 digest for this character string and represent the result as 32 ASCII characters.

Table 4.9 continued

Step	Action
5	Construct a character string by combining the result from step 2, the `nonce` supplied by the server, the `nc` value, the `cnonce` value, the `qop` value, and the result from step 4, all separated by colons (:).
6	Calculate the MD5 digest for the character string obtained in step 5 and represent the result as 32 ASCII characters. This value is the digest.

The client includes this new digest value in its reissued request, along with an appropriate `qop` value. The `qop` parameter indicates that it has accepted the server's proposal to include integrity protection.

```
GET /secret/honeypot.html HTTP/1.1
Authorization: Digest username="pooh",
   realm="users@hundredacrewoods.com",
   qop=auth-int,
   nonce="dcd98bc09f81043d3a8cb935ae393db90674",
   nc=00000001,
   cnonce="32cfe192fd109232aa1b8fe09d18d5efe53",
   uri="/secret/honeypot.html",
   response="dcd98bc09f81043d3a8cb935ae393db90674"
```

When the client accepts a proposal to use integrity protection, the server should do likewise. In the digest for its response, therefore, it includes the entity body of that response in its own digest calculation. It confirms integrity protection with the `qop` value of `auth-int`.

```
HTTP/1.1 200 OK
Authentication-Info: qop=auth-int,
   rspauth="78d98bc09f81ba3d3a8cb935a9993db90674",
   cnonce="32cfe192fd109232aa1b8fe09d18d5efe53",
   nc=00000001
```

Table 4.10 details the digest calculation. The difference is in step 3, where the server calculates A2. Note that this table does not include frequent client protection calculations.

Table 4.10 Server Digest Calculation for Integrity Protection

Step	Action
1	Construct a character string consisting of the username, realm, and password, each item separated by a colon, `pooh:users@hundredacrewoods.com:honey`, for example. (This is string "A1.")
2	Calculate the MD5 digest for this character string and represent the result in hexadecimal as 32 ASCII characters.
3	Construct a second character string consisting of a colon followed by the URI of the client's request, followed by another colon and then the entire entity body prior to any transfer encoding. (This is string "A2.")
4	Calculate the MD5 digest for this character string and represent the result as 32 ASCII characters.
5	Construct a character string by combining the result from step 2, the `nonce` value, the `nc` value, the `cnonce` value, the `qop` value, and the result from step 4, all separated by colons (:).
6	Calculate the MD5 digest for the character string obtained in step 5 and represent the result as 32 ASCII characters. This value is the digest.

4.2 Secure Sockets Layer

Although the HTTP's own procedures offer some important security services, they do not provide complete security for the systems' communications. In particular, they offer no way to encrypt the messages to protect the parties' privacy. That's a significant disadvantage for the World Wide Web. The Web uses the public Internet as its network, and communications traffic on the public Internet is just that—public. Because adversaries are free to observe messages that travel between clients and servers, encrypting those messages so that adversaries cannot understand them is critical to applications such as electronic commerce. Otherwise, valuable and private information such as credit card numbers could be easily intercepted, as figure 4.9 illustrates.

Fortunately, the Web has developed a technology to provide the necessary confidentiality for communication traffic. That technology is not an enhancement to HTTP but, rather, an entirely separate protocol known as the Secure Sockets Layer (SSL). Netscape Communications designed SSL for inclusion in its Web browser, and nearly all Web servers and Web browsers have followed suit. By now, SSL is by far the most popular network security technology deployed in the world.

This section provides a brief introduction to the Secure Sockets Layer protocol. It first shows the relationship between SSL and other protocols, as well as its typical implementation environment. The section then introduces public key cryptography, the crucial cryptographic technology on which SSL is based. The section then shows SSL in operation.

4.2.1 SSL and Other Protocols

As a separate protocol, SSL is available to all applications that use TCP for transport. Figure 4.10 shows its position in the standard protocol stack.

Notice that in the standard case HTTP communicates directly with TCP while, when SSL is involved, HTTP communicates only with SSL, and SSL, in turn, communicates with TCP.

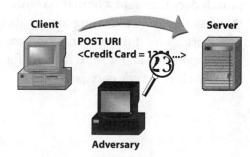

◀ **Figure 4.9**
Without the Secure Sockets Layer (or something equivalent), an adversary can eavesdrop on a communication and uncover confidential information.

Figure 4.10 ▶
The SSL protocol inserts itself between an application like HTTP and the TCP transport layer. TCP sees SSL as just another application, and HTTP communicates with SSL much the same as it does with TCP.

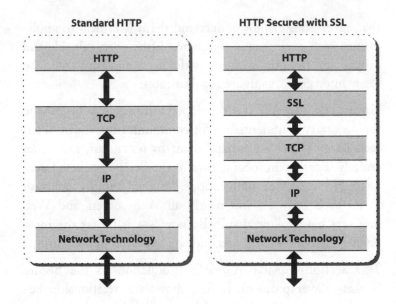

In any communications, particularly the Web, the client decides whether to use SSL or not. For the specific case of SSL in combination with HTTP, the standard URI scheme "https:" indicates a secure session. Users may enter the full URI directly in a browser, or they may be redirected to a secure session by a link. In either case, most browsers provide a convenient way for users to tell if the session is secure. Figure 4.11 shows how Microsoft's Internet Explorer shows a secure site. Notice the padlock icon in the lower right corner of the window.

Although the URI scheme allows explicit specification of a TCP port, HTTP over SSL has a default port of 443. This approach does highlight a limitation with SSL. Each application that has the option of using SSL needs two separate default TCP ports: one for standard, non-secure operation (e.g., HTTP's port 80) and a separate port for secure communications (such as HTTP's port 443).

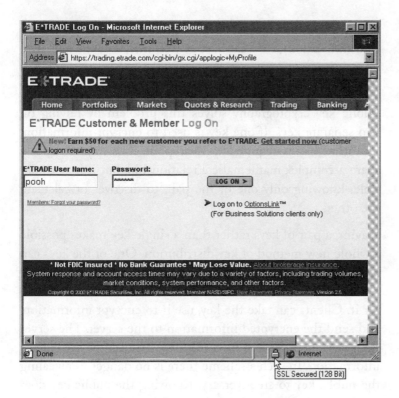

◀ **Figure 4.11**
The padlock icon at the lower right of the browser's window indicates that the session is secured with SSL. Other browsers use similar icons to indicate secure communications.

4.2.2 Public Key Cryptography

Public key cryptography, on which SSL relies, solves a fundamental problem that exists in conventional cryptography: key management. With conventional cryptography, both communicating parties share a single secret value, known as the *key*. In the case of HTTP security discussed in the last section, that key is the user's password. Both the client and the server need to know the password before authentication or integrity protection can succeed.

Keys that must be shared by communicating parties present a serious problem to any security system. How do the parties agree on and exchange the value of the key? It's usually not acceptable to simply send the key using the same communication path that the key will later secure. After all, if there are adversaries in that path waiting to intercept communications, they can just as well intercept the key. And if an adversary possesses the secret key, then securing the communication is not worthwhile.

Public key cryptography solves this problem by relying on two separate keys. If one key is used to encrypt information, the other key is required to decrypt it. The keys obviously share a complex mathematical relationship, but it is not possible, knowing only one of the pair, to discover or calculate the other.

Having a pair of keys rather than a single key makes possible a whole new method of key distribution. One of the keys can be freely published. A server, for example, can send one of its keys, the key known as its *public key*, to any client that asks for it. Clients can take the key, use it to encrypt information, and send the encrypted information to the server. The server then uses its other key, its *private key*, to decrypt the client's information. In such a scheme there is no danger in revealing the public key to an adversary. Knowing the public key does not let an adversary decrypt the confidential information.

Public key cryptography is useful for more than just encryption; it also provides a powerful method of authentication. Public key authentication reverses the roles of the two keys that make up the key pair. A client that wishes to prove its identity, for example, begins with known data and encrypts it using its private key. Anyone with the client's public key can then decrypt the information. If it matches the original known value, then the client is certain to have been the one to encrypt it (because only the client knows its private key).

There is one factor that makes public key cryptography slightly less convenient than the description so far would imply. The complication is ensuring the authenticity of public keys. To return to the earlier example, suppose a client asks for a server's public key. How can the client be sure that the public key really does belong to the server and not an adversary posing as the server? Public key authentication by itself won't help, because that's effective only after the client is sure of the server's public key. Public key cryptography in general, and SSL in particular, resolves this problem by using public key certificates and certificate authorities. A certificate authority is a party that both clients and servers trust, and one for whom they know the legitimate public key. To make its own public key trustworthy, a server presents it to the certificate authority, along with suitable proof of the server's identity. The certificate authority (CA) then encrypts the server's public key using its own private key, a process known as signing. The resulting signed public key is stored in a digital certificate. It is this digital certificate, not just its public key, which the server sends to clients. Those clients who know the certificate authority's public key can verify that the CA did indeed certify the server's public key.

Of course, that still leaves one problem. How do clients and servers learn the public keys of the certificate authority? They can't learn them over an insecure network, as that would allow an adversary to pose as a CA. In this case there is no magic available; communicating parties must learn of the CA through a means other than the network. In the case of the Web, browsers and servers are preloaded by their manufacturer with the public keys of important certificate authorities. Figure 4.12 shows some of authorities that Netscape preinstalls in its browser.

4.2.3 SSL Operation

The Secure Sockets Layer protocol offers three important security services to applications that use it. Those services are authentication, message integrity, and confidentiality. Respectively, those services provide confident answers to three questions: "With whom am I communicating?", "Have I received precisely the information that the other party sent (and vice versa)?", and "Have we ensured that a third party cannot eavesdrop on the communications?"

Figure 4.12 ▶
Commercial Web browsers are
preconfigured with a list of trusted
certificate authorities.

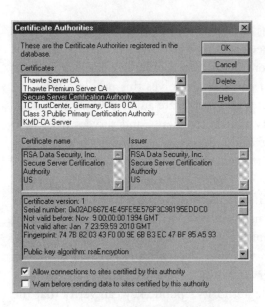

The SSL protocol can provide these services in several ways; however, when securing HTTP communications, particularly on the Web, two scenarios are especially common. Typical electronic commerce sites employ one scenario: SSL authenticates the Web server and encrypts and protects communications between the server and browser. Some specialized sites use the second scenario: In addition to authenticating the server, those sites use SSL to authenticate the client as well.

In both cases the communicating parties exchange a sequence of SSL messages before transferring HTTP information. Figure 4.13 shows the sequence of messages for server-only authentication. Table 4.11 describes each of the messages in the exchange.

Once the nine-step negotiation is complete, application protocols (such as HTTP) can begin exchanging their own messages securely. In the case of HTTP, the client typically follows the SSL negotiation with a GET or POST request. Note that SSL adds its own headers to each application message.

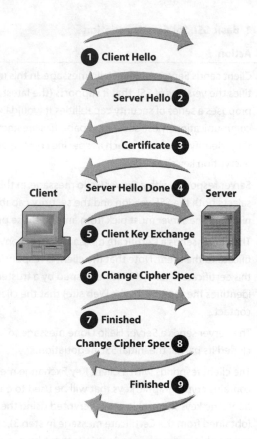

Establishing an SSL session for the first time requires the exchange of several messages. In step 1 the client introduces itself and its capabilities; the server responds in step 2 by selecting the parameters for the session. It then sends the client its public key certificate in step 3, and it ends its part of the initial exchange in step 4. With step 5, the client picks a secret key for the session, encrypts it using the server's public key, and sends it to the server. Since only the server knows its private key, only the server can decrypt the secret key. In the remaining steps, both systems conclude the negotiation phase and activate the session's security.

These headers keep the two parties synchronized, and they provide message integrity protection.

The preceding SSL negotiation is an effective way to authenticate the server, and it establishes a secure communications channel between the server and client. It does not, however, authenticate the identity of the client. That's because, in many applications, SSL isn't needed to verify the client's identity. Consider electronic commerce applications, for example. In a typical transaction the customer provides credit card information, and it is a valid credit card number that validates the user. Other sites ask users to select usernames and passwords, as that combination is far easier for humans to manage than public key technology. In such environments, cryptographic authentication of the client is unnecessary.

Table 4.11 Basic SSL Session Negotiation

Step	Action
1	Client sends Server a Client Hello message. In this message the client identifies the versions of SSL that it supports (the latest version is 3.0), and it proposes a series of security capabilities it would like to employ for the communication. These security capabilities are known as *Cipher Suites*, and they identify parameters such as specific cryptographic algorithms and encryption key sizes.
2	Server responds with a Server Hello message. In this message the server selects both the SSL version and the security capabilities for the communication. The server must pick from among those proposed by the client.
3	The Server sends a Certificate message, which conveys its public key certificate to the client. Note that the client is responsible for ensuring that this certificate is valid, that it was issued by a trusted authority, and that it identifies the server (e.g., the Web site) that the client or user intended to contact.
4	The Server sends a Server Hello Done message to indicate that it has concluded its part of the initial SSL negotiation.
5	The client responds with a Client Key Exchange message. This message contains cryptographic keys that will be used to encrypt the communications. The keys themselves are encrypted using the server's public key (obtained from the Certificate message in step 3), so that only the server will be able to decipher and retrieve these keys.
6	The client sends a Change Cipher Spec message. This message is a signal that the client will encrypt all subsequent communications using the cryptographic keys.
7	The client sends a Finished message, which is encrypted according to the negotiated cryptographic keys and algorithms. The server's ability (or inability) to successfully decrypt this message ensures that the negotiation has been successful.
8	The server sends its own Change Cipher Spec message. As with the client, this message signals that future messages will be encrypted.
9	The server concludes the SSL negotiation with a Finished message of its own which, as is the case for the client's Finished message, is encrypted according to the negotiated parameters. Once the client has successfully decrypted this message, it is assured that the negotiation has succeeded.

In some specialized implementations, however, cryptographic authentication is useful. The SSL protocol supports this type of operation as well. Figure 4.14 shows the message exchange for client authentication. The figure highlights those messages that differ from typical server-only authentication. Table 4.12 describes those steps.

◀ Figure 4.14
Clients can also use SSL to authenticate themselves to the servers. The server requests such authentication by sending a certificate request, as in step 4. The client honors this request in step 6, and then, in step 8, it sends a special message that verifies its knowledge of the corresponding private key. The rest of the exchange is the same as in figure 4.13.

Table 4.12 Additional Steps for Client Authentication

Step	Action
4	The server sends a Certificate Request message after sending its own certificate. This message tells the client that the server wants to authenticate the client using SSL, and it is the trigger for SSL's client authentication.
6	The client provides its public key certificate in a Certificate message.
8	The client sends a Certificate Verify message, in which it encrypts some known information using its private key. The server can decrypt the information using the public key from the client's certificate. Successful decryption verifies that the client truly possesses the private key corresponding to the public key certificate.

There are two important items to note about client authentication using SSL. First, the client has to possess a public key certificate, and it must be one that the server can trust. Often the server itself (or the same organization that operates the server) issues client certificates. Secondly, SSL client authentication tends to authenticate the system acting as the client; it is not normally effective at authenticating the user of that system. Because public key certificates are far too complex for humans to conveniently store and remember, clients rely on the computer systems to store and manage them, and computer systems are frequently vulnerable to unauthorized users. For this reason electronic commerce sites do not normally use SSL client authentication to validate their users.

Something that figures 4.13 and 4.14 highlight is that SSL negotiation can add significant overhead to a communication. Not only must the parties exchange several SSL messages, they must perform processor- and time-intensive public key encryption. (See the "Public Key Disadvantages" sidebar on page 160.) For a Web site struggling to serve millions of users, SSL overhead can have a significant impact on performance. Using HTTP persistence helps, as it lets clients issue multiple HTTP requests without renegotiating the SSL pa-

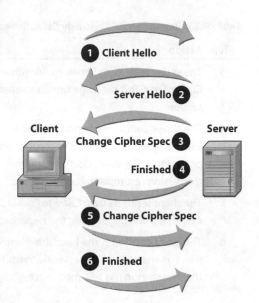

◀ Figure 4.15
If they have previously established an SSL session, clients and servers can reuse that session's parameters and avoid a full SSL negotiation process. The client proposes to resume an earlier session in its hello message. If the server agrees, it accepts the proposal in its hello reply.

rameters. The SSL protocol also provides its own form of persistence, however, which may be useful for applications that do not support persistence or in cases where persistence is impractical. The approach is relatively straightforward. With each negotiation, the server may, if it chooses, assign a Session ID to the results. When the client later wants to reestablish secure communications, it can include the Session ID in its Client Hello message. If the server agrees to reuse the previously negotiated parameters, it replies with the same Session ID in its Server Hello. Figure 4.15 illustrates the complete exchange, and table 4.13 describes each step.

Table 4.13 Resuming a Previously Established SSL Session

Step	Action
1	The client sends a Client Hello message containing a previously established SSL Session ID. Note that the client should also include a full set of proposed cryptographic parameters in case the server decides not to reuse the session.
2	The server responds with a Server Hello message also containing the Session ID, indicating that it is willing and able to resume the SSL session.

continues…

Table 4.13 Resuming a Previously Established Session (continued)

Step	Action
3	The server follows its Server Hello with an immediate Change Cipher Spec. This message signals the resumption of the secure session.
4	The server concludes its part of the negotiation by sending a Finished message, which is encrypted according to the session parameters. The client decrypts this message to make sure that the session resumption has succeeded.
5	The client sends its own Change Cipher Spec message to indicate that it will begin using the negotiated session parameters.
6	The client concludes the handshake with a Finished message, which is encrypted. The server decrypts this message to verify that the session has resumed successfully.

4.3 Transport Layer Security

The Secure Sockets Layer protocol was designed by Netscape Communications. And, although Netscape did involve the Internet community in its development, SSL technically remains a proprietary protocol. To ensure that Web security can be supplied by a true, open standard, the Internet Engineering Task Force (IETF) took over responsibility for enhancements and updates to SSL and, as part of the transition, gave the protocol a new name: Transport Layer Security, or TLS.

4.3.1 Differences from SSL

Despite the new name, TLS is really nothing more than the next revision of SSL. Indeed, it is a relatively minor revision. Its designers acknowledge the modesty of their changes in the protocol version number; TLS messages indicate their protocol version as 3.1. (The last version of SSL is version 3.0.)

Other than a new version number, TLS makes only two real changes to SSL. First, it almost doubles the number of error

Version Number Confusion

Although the protocol messages advertise a protocol version of "3.1," the TLS protocol itself is officially known as TLS version 1.0. That's because even though TLS is effectively version 3.1 of SSL, it is technically the first version of Transport Layer Security. Presumably, version 2 of TLS will advertise itself as protocol version "4.0" in its messages. This approach is perhaps an unfortunate one, as it may cause confusion for the life of the protocol. The IETF could resolve this confusion by making the next version of TLS version 4 rather than version 2.

message types; this increase should help identify and isolate interoperability problems. Second, TLS makes slight adjustments to the complex cryptographic calculations to eliminate some minor theoretical weaknesses.

4.3.2 Control of the Protocol

The real significance of the migration from SSL to TLS is control of the protocol. With TLS that control rests with an international standards organization, the IETF, rather than Netscape. The IETF provides a much more open and understandable process for adding to TLS, particularly in its cipher suites. A cipher suite specifies the cryptographic parameters of a secure communication, including elements such as the encryption algorithm and key size. The IETF has already accepted proposals to increase the number of cipher suites supported by TLS. Those proposals adopt existing security systems such as Kerberos, and they add advanced new technology such as elliptic curve cryptography, technology that is particularly well suited for low-power devices such as mobile phones and personal digital assistants. These advances will help bring TLS—and with it secure HTTP—to all manner of devices and systems.

4.3.3 Upgrading to TLS within an HTTP Session

There is another significant effect of IETF control over TLS. Because the IETF also controls HTTP, much closer coordination between the two protocols is possible. Indeed, such cooperation is already apparent. One of the problems with SSL is that it requires a separate TCP port for each application it secures. That is why the Web uses port 80 for standard HTTP and port 443 for HTTP secured by SSL. With TLS, however, it is now possible to support both secure and non-secure operation on the same port. This conserves TCP port numbers, which can be a limited resource on many systems.

To support a single port the communicating systems begin their HTTP connection without security. Then, while the connection remains active, they upgrade to a secure session. The upgrade can be initiated either by the client or the server. The client begins the upgrade process by including the Upgrade and Connection headers in its message, as in the following example.

```
GET http://www.bank.com/acct.html?7493948 HTTP/1.1
Host: www.bank.com
Upgrade: TLS/1.0
Connection: Upgrade
```

The server can respond to this request with a 101 status.

```
HTTP/1.1 101 Switching Protocols
Upgrade: TLS/1.0, HTTP/1.1
Connection: Upgrade
```

After this exchange, the two parties carry out a TLS handshake negotiation. Once that has succeeded, the server replies to the client's original GET request.

One potential problem with this approach is that the server can choose not to perform the requested upgrade. In that case, it will still respond to the client's GET request; the response, however, will not be secured by TLS. Because of this possibility, clients should include the upgrade request directly in a GET message only if it is acceptable for the server to respond to the GET without security. In effect, the client's request to upgrade to TLS is optional.

To avoid this behavior, the client can request the upgrade before it issues a critical GET request. Clients should also do this if the GET message itself includes data that should be kept confidential. To upgrade before committing to a GET or POST exchange, clients can use an OPTIONS message.

```
OPTIONS * HTTP/1.1
Host: www.bank.com
Upgrade: TLS/1.0
Connection: Upgrade
```

The server responds as before, either accepting the upgrade or not. This time, however, the client has the benefit of the server's response before it sends a GET message. If the server does not upgrade to TLS, the client can simply terminate the connection without sending a GET.

A server can indicate its willingness to upgrade to TLS in any response other than a 101 or 426. It simply includes the Upgrade and Connection headers in that response.

```
HTTP/1.1 200 OK
Upgrade: TLS/1.0, HTTP/1.1
Connection: Upgrade
```

Actual initiation of the upgrade is still up to the client, and the client does so using either of the techniques above. The client will know in advance, however, that the server can support a TLS upgrade.

If the server wishes to force the client to initiate an upgrade, it can respond with a 426 Upgrade Required error status.

```
HTTP/1.1 426 Upgrade Required
Upgrade: TLS/1.0, IITTP/1.1
Connection: Upgrade

<HTML>
<BODY>
<P>Secure connection required. Please follow <A
HREF="https://www.bank.com/acct.html?749394889300"
>this link</A>.
</BODY>
</HTML>
```

Notice that the message body includes an HTML page that describes the problem for a human user and gives that user an alternative link to click. Any 426 response should include both these items to support Web browsers that may not understand the upgrade request.

If the client does understand the upgrade request, it can initiate the upgrade as above. Note that the client does not immediately begin the TLS handshake.

One final issue for TLS upgrades is support for proxy servers. If a client used the approach described above when communicating through a proxy, it would secure the communication only to that proxy. Once the data passed beyond the first proxy, it would no longer be secured by TLS. Because a client requesting a TLS upgrade presumably wants to establish the TLS session with the ultimate host, not with an intermediate proxy, it should use the CONNECT method to create a tunnel to the final host. Once the tunnel is established, the TLS upgrade and handshake can proceed.

4.4 Secure HTTP

At the same time Netscape was developing the initial version of the Secure Sockets Layer protocol, other engineers were working on an alternative security protocol known as secure HTTP. Although SSL has clearly established itself as the preferred approach for securing HTTP sessions on the Web, Secure HTTP has been published as an experimental IETF standard.

Secure HTTP provides the same security services as SSL: authentication, message integrity protection, and confidentiality (through encryption). Unlike SSL, however, secure HTTP messages have the same general syntax as HTTP. As the following example shows, the protocol is referred to as Secure-HTTP, the version is 1.4, and the main method is SECURE.

```
SECURE * Secure-HTTP/1.4
Content-Type: message/http
Content-Privacy-Domain: CMS
```

Secure HTTP itself defines four headers. It also defines several additional options for HTTP messages that it encapsulates. Table 4.14 lists the secure HTTP headers; table 4.15 lists the HTTP options that are not related to cryptographic negotiations, and table 4.16 lists the HTTP options that the parties use to negotiate cryptographic parameters.

Table 4.14 Secure HTTP Headers

Header	Use
Content-Privacy-Domain	Indicates the format of the cryptographic information; either `CMS` for the IETF's Cryptographic Message Syntax or `MOSS` for MIME Object Security Services used with secure email.
Prearranged-Key-Info	Identifies keys that have been previously established between the parties; this header allows Secure HTTP to support traditional, shared key cryptography as well as public key cryptography.
Content-Type	Identifies the type of content protected by Secure HTTP; all Secure HTTP messages have the content-type of `message/http`.
MAC-Info	Carries a message authentication code for the message, which is used to provide message integrity protection.

Table 4.15 HTTP Options for Secure HTTP

Option	Use
Key-Assign	Assigns an identifier to a cryptographic key (so that key may be conveniently referenced later).
Encryption-Identity	Identifies the party for whom a message should be encrypted.
Certificate-Info	Identifies a public key certificate.
Nonce	Contains a random value used to vary message contents and therefore improve security.
Nonce-Echo	Returns a previously provided nonce value.

Table 4.16   Secure HTTP Cryptographic Negotiation Options

Option	Use
SHTTP-Cryptopts	Contains general cryptographic options.
SHTTP-Privacy-Domains	Indicates the format of the cryptographic information; either CMS for the IETF's Cryptographic Message Syntax or MOSS for MIME Object Security Services used with secure email.
SHTTP-Certificate-Types	Identifies the format of public key certificates.
SHTTP-Key-Exchange-Algorithms	Identifies a cryptographic algorithm used to exchange keys.
SHTTP-Signature-Algorithms	Identifies a cryptographic algorithm used to digitally sign messages.
SHTTP-Message-Digest-Algorithms	Identifies a cryptographic algorithm used to calculate the digest of a message.
SHTTP-Symmetric-Content-Algorithms	Identifies a cryptographic algorithm used to encrypt message contents.
SHTTP-Symmetric-Header-Algorithms	Identifies a cryptographic algorithm used to encrypt message headers.
SHTTP-Privacy-Enhancements	Lists privacy enhancements desired or used for a message.
Your-Key-Pattern	Identifies a cryptographic key using a general, pattern-matching syntax.

Secure HTTP, like SSL, has its own protocol designator for URLs. In the case of secure HTTP, that designator is "shttp" (which, unfortunately, is close enough to SSL's designator of "https" to create some confusion). Because secure HTTP uses the same syntax as HTTP, however, secure HTTP does not require its own default TCP port. Instead, Secure HTTP and HTTP messages can be safely intermingled on the same port, port 80 by default.

CHAPTER 5

Accelerating HTTP — Improving Users' Web Experience

Not long after the first Web sites appeared on the Internet, engineers began looking for ways to make those sites perform faster. Their efforts have led to several approaches that accelerate HTTP, including load balancing, advanced caching, SSL acceleration, and TCP multiplexing. This chapter takes a more detailed look at the technologies behind those acceleration techniques.

The two most widely used technologies for accelerating HTTP are load balancing and caching, and these two topics form the bulk of this chapter. The final sections, however, describe some additional techniques for improving Web performance—TCP multiplexing and SSL acceleration.

5.1 Load Balancing

As the popularity of early Web sites grew and the demand on their servers increased, site administrators quickly discovered that load balancing was a simple way to improve their sites' scaleability and performance. The concept of load balancing is quite simple: Let many different Web servers act as a single Web site. As Web technology has matured, load balancing has itself grown more complex and more powerful. This section considers three key aspects of load balancing implementations. The first consideration is the location of the servers to be balanced. Next we look at the various ways that an implementation can direct the client to an appropriate server. The final section describes how load balancing implementations decide which server is appropriate for a particular request.

5.1.1 Locating Servers

The simplest load balancing configuration places multiple servers right next to each other, as in figure 5.1. HTTP requests from the Internet are directed to one of these local servers. Even in this simple configuration, load balancing offers significant benefits. As traffic demand increases, the site administrator simply adds more servers. The new servers reduce the load on the existing systems, improving their performance and, ultimately, the end user's experience. Local load balancing can also improve a site's reliability, particularly if the implementation's technique for allocating servers can

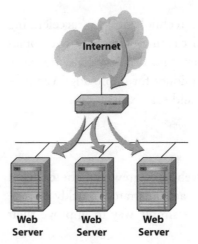

Figure 5.1 ▶
Load balancing distributes requests among many physical servers. The Web site's overall performance becomes the sum of that of the physical servers.

automatically account for failed systems. And even if adding or deleting servers requires manual configuration, load balancing facilitates taking servers out of service for scheduled maintenance.

Local load balancing focuses on the Web servers, and most of its benefits are targeted to servers. (Of course, any improvement of server performance also improves the user's experience, so clients can gain considerable indirect benefit from local load balancing.) A different type of load balancing implementation, however, provides direct benefits to Web clients. That implementation is frequently called global load balancing.

With global balancing, as figure 5.2 shows, the various Web servers are distributed around the Internet; unlike the case for local load balancing, the servers do not share the same facilities and infrastructure.

The primary advantage of global load balancing is that it allows the client to interact with a server that is physically nearby. This benefit is particularly important for international Web sites. End users in Europe can retrieve their content from servers in Europe, while clients in the Pacific communicate with servers in the same region. To appreciate the significance of this optimization, consider the limits of

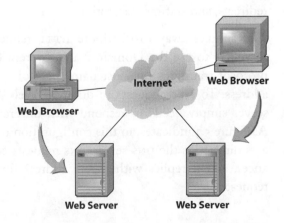

◀ **Figure 5.2**
Global load balancing locates servers at different locations around the Internet. In addition to combining the performance of multiple servers into one site, this architecture allows clients to communicate with the nearest server, improving the site's responsiveness to diverse clients.

basic physics. The speed of light in fiber imposes a round trip delay of nearly 100 milliseconds for traffic that must cross the Atlantic Ocean. Yet it takes only about 60 milliseconds to deliver a typical Web page over a dial-up ISDN connection; for ADSL connections the delivery time is around 10 milliseconds. Clearly, moving the content closer to the end user can have a significant effect on that user's experience.

Global load balancing provides benefits to more than just the end user. Servers also benefit. By distributing servers across the Internet, the Web site reduces the bandwidth requirements of any individual site. Global load balancing also improves site availability. While local load balancing can be used to route around failed servers, it offers no protection against the failure of an entire physical site. Unfortunately, site failures are not necessarily rare events, as anything from a power failure to loss of network connectivity can effectively shut down a location. Global load balancing, however, protects against a physical site failure; if one of the servers is unavailable, another server, distantly located, can still function.

5.1.2 Distributing Requests

Once a Web site has established multiple servers for load balancing, the site must then determine how to distribute HTTP requests among those servers. Several approaches are possible, including Domain Name Service responses, HTTP redirects, and traffic interception.

The simplest way to distribute HTTP requests to multiple servers is to use the Domain Name System (DNS). The DNS protocol translates the host name part of a URL into an IP address. To send requests to different Web servers, the DNS server simply needs to respond with different IP addresses. As figure 5.3 indicates, in this configuration the load balancer acts directly as the DNS server. DNS requests come to the balancer, and it replies with the IP address for that particular request.

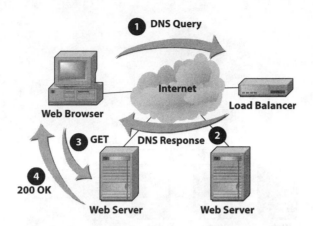

◀ **Figure 5.3**
A global load balancing system may act as a DNS server for a site. It can vary the IP address in its DNS responses based on the location of the requesting client.

Another approach to redirection is to use HTTP itself. The load balancer acts as a Web server itself. Instead of returning pages, however, the server responds to requests with HTTP messages that point the client to a new server. Figure 5.4 shows the general operation. Load balancers commonly return a 302 status, with the Location: header pointing to the real Web server for the client.

Global load balancers can use both DNS responses and HTTP redirection to distribute requests to different Web servers. A third technique, traffic interception, is effective only for local load balancing. Traffic interception requires the load balancer to be positioned between the Internet and the Web servers, as figure 5.5 shows.

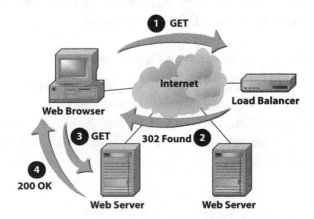

◀ **Figure 5.4**
A global load balancing system can also act as the primary HTTP server for a site. In that role it uses HTTP redirection to route clients to the actual Web site.

Figure 5.5 ▶

Traffic interception, sometimes called layer 4 or layer 7 switching, acts transparently to HTTP clients and servers. Requests passing through the load balancer are routed directly to an appropriate server.

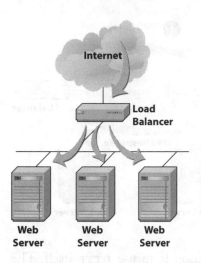

Because all HTTP requests pass through the load balancer, it has complete control over their ultimate destination. Traffic interception does place much greater demands on the load balancer, however. With DNS responses and HTTP redirection, the load balancer can "redirect and forget." Once it sends a request to a particular server, the load balancer doesn't have to keep track of the request or its session. With traffic interception, however, the load balancer is, in effect, pretending to be the Web server. To keep from confusing the client, the load balancer must maintain that pretense for the life of the client's session. And, in the case of communications encrypted with SSL, the load balancer may have to track activity across multiple HTTP sessions.

5.1.3 Determining a Target Server

The final element of a load balancing strategy is determining which Web server is best suited to respond to a particular request. As the technology has developed, load balancers have gotten more and more sophisticated in their ability to make that decision.

The earliest load balancing implementations used a simple round-robin algorithm to route the requests. With a round robin, the first request is sent to host A; the next request is sent to host B, and so on. The process continues through all the Web servers and then starts over again at server A. This approach is particularly easy to implement with DNS-based redirection. Most DNS servers can be configured to use a round-robin algorithm in returning IP addresses. In such a configuration, a standard, "off-the-shelf" DNS server can act as a load balancer.

With a round-robin algorithm, the load balancer need not consider the Web servers or the requesting clients. It needs only to remember the last redirection with which it, itself, responded. That approach clearly has some significant limitations, however. Round-robin load balancers don't track, and therefore don't know, the status of individual servers. If a Web server fails or loses connectivity to the Internet, the load balancer won't know that and will continue to send clients its way. Also, the round-robin approach is effective only if each request places a similar burden on the server. If some requests require more server resources than others, a round-robin load balancer, not knowing any better, may send the bulk of those requests to one server, loading it disproportionately.

More advanced load balancers, particularly local load balancers using traffic interception, can take a more active interest in the health of the Web servers they support. Because such balancers see all the requests and responses from the Web servers, they are in an excellent position to evaluate the health of individual servers and adjust their redirection appropriately. Table 5.1 lists some of the factors a traffic interception load balancer can consider in determining a target server.

Table 5.1 Monitoring Web Server Health

Factor	Approach
Passive Monitoring	Load balancer measures the traffic flowing to and from individual servers to estimate their current load and health.
Active Requests	Load balancer issues its own requests to the servers periodically; these requests can be as simple as an Internet Control Message Protocol (ICMP) echo request (ping) or as sophisticated as a request for an actual Web page.
Network Monitoring	Load balancer uses a standard network management protocol such as the Simple Network Management Protocol (SNMP) to gather performance statistics for each server.
System Monitoring	Load balancer uses a system monitoring protocol (such as Windows 2000 performance monitor) to gather performance statistics for each server.

Global load balancers, because they manage a distributed set of Web servers, have an even greater opportunity to distribute traffic. In addition to maintaining its own information and monitoring the status of the Web servers, a global balancer can take the client itself into account in determining a request's target. Indeed, that's the main point of global load balancers that strive to match a client to the best server for it. The technique may seem a bit complicated, but, taken a step at a time, it is straightforward. Figure 5.6 illustrates the process. In the figure, we've assumed that the global load balancer uses HTTP redirection to send the client to the best server.

The process begins in step 1, when the Web browser requests a Web page. This request goes to the global load balancer, which is acting as a virtual Web server for the Web site. In step 2, the global balancer communicates with the local load balancers at all of the physical sites. The communication is a probe request; in effect, the global load balancer is asking each local load balancer to measure its distance to the client.

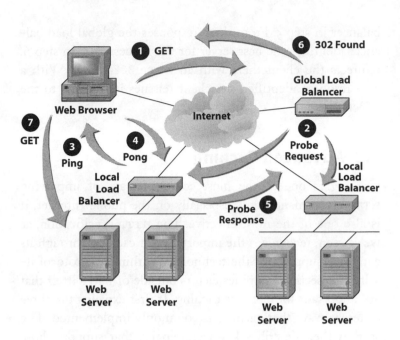

◄**Figure 5.6**
Sites can combine local and global load balancing in a coordinated manner. In this example, the global balancer queries the local load balancers when it receives a client's request; the query asks each local balancer to assess the performance between it and the client. The local load balancers report the results back to the global balancer so it can redirect the client appropriately.

Note that there are no standard communication protocols for step 2 (or the response in step 5), only proprietary ones. Consequently, the global and local load balancers usually must be from the same vendor.

In the next step, each local load balancer assesses its performance relative to the client. For clarity, figure 5.6 shows only the actions of the left-most local balancer, but the local balancer on the right takes similar actions. In the figure, the local balancer issues an ICMP echo request to the client; in step 4 the client replies with an ICMP echo response. The time between the request and the response can serve as an estimate of the round-trip latency between the client and the local balancer. Other approaches are possible as well. The local balancer could initiate a trace route to the client to measure the number of intervening routers. Alternatively, the local balancer could consult its own routing information (e.g., Border Gateway Protocol paths) to appraise the network topology between it and the client. In all cases, the local load balancers report their results to the global load balancer in step 5. From these responses the global load balancer identifies the best server for the request and, in step 6, redirects the client there with an HTTP 302 status. With a new resource identifier, the client reissues its request to the selected server.

5.2 Advanced Caching

Caching is one of the most common ways of improving HTTP performance, and, especially on the public Internet, it is also one of the most effective. The HTTP specification, as we've seen, recognizes the importance of caching through its extensive support for the technology within the protocol itself. This section examines factors outside of HTTP itself that are important for effective caching. It first explains the three different ways that caching is commonly implemented. The section then describes key technologies that support those implementations.

5.2.1 Caching Implementations

The Internet includes many participants—individual users, enterprises, Web sites, service providers, and others—almost all of whom can benefit from HTTP caching. Supporting each of these parties effectively, however, leads to significantly different caching implementations. All implementations rely on the HTTP headers and options that chapter 3 describes, but differ in the location of cache servers and the additional technology supporting those servers. The three implementation approaches are known as proxy caches, transparent caches, and reverse proxy caches. Table 5.2 summarizes the approaches; we'll look at each in more detail in the rest of this subsection. The following subsections examine the supporting technologies.

Table 5.2 Caching Implementations

Implementation	Benefits	Technologies
Proxy Caches	Enterprises reduce the bandwidth required for their Internet connections and improve performance for their users.	PAC, WPAD
Transparent Caches	Internet Service Providers reduce the bandwidth required for their inter-provider connections and improve performance for their customers.	WCCP, NECP
Reverse Proxy Caches	Web sites reduce the load on their Web servers and improve performance for their users.	ICP, HTCP, CARP

The most straightforward implementation of HTTP caching is with proxy cache servers. Proxy caches are most common in enterprises and other organizations that connect many users to the Internet. As figure 5.7 shows, the organization

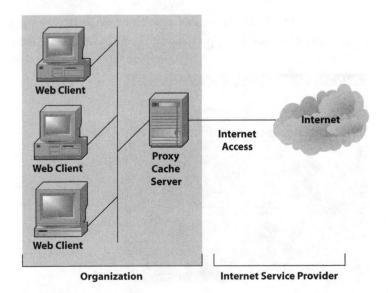

◀ Figure 5.7
Organizations with Internet connections can run their own proxy cache server to improve performance for their users and to reduce the bandwidth the Internet connection needs.

deploys the proxy cache as the gateway to the Internet connection. (In many cases, the proxy server system is also an Internet firewall.)

To exploit the proxy cache server, users within the organization direct their Web browsers to use the proxy for Internet access. All popular Web browsers include the ability to specify a proxy server; figure 5.8 shows the relevant configuration screen for Microsoft's Internet Explorer.

Properly configured, the users' browsers will send their HTTP requests to the proxy cache server rather than to actual Web sites. If the proxy has previously cached the content it will, as in figure 5.9, return the appropriate HTTP response to the client immediately.

Notice that the proxy cache server is able to return the appropriate HTTP response without sending any traffic to the Internet. This behavior not only saves the organization money by reducing the bandwidth requirements for its Internet access connection, it also gives the user improved performance. The proxy cache is able to respond to the user immediately, without the delay associated with communications across the Internet.

One of the practical challenges associated with deploying a proxy cache server is appropriately configuring the users'

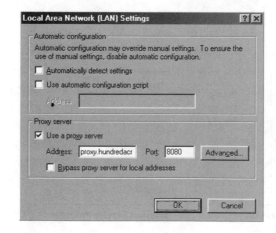

Figure 5.8 ▶

Users configure their Web browsers to send requests to a proxy server rather than directly to the Internet.

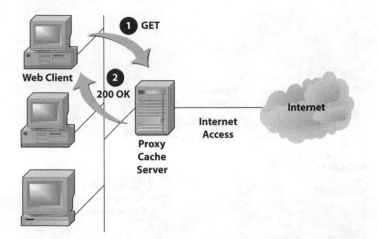

If a proxy server already has a copy of a resource in its local cache, it can respond directly to the client without communicating with the origin server.

Web browsers. Some browsers allow organizations to pre-configure proxy services (along with several other options) and distribute the preconfigured version within the organization. Preconfiguration is not always simple, however, and users that download the latest browser version directly from the Internet quickly defeat the organization's efforts. A more foolproof approach relies on Proxy Auto Configuration (PAC) scripts and the Web Proxy Auto-Discovery Protocol (WPAD). A PAC script is a simple JavaScript file with proxy configuration instructions, and WPAD is a simple communication protocol that allows browsers to automatically discover and access PAC scripts stored on a network. Later subsections look at each in more detail.

Internet Service Providers (ISPs) can also realize significant benefits from HTTP caching. The benefits are similar: ISPs reduce the amount of bandwidth they require for their connections to other ISPs or the Internet backbone, and they provide more responsive Web browsing to their customers. Figure 5.10 shows a typical cache server deployment at an ISP; notice that the cache server is located on the ISP's network rather than the organization's. Also, the figure shows an Internet connection for an enterprise or other organization to highlight the differences with figure 5.7. The technique is

Figure 5.10 ▶

Transparent cache servers are often administered by Internet access providers rather than user organizations. They avoid forcing users to configure their browsers with proxy server information.

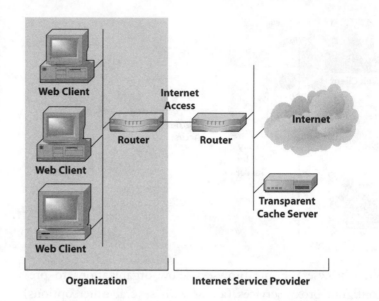

equally effective, however, for ISPs serving dial-up or other individual users.

The most significant difference between figures 5.10 and 5.7 is the type of cache server. Instead of a proxy cache server, ISPs typically use transparent cache servers. The reason for the difference is the configuration burden. Unlike an enterprise or organization, ISPs cannot easily mandate that all Web users configure the appropriate proxy settings in their browsers. Furthermore, PAC scripts and the WPAD protocol are generally effective only within a single local network, so ISPs cannot benefit from their use.

Transparent cache servers compensate for these restrictions. As the name implies, transparent caches are invisible to the end users. Web browsers don't need any special configuration to use a transparent cache; they simply access remote Web sites normally. The key to the operation of a transparent cache is cooperation between the ISP's routers and the cache server. As figure 5.11 shows, each access router continuously examines traffic from the ISP's customers, looking for HTTP messages. (Routers recognize those requests by their TCP

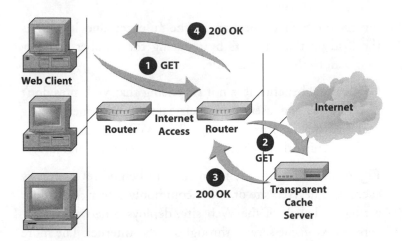

◀**Figure 5.11**
To force user requests to traverse a transparent cache server, a router (or switch) must explicitly reroute those requests to the cache.

port number; generally 80.) When the router detects an HTTP message, it intercepts the message and, in effect, sends it on a detour to the transparent cache server. If the cache server has a local copy of the content, it can respond immediately as in figure 5.11. Otherwise it sends the request on to the actual Web server. (A slight variation relies on HTTP switches, rather than routers, to redirect HTTP messages. The effect is the same, however.)

The key to effective transparent caching is coordinating the operation of the access router and the cache server. Cisco's proprietary Web Cache Communication Protocol (WCCP) is one approach for this coordination; the Network Element Control Protocol (NECP) is a newer, but standard, protocol with similar functions.

The third type of cache implementation, reverse proxy caching, moves control over caching to Web sites. Although it's easy to see the improvement caching offers to end users—quicker, more responsive Web browsing—caching can also benefit Web sites. Indirectly, of course, the Web site's image improves whenever end users' experiences improve. In addition, whenever a cache provides HTTP content on behalf of an origin server, the server itself has one less HTTP exchange to process. Caching reduces the bandwidth required by Web

Cache Controversies

Although transparent caching has obvious benefits to both ISPs and end users, it is not free from controversy. Many in the Internet community object to the very idea behind transparent caches—users' requests are redirected from their intended destination without the users' knowledge or consent. HTTP acceleration is generally considered a beneficial application of this technology, but it is easy to imagine more disreputable uses. Users attempting to access a Web site could be "detoured" to a Web site of a competitor, for example, or they could be redirected to a phony version of the intended site. Despite the controversy, ISPs are expected to continue to deploy transparent cache servers in their networks.

servers for their connection to the Internet, and it reduces the load on those servers by reducing the number of HTTP transactions they must handle.

Given these benefits, it is not surprising that Web sites don't just rely on end users and their ISPs to implement HTTP caching. Reverse proxy caching allows Web sites to take control of caching themselves, independently of users and ISPs.

Figure 5.12 illustrates the main concept behind reverse proxy caching. The Web site or, more commonly, a service provider acting on behalf of the Web site, deploys a network of reverse proxy cache servers throughout the Internet. The more widely they can be dispersed, and the farther away from the origin server, the better.

Once the cache servers are in place, end users can receive the Web site's content directly from the nearest cache. As figure 5.13 indicates, different users are likely to communicate with

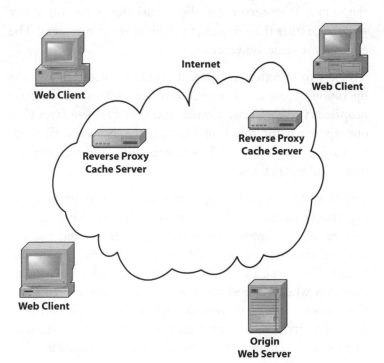

Figure 5.12 ▶
Web sites or Web hosting providers can deploy a network of reverse proxy cache servers throughout the Internet.

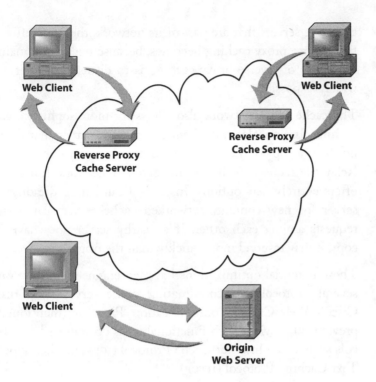

◀ Figure 5.13
With a network of reverse proxy cache servers in place, a Web site's users can be effectively serviced by nearby servers. Since the cache servers are closer to the clients, they can respond more quickly. Cache servers also relieve some of the processing burden on the origin server, and they reduce that server's bandwidth requirements.

different cache servers, depending on their location on the Internet.

This discussion is probably starting to sound a lot like our description of global load balancing, and, indeed, the distinction is not very fine. At the risk of exaggerating differences between the two, we note that global load balancing typically relies on multiple Web sites with full-featured Web servers, while reverse proxy caches are often special-purpose devices tailored for caching. Also, the Web sites that support global load balancing tend to be run by organizations and Web hosting providers; reverse proxy servers, on the other hand, are most effective if they are located on the networks of Internet access providers.

There is one aspect of reverse proxy caching that makes it significantly different from other forms of caching: Reverse proxy caching relies on a network of cache servers. Indeed,

Status of Caching Protocols

As of this writing, HTTP caching and caching protocols are rapidly evolving technologies. Although a few protocols have been standardized, the industry acknowledges that those protocols have several deficiencies. New protocols with essential new functionality, however, are still in the early stage of their development. In these circumstances, it does not seem appropriate to describe the details of each protocol. This text, therefore, focuses on an overview of the protocols' operation rather than details. Readers are encouraged to consult the "References" section of this book for information on obtaining the latest versions of each protocol specification.

the more servers that are part of its network, the more effective reverse proxy caching becomes, because one of the main objectives of reverse proxy caching is to disperse content as widely as possible.

The cache server network also allows for more sophisticated caching. In an isolated deployment, a cache server that does not have a copy of the requested content has only one choice: Relay the request to the origin server. A network, however, offers entirely new options. Instead of burdening the origin server for new content, networked cache servers can pass requests among each other. If a nearby server does have a copy, it may respond more quickly than the origin server.

These potential optimizations have led engineers to develop several protocols for coordinating cache server networks. Cisco's Web Cache Communication Protocol (mentioned previously) provides such functionality, as do standard protocols such as the Internet Cache Protocol (ICP) and the Hyper Text Caching Protocol (HTCP).

5.2.2 Proxy Auto Configuration Scripts

One of the major problems facing any deployment of traditional proxy servers is configuring end users' browsers appropriately. Figure 5.8 shows the standard dialog box for Microsoft's Internet Explorer. That setting alone is complicated enough for end users to find and understand, but imagine the difficulties if an installation requires the "Advanced" setting at which that dialog box hints. A dialog box such as the one in figure 5.14 will certainly challenge average users.

To save end users from having to manually configure their proxy settings, and to give network administrators much more flexibility in defining proxy configurations, Netscape created the concept of a Proxy Auto Configuration (PAC) script. Other browser manufacturers have agreed to support PAC scripts as well. There are, however, slight differences in

◀ **Figure 5.14**
Manually configuring the full range of proxy services for a browser can be complicated, as this dialog box shows.

the more subtle and advanced aspects of the PAC format, so anyone developing PAC scripts for multiple browsers should stick to the basic PAC capabilities.

The PAC format itself is a file containing JavaScript code. The file can contain any number of functions and variables, but it must include the function `FindProxyforURL()`. The browser will call this function with two parameters, `url` and `host`, before it retrieves any URL. The `url` parameter contains the URL that the browser wants to retrieve, and the `host` parameter contains the host name from that URL. (This second parameter is actually redundant, but, because extracting the host from the URL is an extremely common operation, the PAC format makes it a separate parameter as a convenience to PAC developers.)

The `FindProxyForURL()` function returns a single character string. That string lists, in order, the methods that the browser should use to retrieve the URL; table 5.3 lists the possible values. The string separates individual methods by semicolons. If the string is empty, the browser should contact the host directly.

Table 5.3 PAC Retrieval Options

Option	Meaning
DIRECT	Connect to the host directly without using a proxy.
PROXY host:port	Connect to the indicated proxy server.
SOCKS host:port	Retrieve the URL from the indicated SOCKS server.

An example PAC file, shown below, simply returns the name of a proxy server for any URL.

```
function FindProxyForURL(url, host)
{
    return "PROXY proxy.hundredacrewoods.com:8080";
}
```

In addition to identifying the FindProxyForURL() function, the PAC format defines several functions that the browser can provide on behalf of a PAC script developer. These functions, listed in table 5.4, provide many utilities that PAC script developers are likely to find useful.

Table 5.4 PAC Helper Functions

Function	Use
isPlainHostName()	Indicates if a host name is not a domain name (e.g., has no dots).
dnsDomainIs()	Indicates if the domain of a host name is the indicated domain.
localHostOrDomainIs()	Indicates if a host name is the same as a local name or domain name.
isResolvable()	Indicates if a host name can be resolved to an IP address.
isInNet()	Indicates if a host name or IP address belongs to the indicated network.
dnsResolve()	Resolves a host name to an IP address.
myIpAddress()	Returns the IP address of the client browser.

Table 5.4 continued

Function	Use
`dnsDomainLevelIs()`	Indicates the level in the DNS hierarchy of a host name.
`shExpMatch()`	Indicates if a string matches a specified shell expression.
`weekdayRange()`	Indicates if the current date is within the specified range of weekdays.
`dateRange()`	Indicates if the current date is within the specified range.
`timeRange()`	Indicate if the current date is within the specified time.

The following example shows how a PAC developer might use these helper functions. The example directs browsers to a proxy unless the requested URL is for a host in the hundredacrewoods.com domain or for a host that is local (in other words, has no domain name).

```
function FindProxyForURL(url, host)
{
   if (isPlainHostName(host) ||
       dnsDomainIs(host, ".hundredacrewoods.com"))
       return "DIRECT";

   else
       return
         "PROXY proxy.hundredacrewoods.com:8080";
}
```

Once a network administrator has created a PAC script, users configure their browsers to locate and retrieve the script from a server on the network. Typically, browsers allow users to specify the location of a PAC script via a URL, as figure 5.15 shows.

5.2.3 Web Proxy Auto-Discovery

Proxy Auto Configuration scripts allow network administrators to hide some of the complexity of proxy configuration from end users, but, as figure 5.15 shows, those users must

Figure 5.15 ▶

To simplify proxy server configuration, users can tell their browsers to automatically retrieve proxy settings from a network server. This dialog box tells the browser where to find its PAC script.

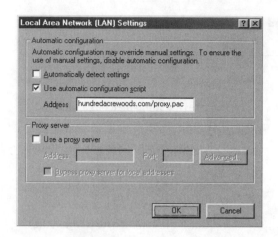

still configure their browsers with the URL for the PAC script. Even that minimal configuration introduces the possibility of a configuration error. To simplify proxy configuration even further, newer browsers support a technique known as Web Proxy Auto-Discovery (WPAD). With WPAD, browsers discover the location of their PAC script automatically, without any user configuration.

Although it's often referred to as a protocol, WPAD is not a separate communications protocol itself. Rather, it is a set of rules for using various existing protocols. Each of these protocols can provide a PAC script location; WPAD simply defines a consistent and unambiguous procedure for using them.

Table 5.5 Web Proxy Auto-Discovery Rules

Step	Use	Procedure
1	Required	Check for a PAC location (option code 252) in a Dynamic Host Configuration Protocol (DHCP) message.
2	Optional	Query for a PAC location using the Server Location Protocol (SLP).
3	Required	Query the Domain Name System (DNS) for the address (A) record for wpad.target.domain.name.com, where target.domain.name.com is the domain name of the client.

Table 5.5 continued

Step	Use	Procedure
4	Optional	Query DNS for the server (SVR) record for wpad.tcp.target.domain.name.com.
5	Optional	Query DNS for the text record (TXT) for wpad.target.domain.name.com.
6		Remove the left-most component of the domain name (so that target.domain.name.com becomes domain.name.com) and repeat steps 3-6, continuing until the minimal domain name is reached (i.e., don't try wpad.com).

When a client obtains the location of its PAC script using the WPAD procedure, it may find that the information is not complete. The Domain Name System, for example, can return a host name or address, but it cannot provide a protocol, port number, or path. To fill in any missing information, the WPAD client uses values from table 5.6.

Table 5.6 Default Values for PAC Location from WPAD

Component	Default Value (if not obtained via WPAD)
Protocol	http
Host	No default; must be obtained from WPAD procedure.
Port	80
Path	/wpad.dat

Once the client forms the complete URL for its Proxy Auto Configuration script, it retrieves the PAC script and configures its proxy settings appropriately. As part of the retrieval process, the client may receive various HTTP headers, including, for example, an expiration time for the PAC script. The client should honor all of the HTTP headers that are appropriate for a PAC script. If, for example, the script expires, the client should restart the entire WPAD procedure. It must not simply reuse the previously discovered PAC URL.

The latest versions of most Web browsers default to using WPAD to discovery proxy configuration. Figure 5.16 shows the dialog box that enables WPAD for Internet Explorer.

5.2.4 Web Cache Communication Protocol

Both Proxy Auto Configuration scripts and Web Proxy Auto-Discovery help network administrators automatically configure client browsers to use proxy cache servers. They both require some amount of control over the users, however (if for no other purpose, then at least for preventing users from overriding the WPAD process by, for example, clearing the checkbox in figure 5.16). Other organizations that can benefit from caching, particularly Internet Service Providers, don't have that level of control over their users. To employ caching for their customers, ISPs typically rely on transparent caching.

The Web Cache Communication Protocol (WCCP) is one important protocol for supporting transparent caching. Cisco Systems developed WCCP as a way for routers to learn of the existence of cache servers and to learn how to redirect HTTP requests to those caches.

Figure 5.17 shows the environment in which WCCP operates. The Internet Service Provider deploys one or more cache

Figure 5.16 ▶
Modern Web browsers can automatically search for proxy server configuration settings. This dialog box lets users enable or disable Web proxy auto-discovery.

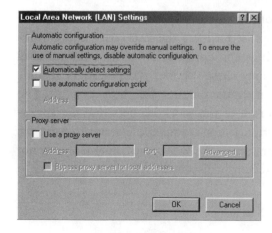

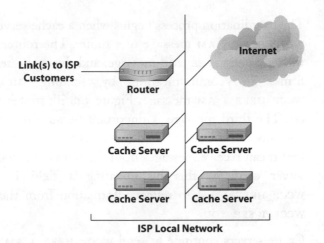

Link(s) to ISP
Customers

Router

Internet

Cache Server   Cache Server

Cache Server   Cache Server

ISP Local Network

WCCP coordinates the operation of
an access router with a collection of
transparent cache servers. This
figure shows a typical
configuration, in which the access
router and the cache servers belong
to an Internet service provider.

servers on the same local network as their access routers.
These access routers provide Internet connectivity to the
isp's customers, and HTTP requests from the customers' clients pass through the access routers. The goal, of course, is
for access routers to detect the HTTP requests and redirect
them to the cache servers. Routers and cache servers can use
wccp to meet that goal.

Table 5.7 summarizes the three types of messages that wccp
defines. The rest of this subsection describes their use.

Table 5.7 WCCP Messages

Message	Use
WCCP_HERE_I_AM	A cache server sends this message to a router to identify itself to the router.
WCCP_I_SEE_YOU	The router acknowledges the presence of a cache server with this message; it provides its current WCCP configuration to the cache server at the same time.
WCCP_ASSIGN_BUCKETS	A cache server tells the router how to redirect HTTP traffic, indicating how much (in relative terms) each cache server should receive.

The coordination process begins when a cache server sends a WCCP_HERE_I_AM message to a router. The router responds with a WCCP_I_SEE_YOU message, and the cache server confirms the communication by sending an updated WCCP_HERE_I_AM message. Figure 5.18 illustrates the process. The third message is important because it verifies that not only can the server send messages to the router, but also that it can receive messages from the router successfully. The server confirms this by updating a field in its own WCCP_HERE_I_AM to reflect information from the received WCCP_I_SEE_YOU.

Cache servers continue to send WCCP_HERE_I_AM messages even after the router has recognized them. The router uses those messages to determine if a cache server remains healthy. If the router does not receive a WCCP_HERE_I_AM message within a certain time interval (generally, long enough so that the router must miss three successive messages from the server), the router considers the cache server to be unusable.

Once the router has learned of participating cache servers, those servers can tell the router how to redirect HTTP traffic. A cache server does so with an WCCP_ASSIGN_BUCKETS message, which figure 5.19 illustrates. There is no special message to acknowledge this information, but WCCP_I_SEE_YOU messages from the router confirm the assignment by including the redirection table explicitly. Although routers accept

Figure 5.18 ▶
Cache servers announce themselves to an access router. The router responds, and the cache server acknowledges that response in a subsequent message.

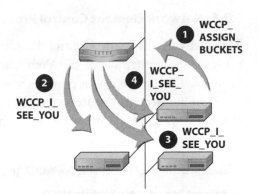

◀Figure 5.19
Once the access router and cache servers have recognized each other, a cache server can tell the router how to divide requests among the participating caches. The router acknowledges this assignment in WCCP messages to all cache servers.

WCCP_ASSIGN_BUCKETS from any cache server, generally only one server controls the redirection. As figure 5.19 indicates, though, the router confirms the redirection with WCCP_I_SEE_YOU messages to all servers.

Once HTTP redirection is active, the router intercepts all traffic to TCP port 80. It calculates a hash on the destination IP address, resulting in a value between 0 and 255. Based on this value and the WCCP_ASSIGN_BUCKETS message from the cache server, the router identifies a cache server for the traffic. Alternatively, the WCCP_ASSIGN_BUCKETS message could indicate that traffic with a particular hash value should not be redirected at all but forwarded to the actual destination. Traffic that is to be redirected is encapsulated according to the Generic Routing Encapsulation (GRE) specification using a protocol number of (hexadecimal) 883E.

As this description indicates, WCCP is a fairly simple protocol. It does not support sophisticated services such as redirection of traffic other than to TCP port 80; nor does it allow the cache servers to direct specific traffic to a specific server. (The WCCP specification does not define the actual hash function the router uses, so it is impossible to predict which server will receive particular traffic.) The buckets mechanism effectively randomly distributes traffic to the set of cache servers.

WCCP version 2

In 1999, Cisco released products that support version 2 of the Web Cache Coordination Protocol. Cisco promotes WCCP version 2 as having several enhancements over version 1, most notably a security feature comparable to that of NECP. As of this writing, however, Cisco has not published the details of WCCP version 2.

5.2.5 Network Element Control Protocol

The Network Element Control Protocol (NECP) addresses many of the limitations of the Web Cache Communication Protocol. Like WCCP, NECP provides a way for cache servers to communicate with routers, switches, and other network elements. As table 5.8 indicates, NECP has three significant enhancements compared to WCCP.

Table 5.8 Differences between the WCCP and the NECP

Additional Features Available in NECP

- Servers can specify which traffic is redirected by the network element (by protocol and destination port).
- Servers can distinguish specific traffic (by source IP address and other characteristics) which should not be redirected.
- Communications between servers and network elements may be secured so that the identities of the communicating systems are authenticated.

The first significant difference between NECP and WCCP is that NECP allows cache servers to indicate which traffic should be redirected. Servers specify the protocol identifier (usually TCP or UDP) and destination port. In contrast, WCCP always redirects TCP traffic to port 80.

As a further refinement, NECP allows servers to specify exceptions, traffic that the network element should not redirect, even though it otherwise matches a redirection request. Cache servers identify exceptions by any combination of the traffic's source (either by IP address or network mask), destination, protocol identifier, and port.

The final enhancement is especially important; NECP includes mechanisms to secure the communication between network elements and cache servers. Specifically, all messages between the two systems may include authentication credentials that are based on a secret value (like a password) shared by the server and network element. These mechanisms protect against an adversary hijacking communications by redirecting traffic. As long as the adversary doesn't know the network element's password, its requests for redirection will be rejected.

Although NECP is flexible enough to support many applications, its primary focus is on the same environments as WCCP—a set of transparent cache servers deployed by an Internet Service Provider. Unlike WCCP, NECP intends to support general network elements in addition to routers, particularly application layer switches. As figure 5.20 shows, the cache servers are likely to be in close proximity to the network element.

The NECP specification defines a total of 16 different messages, which table 5.9 lists. These messages are used in pairs; each of the 8 primary messages has its own acknowledgment.

When a cache server starts operation, it establishes a TCP connection with the network element and sends an NECP_INIT message, as in figure 5.21. The network element responds with an NECP_INIT_ACK. The systems maintain the TCP connection even after the initial message exchange; they use it for subsequent message exchanges.

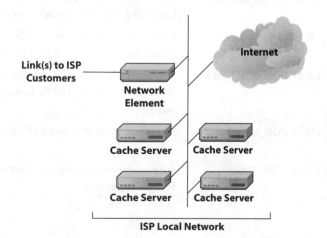

◀ **Figure 5.20**
The Network Element Control Protocol is a more general form of WCCP. It supports general network elements such as switches and network access servers, as well as access routers. The concept is the same, though. The protocol coordinates the operation of these network elements with a set of cache servers.

Table 5.9 NECP Messages

Message	Use
NECP_INIT	A server indicates to a network element that it is up and running.
NECP_INIT_ACK	A network element acknowledges a server's initialization.
NECP_KEEPALIVE	Either system queries the other for its health.
NECP_KEEPALIVE_ACK	A system responds to a health query from its peer.
NECP_START	A server asks a network element to begin forwarding traffic to it.
NECP_START_ACK	A network element acknowledges a forwarding request.
NECP_STOP	A server asks a network element to cease forwarding traffic.
NECP_STOP_ACK	A network element acknowledges a server request to cease forwarding.
NECP_EXCEPTION_ADD	A server defines an exception to traffic forwarding.
NECP_EXCEPTION_ADD_ACK	A network element acknowledges the definition of a traffic forwarding exception.
NECP_EXCEPTION_DEL	A server removes a traffic forwarding exception.
NECP_EXCEPTION_DEL_ACK	A network element acknowledges the removal of a traffic forwarding exception.
NECP_EXCEPTION_RESET	A server requests the removal of all traffic forwarding exceptions defined by the server.
NECP_EXCEPTION_RESET_ACK	A network element acknowledges the deletion of all of a server's traffic forwarding exceptions.
NECP_EXCEPTION_QUERY	A server asks for all active traffic forwarding exceptions.
NECP_EXCEPTION_RESP	A network element returns all active traffic forwarding exceptions.

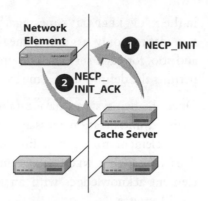

◀ **Figure 5.21**
Cache servers first introduce themselves to network elements with an NECP_INIT exchange. The cache server begins the exchange as in this example's first step. The network element acknowledges it in step 2.

To reassure each other that they're still functioning, both systems periodically send NECP_KEEPALIVE messages to the other. A system that receives this message replies with an NECP_KEEPALIVE_ACK. Either system can initiate this exchange; figure 5.22 shows the network element starting the exchange.

In addition to checking the overall health of a device, the keep-alive exchange can determine the health of a specific protocol in a device. With each NECP_KEEPALIVE message, the sender may include a list of protocol identifier and port number pairs. By including them, the sender asks the peer system to report the health of that service. For example, a query for the health of TCP port 80 would ask a cache server for the health of its HTTP service. A queried system responds

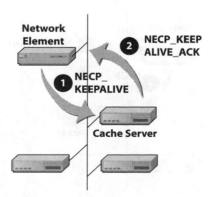

◀ **Figure 5.22**
NECP systems maintain their TCP connection by periodically sending NECP_KEEPALIVE messages; these exchanges also reassure each party that the other is still alive and functioning.

in the NECP_KEEPALIVE message. The current NECP specification defines only a general measure, an integer between 0 and 100, for each service. The protocol framework, however, permits the definition of a much more specific response.

Once the two systems have established a connection and exchanged initialization messages, the server can ask the network element to begin redirecting traffic to it. The server does that with a NECP_START message, which the network element acknowledges with an NECP_START_ACK, as figure 5.23 illustrates.

The NECP_START message includes a list of services that the network element should begin redirecting to the cache server. Services are identified by their protocol identifier (TCP or UDP) and destination port. The cache server also indicates a forwarding method for each service. Options include layer 2 forwarding (in which packets are delivered unchanged directly to the server), Generic Routing Encapsulation (the same approach used by WCCP), or layer 3 forwarding (in which the network element replaces the packet's destination IP address with that of the server).

The NECP_STOP message halts traffic redirection. The network element acknowledges this message by returning an NECP_STOP_ACK message.

Figure 5.23 ▶
The NECP_START message includes a list of services that the network element should begin redirecting to the cache server. As with all NECP messages, the receiving system (in this case the network element) acknowledges with a response.

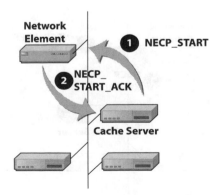

In addition to having network elements blindly forward all traffic of a particular service, NECP lets cache servers define exceptions to the normal forwarding behavior. Network elements do not redirect exception traffic to the cache server but, instead, send it directly to its real destination.

To inform a network element of an exception, a server sends it an NECP_EXCEPTION_ADD message, to which the network element responds with an NECP_EXCEPTION_ADD_ACK. Figure 5.24 illustrates the exchange. One message can list several exceptions, each of which is identified by the parameters table 5.10 lists.

Servers remove exceptions by sending NECP_EXCEPTION_DEL messages to network elements. A network element acknowledges the deletion with an NECP_EXCEPTION_DEL_ACK message. A server can also delete all of its exceptions at once with an NECP_EXCEPTION_RESET message, which elements acknowledge with an NECP_EXCEPTION_RESET_ACK.

Servers can also query a network element to find out what exceptions the element has in force. The message that does this is the NECP_EXCEPTION_QUERY, and the network element's response is contained in an NECP_EXCEPTION_RESP.

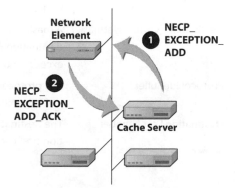

◀ **Figure 5.24**
Cache servers can list exceptions to redirected services in NECP_EXCEPTION_ADD messages. The network element ceases to redirect for these exceptions.

Table 5.10 Defining a Forwarding Exception

Parameter	Meaning
Scope Advisory	Indicates whether the exception applies only to traffic that would be forwarded to this server or whether the exception should apply to all traffic that passes through the network element; network elements may choose to ignore a global scope if, for example, the server isn't trusted to speak for all cache servers.
TTL	The length of time (in seconds) that the exception should be considered valid; if this period of time passes without an update from the server, the network element should consider the exception to have expired.
Source IP Address	Source IP address(es) for exception traffic.
Source Address Netmask	A mask indicating which bits in the source IP address are relevant for exception traffic (e.g., a source address of 192.168.0.0 and netmask of 255.255.0.0 mean that packets with a source address of 192.168.x.x, where x is any value, should be considered exception traffic).
Destination IP Address	Destination IP address(es) for exception traffic.
Destination Address Netmask	A mask indicating which bits in the destination IP address are relevant for exception traffic.
Protocol Identifier	The protocol identifier for exception traffic, generally UDP or TCP.
Destination Port Number	The destination port number for exception traffic (e.g., 80 for HTTP).

In the query message the server can refine the set of exceptions in which it is interested by specifying exception parameters, as well as the IP address of the server that initiated the exception. If a server omits the initiator's address, or if it specifies an address other than its own, the server can discover exceptions installed by other cache servers.

An important characteristic of all requests that servers make of network elements is their effect on existing traffic sessions. Requests, whether to start or stop forwarding or add or delete exceptions, have no impact on sessions already in progress. If, for example, a client has already begun an HTTP session with the actual destination, a cache server's request to receive redirected HTTP traffic will have no effect on that client's session. New sessions begun by this client (or any other) will be forwarded appropriately, but existing sessions continue unchanged.

This behavior has two important consequences for network elements and cache servers. First, it means that network elements must keep track of individual user sessions that pass through them. This requirement places a significant burden on the network element. Second, this behavior means that a cache server should not abruptly terminate its operation. A more graceful approach—in which the server stops future forwarding but continues to support existing sessions until those sessions terminate naturally—provides a much better service to users.

Perhaps the most important aspect of NECP's operation is its security support. With NECP, cache servers and network elements can negotiate the use of authentication on all messages they exchange. The authentication procedure relies on a secret value that the network element and cache server share. It is effectively a network element password that a cache server must know before its messages will be accepted by the network element.

When authentication is in use, a system that wishes to send an NECP message takes that message, adds the shared secret to the end of it, and computes a cryptographic digest of the result. It then replaces the shared secret with the output of the digest and transmits the resulting NECP message. Figure 5.25 illustrates the process. The current version of NECP specifies the Secure Hash Algorithm (SHA-1) function for the cryptographic digest calculation.

When a network element receives an authenticated message, it performs the same cryptographic digest calculations. If the results match, then the network element is assured that the sending cache server knows the shared secret. If the results don't match, the network element rejects the message.

5.2.6 Internet Cache Protocol

So far we've looked at protocols that cache servers can use to communicate with clients and with network elements such as routers. Equally important in some configurations is how cache servers communicate with each other. Of particular

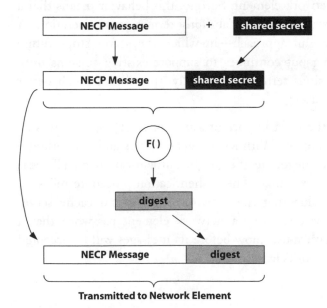

Figure 5.25 ▶
To protect against malicious parties gaining control of a network element (and "hijacking" sessions passing through it), the network element and its cache servers share a secret password. All systems combine this password with their NECP messages to create a cryptographic digest, which they transmit along with the message proper.

interest is what happens when a client requests an object for which the cache server has no local copy. Of course, the cache server could simply request the object from the actual destination, but that may not be an optimal approach. There could well be another cache server nearby that does have the object, and requesting it from that cache server would be much quicker than asking the actual destination. A cache server must answer two questions before it can take advantage of this optimization, however. First, how does it know which other cache servers have a local copy of the object? Second, if multiple servers have a copy, how can it determine which is the closest? The Internet Cache Protocol (ICP) provides answers to both.

The Internet Cache Protocol is actually a very simple protocol. It is designed specifically for a deployment like that of figure 5.26. In that figure, the user's HTTP GET request arrives at Cache Server A. That server doesn't have the object, so it

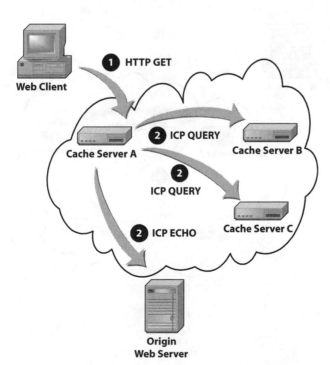

◀ Figure 5.26
A cache server can use the Internet Cache Protocol to query other cache servers on the network. At the same time, it can send a simple echo message to the origin server.

immediately sends three messages simultaneously. It sends ICP queries to each of the cache servers it knows about, and it sends an ICP echo message to the actual destination, the origin Web server for the object.

When the cache servers and origin server receive these ICP messages, they respond as in figure 5.27. The first response arrives from Cache Server B. That response indicates that Server B does not have a local copy in its cache. The next response, from Cache Server C, indicates that Server C does have a local copy. The final response is from the origin server; it is simply an echo of Cache Server A's original message. (The ICP echo message is transmitted to the server's UDP echo port, so that even servers that don't understand ICP will respond.)

With these responses, Cache Server A now knows that Server C has a copy of the object and that Server C was able

Figure 5.27 ▶
Cache servers respond to ICP queries with an indication of whether the requested object is in their local cache. The origin server merely responds to the echo request (because it should always have a copy of the object). In this example cache server B responds first, but it indicates a cache miss. Cache server C is the next to respond, and it does have a copy of the object.

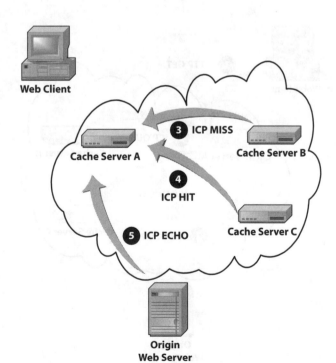

to respond more quickly than the origin server. Server A can assume, therefore, that the quickest way to retrieve the object is by requesting it from Server C. As figure 5.28 shows, Server A does exactly that and then returns the requested object to the client.

One of the important assumptions behind ICP is that the ICP query exchange can be very quick. Otherwise, the time taken for the ICP query would cancel out any time saved by querying a nearby cache server. For that reason, ICP messages are short, simple, and carried in UDP datagrams rather than TCP connections.

Table 5.11 lists the ICP message types and their use. By design, ICP is a simple protocol, and there are few complications in its operation. One extra feature that isn't obvious from the table is round-trip time measurements. When a cache server sends an ICP query, it can ask the responders to report their

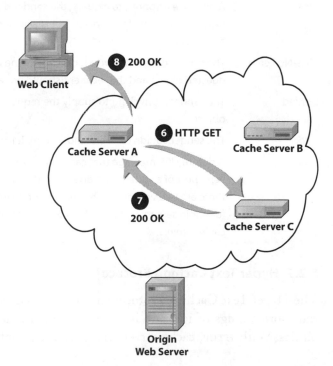

◀ **Figure 5.28**
The original cache server routes the request to the system with the object that responded the quickest. Here, that was cache server C. Cache A, therefore, forwards the request to C and relays C's response to the client.

Shortcomings of ICP

Unlike most of the other protocols this section describes, ICP is relatively stable and has been implemented in many products. Unfortunately, it is rather primitive and suffers from several shortcomings when applied to HTTP caching. The major problem is that ICP includes only the requested object in its queries. Most notably, it does not include the HTTP headers that the client included in its original HTTP request. In some cases those headers are critical to the response and may determine the content of the returned object. Web servers often use cookies, for example, to identify a returning user and provide personalized content. Obviously, in those cases, ICP will interfere with the server's intentions.

round-trip time to the origin server. This value allows the original requesting server to estimate how long it would take for those servers to retrieve the object should they not have a copy in their local caches.

Table 5.11 ICP Messages

Type	Use
Query	Asks if the recipient has a copy of an object, identified by a URL, in its local cache; this message also includes the IP address of the original requester (the HTTP client) and an indication of whether the sender is willing to receive the entire requested object in an ICP response.
Hit	A positive response to a query; the sender does have a local copy of the object.
Hit/Object	Not only does the sender have a local copy of the requested object, it is including that object in its response.
Miss	A negative response to a query; the sender does not have a local copy of the object (but is willing to get one if asked).
Miss/No Fetch	The sender does not have a local copy of the requested object and the recipient should not ask for it.
Denied	The sender is unwilling to supply the requested object.
Error	The sender couldn't understand a query it received.
Echo	A dummy ICP message that can be sent to the UDP echo port of a system that doesn't understand ICP; there are two versions of this message, one intended for origin servers and the other intended for remote cache servers.

5.2.7 Hyper Text Caching Protocol

The Hyper Text Caching Protocol (HTCP) addresses some of the shortcomings of ICP, and it adds a few additional capabilities. With HTCP, cache servers can probe the contents of other cache servers to find out if an object can be retrieved more quickly from a nearby cache rather than the origin server. Unlike ICP, HTCP allows the sending server to include a copy of all the HTTP headers in the client's original request, so the responding server can more accurately determine if its local copy really satisfies the client. In addition, HTCP allows cache servers to actively monitor the contents of each other's caches; with this feature they can tell when a neighbor adds new objects to its cache, modifies objects in its cache, or deletes objects from its cache. Through HTCP, servers can also actively modify the contents of another's cache, adding objects to that cache or deleting them from it. Because HTCP can be used to modify the content of a server's local cache, its messages may include authentication information that validates the identity of the sender.

Table 5.12 lists the different types of HTCP messages. In contrast with ICP, HTCP doesn't have separate acknowledgment message types. Rather, each message includes a flag that indicates whether it is a request or a response.

Table 5.12 HTCP Messages

Type	Use
NOP	No operation, although this can be used to probe the round-trip time between servers.
TST	Test, used to determine if an object is present in a server's local cache.
MON	Monitor, used to monitor activity in a server's local cache; a MON request initiates a monitoring session, while MON responses report additions to, deletions from, replacements, and refreshes of the monitored server's cache.
SET	Sends information about an object to a cache server including, for example, updated cache or expiration headers.
CLR	Clear, directs a server to delete an object from its local cache.

The Test exchange resembles the ICP query. As figure 5.29 shows, a cache server initiates it when a client requests an object that is not in its local cache. That server sends simultaneous TST request messages to all its neighbor caches, specifying both the object requested and any HTTP headers in the client's original request. In the example of the figure, server B replies with a TST response that indicates the object is not present in its cache while, a short time later, server C's TST response indicates that it does have a copy. With this information, cache server A can send an HTTP request to server C requesting the object.

The HTCP TST response not only indicates whether the sender has a copy of the object; it can also provide information about that object. Most notably, the response indicates the HTTP method, URI, version, and headers used to request the object, as well as the HTTP headers included in the origin server's response. The TST response may also include special cache information listed in table 5.13.

Figure 5.29 ▶
The Hyper Text Caching Protocol is a more sophisticated version of the Internet Cache Protocol, but its basic operation is very similar. A cache server sends HTCP TST messages to other cache servers to try to locate a nearby source for the requested object.

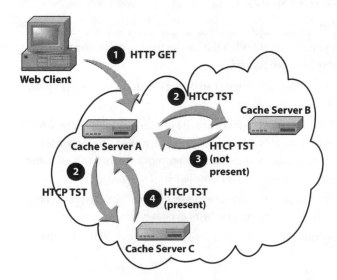

Table 5.13 Cache Information HTCP May Provide

Item	Meaning
Cache-Vary	The content of the object varies depending on the value of the indicated HTTP headers.
Cache-Location	The indicated cache servers have a copy of this object.
Cache-Policy	The object may not be cacheable or shareable among cache servers, or its content could change depending on HTTP cookies.
Cache-Flags	The server doesn't know all the HTTP response headers that apply to the object.
Cache-Expiry	The object expires at the indicated time.
Cache-MD5	A cryptographic checksum of the contents of the object.
Cache-to-Origin	The round-trip time to the origin server.

A unique feature of HTCP is the ability for one cache server to monitor the contents of another server's local cache. A cache server that is quite remote from an origin server, for example, can monitor another cache server that is local to the origin. The local server, especially if it is positioned between the Internet and the origin server, may be able to track all requests for objects. Such a local server would be well positioned to know about all objects on the origin server, so by monitoring its cache, the remote cache server could keep up to date with the origin server's content.

Figure 5.30 shows this scenario. The process begins when the remote server sends an HTCP MON request to the local server. This request identifies a channel through which the local server should inform the remote server of any changes to its cache contents. The MON request includes a time period for the channel. If the remote server doesn't renew the channel (with another MON request) within that time, cache updates from the local server automatically cease.

Once the channel is established, the local cache server sends a MON response to the remote server every time its cache

Figure 5.30 ▶
HTTP allows one cache server to monitor another's contents. As content on the local cache server changes, the server sends MON responses to the remote cache server. This operation can help the remote server keep its cached contents up to date even before a client requests an object.

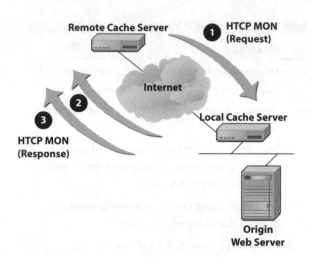

contents change. Each MON response includes the time remaining for the life of the channel, the action that occurred in the local cache, the reason for the action, and the identity of the object affected, as table 5.14 indicates.

Table 5.14 HTCP Monitor Responses

Field	Meaning
TIME	How many seconds remain in the monitor channel's life (unless refreshed).
ACTION	The change that has occurred in the local cache.
	0 An object has been added to the cache.
	1 An object in the cache has been refreshed.
	2 An object in the cache has been replaced.
	3 An object in the cache has been deleted.
REASON	The reason for the change in the cache.
	0 Unspecified reason.
	1 A client fetched the object.
	2 A client fetched the object with caching disallowed.
	3 The cache server prefetched the object.
	4 The object expired, as per its headers.
	5 The object was purged to conserve cache space.

Table 5.14 continued		
Field	**Meaning**	
IDENTITY	The object in the local cache that changed.	
	METHOD	The HTTP method used to access the object.
	URI	The object's Uniform Resource Identifier.
	VERSION	The HTTP version used to access the object.
	REQ-HDRS	The HTTP headers included in the request for the object.
	RESP-HDRS	The HTTP headers included in the response to the request.
	ENTITY-HDRS	HTTP headers applying to the object.
	CACHE-HDRS	Cache information about the object.

The HTCP MON exchange allows a cache server to ask for updates to another's cache. The protocol can also operate in reverse: Cache servers can, without invitation, tell other servers to modify their caches. The messages to do that are SET and CLR. As figure 5.31 shows, even an origin Web server can use HTCP to keep cache servers supporting it up to date. The SET and CLR messages are tools that the origin server could use to do so. A SET message updates the headers corresponding to an object including, for example, its expiration time. A

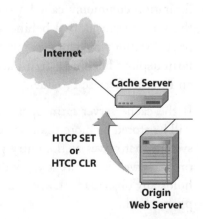

◄ Figure 5.31
Origin servers may use HTCP to proactively update cache servers, telling them, for example, when HTTP headers corresponding to a cached object have changed.

CLR message asks a cache server to remove the object from its cache entirely.

Because the SET and CLR messages allow an external system to modify the contents of a server's cache, it is important to be able to verify the identity of the system that sends them. To provide that verification, HTCP defines a mechanism for authenticating system identity. The approach is very similar to that of the Network Element Control Protocol. The communicating systems must first share a secret value. A sending system adds the contents of the message to the secret key, computes a cryptographic digest of the combination, and appends that digest result to the message. The receiving system performs the same computation and makes sure that the digest results match. If they don't match, the receiving system rejects the HTCP message.

5.2.8 Cache Array Routing Protocol

Another protocol that can enhance the performance of HTTP caching is the Cache Array Routing Protocol (CARP). This protocol allows a collection of cache servers to coordinate their cache contents in order to use their cache resources more efficiently. The typical environment for CARP, shown in figure 5.32, is somewhat different from the configurations we've previously considered. That environment assumes a collection of cache servers co-located with each other, a configuration commonly called a server farm. The figure shows the server farm located behind a proxy server on an Enterprise location; the same principles apply to a cache server farm deployed behind a transparent cache on the premises of an Internet Service Provider.

If the cache server farm operates most efficiently, no object will be stored by more than one cache server. In addition, the system that serves as the entry point to the server farm (the proxy server in figure 5.32) will know which cache server holds any object. The Cache Array Routing Protocol accomplishes both.

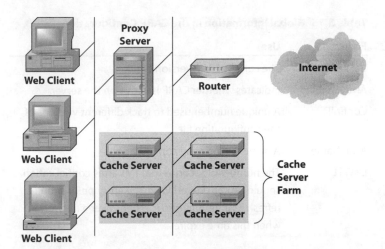

◀ **Figure 5.32**
The Cache Array Routing Protocol (which isn't really a communications protocol at all) defines a set of rules that coordinate the operation of a collection of cache servers, primarily to avoid redundant caching.

Interestingly, CARP is not actually a communication protocol at all. It achieves its goals without any explicit communications between the entry point and cache servers, or among the cache servers themselves. Instead, CARP is a set of rules for the entry point to follow. The rules consist of an array configuration file and a routing algorithm. The configuration file tells the entry point which cache servers are available, and the routing algorithm tells the entry point which cache server should be queried for any particular object.

Note that the cache servers themselves don't necessarily have to do anything special to support CARP. They simply operate as regular cache servers. When a request arrives for an object not in the local cache, the server retrieves it and then adds it to the cache. The key to CARP is the routing algorithm. Entry points that use it correctly always ask the same cache server for the same object. Subsequent client requests for an object will always be directed to the cache server that has already retrieved that object.

The entry point reads its CARP configuration file when it begins operation. That file consists of global information, shown in table 5.15, and a list of cache servers.

Table 5.15 Global Information in the CARP Configuration

Field	Use
Version	The current CARP version is 1.0.
ArrayEnabled	Indicates whether CARP is active on the server.
ConfigID	A unique number used to track different versions of the configuration file.
ArrayName	A name for the array configuration.
ListTTL	The number of seconds that this array configuration should be considered valid; the entry point should refresh its configuration (perhaps over a network) when this time expires.

Table 5.16 lists all the information the file contains about each cache server, but the important parameters are the server's identity and a value called the *Load Factor*. The Load Factor is important because it influences the routing algorithm. Cache servers with higher load factors are favored over servers with lower load factors. An administrator configuring a CARP server farm, for example, should assign higher load factors to those cache servers with larger caches and faster processors.

Table 5.16 Server Information in CARP Configuration File

Field	Use
Name	Domain name for the cache server.
IP address	IP address of the cache server.
Port	TCP port on which the cache server is listening.
Table URL	URL from which the CARP configuration file may be retrieved.
Agent String	The vendor and version of the cache server.
Statetime	The number of seconds the cache server has been operating in its current state.
Status	An indication of whether the cache server is able to process requests.
Load Factor	How much load the server can sustain.
Cache Size	The size (in MB) of the cache of this server.

Table 5.17 details the CARP routing algorithm. Note that steps 1 and 2 are performed before the entry point begins redirecting HTTP requests; they are not recalculated with each new request.

Table 5.17 The CARP Routing Algorithm for Entry Points

Step	Action
1	Convert all cache server names to lowercase.
2	Calculate a hash value for each cache server name.
3	As an HTTP request arrives, convert the full URL to lowercase.
4	Calculate a hash value for the complete URL.
5	Combine the URL's hash value with the hash values of each cache server, biasing the result with each server's load factor; the resulting values are a "score" for each cache server.
6	Redirect the request to the server with the highest score.

5.3 Other Acceleration Techniques

While load balancing and caching are the two most popular techniques for accelerating HTTP performance, Web sites have adopted other acceleration techniques as well. Two particularly effective approaches are specialized SSL processing and TCP multiplexing. Strictly speaking, neither actually directly influences the HTTP protocol operation; however, both techniques are so closely associated with Web performance that any HTTP developer should be aware of their potential.

5.3.1 Specialized SSL Processing

As section 4.2 explains, the Secure Sockets Layer (SSL) is the most common technique—by far—for securing HTTP sessions. Unfortunately, SSL relies on complex cryptographic algorithms, and calculating those algorithms is a significant burden for Web servers. It can require, for example, one thousand times more processor resources to perform SSL calculations than to simply return the requested object. A secure

Web server may find that it is doing much more crypto-graphic processing than returning Web pages.

To address this imbalance, several vendors have created spe-cial-purpose hardware that can perform cryptographic calcu-lations much faster than software. Such hardware can be included in add-in cards, on special-purpose modules that interface via scsi or Ethernet, or packaged as separate net-work systems. In all cases, the hardware performs the ssl calculations, relieving the Web server of that burden.

Figure 5.33 compares a simple Web server configuration with one employing a separate network system acting as an ssl processor. The top part of the figure emphasizes the fact that a simple configuration relies on the Web server to perform both the ssl and the http processing. In contrast, the bot-tom of the figure shows the insertion of an ssl processor. That device performs the ssl processing. After that process-ing, the device is left with the http connection, which it merely passes through to the Web server. To the Web server, this looks like a standard http connection, one that does not require ssl processing. The ssl processor does what it does best—cryptographic computations—while the Web server does its job of responding to http requests.

Figure 5.33 ▶
An external SSL processor acts as an endpoint for clients' SSL sessions, but it passes the HTTP messages on to the Web server. This configuration offloads SSL's cryptographic computations from the Web server and onto special purpose hardware optimized for that use.

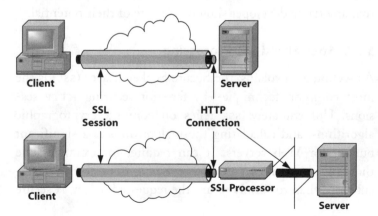

5.3.2 TCP Multiplexing

Although the performance gains are not often as impressive, TCP multiplexing is another technique for relieving a Web server of non-essential processing duties. In this case, the non-HTTP processing is TCP. Take a look at the simple Web configuration of figure 5.34. In that example, the Web server is supporting three clients. To do that, it manages three TCP connections and three HTTP connections.

Managing the TCP connections, particularly for simple HTTP requests, can be a significant burden for the Web server. Recall from the discussion of section 2.1.2 that, although it always takes five messages to create and terminate a TCP connection, an HTTP GET and 200 OK response may be carried in just two messages. In the worst case, a Web server may be spending less than 30 percent of its time supporting HTTP.

External TCP processors offer one way to improve this situation. Much like an SSL processor, a TCP processor inserts itself between the Internet and the Web server. As figure 5.35 indicates, the TCP processor manages all the TCP connections to the clients while funneling those clients' HTTP messages to the Web server over a single TCP connection. The TCP processor takes advantage of persistent HTTP connections and pipelining.

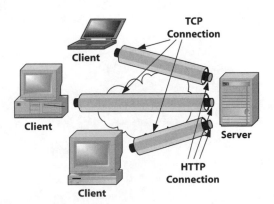

◀ **Figure 5.34**
Each HTTP connection normally requires its own TCP connection, forcing Web servers to manage TCP connections with every client. For Web sites that support millions of clients, this support can become a considerable burden.

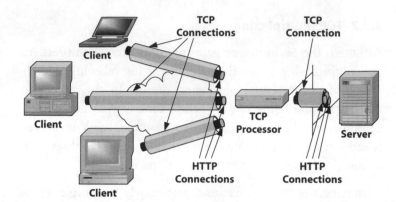

Figure 5.35 ▶

A TCP processor manages individual TCP connections with each client, consolidating them into a single TCP connection to the Web server. This single connection relies heavily on HTTP persistence and pipelining.

External TCP processors are not effective in all situations. They work best for Web sites that need to support many clients, where each client makes simple HTTP requests. If the Web server supports fewer clients, or if the clients tend to have complex or lengthy interactions with the server, then TCP processors are less effective. In addition, the TCP processor must be capable of processing TCP faster than the Web server, or it must be capable of supporting more simultaneous TCP connections than the Web server.

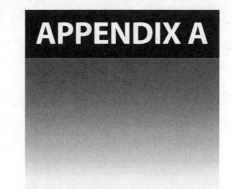
HTTP Versions — Evolution & Deployment of HTTP

Until now, this book has described version 1.1 of http. That version, however, is actually the third version of the protocol. This appendix takes a brief look at the protocol's evolution over those three versions and the differences between them. The last subsection assesses the support for the various features of version 1.1 by different implementations.

A.1 HTTP's Evolution

The Hypertext Transfer Protocol has come to dominate the Internet despite a rather chaotic history as a protocol standard. As we noted in chapter 1, HTTP began as a very simple protocol. In fact, it could hardly be simpler. The original proposal by Tim Berners-Lee defined only one method—GET—and it did not include any headers or status codes. The server simply returned the requested HTML document. This protocol is known as HTTP version 0.9, and despite its simplicity, it occasionally shows up in Internet traffic logs even today.

Vendors and researchers quickly realized the power of the hypertext concept, and many raced to extend HTTP to accommodate their own particular needs. Although the community worked cooperatively and openly enough to avoid any serious divergences, the situation evolved much as figure A.1 depicts, with many different proprietary implementations claiming to be compatible with HTTP 1.0.

Without a true standard, however, developers grew increasingly concerned about the possibility of HTTP fragmenting into many incompatible implementations. Under the auspices of the Internet Engineering Task Force (IETF), leading HTTP implementers collected the common, and commonly used, features of many leading implementations. They defined the resulting specification as HTTP version 1.0. In some

Figure A.1 ▶
HTTP diverged from the original version 0.9 specification into many vendors' proprietary implementations. The specification for HTTP version 1.0 attempted to capture the most common implementation practices. Although vendors have continued to create their own implementations based on incomplete versions of the HTTP 1.1 specification, it is hoped that the final release of HTTP version 1.1 specifications will allow implementations to converge on a single standard.

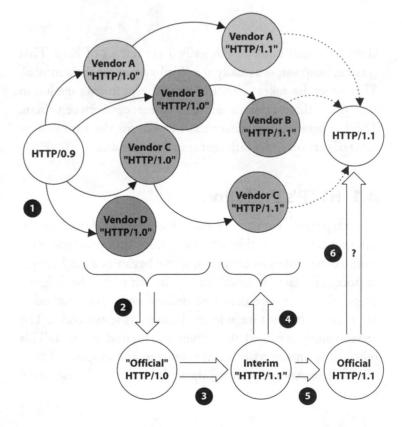

ways, writing the specification after products are already widely deployed seems backwards, but it did allow the working group to take into account a lot of operational experience. The working group then embarked on an effort to create a true HTTP standard, which would be called HTTP version 1.1.

Unfortunately, the effort to define HTTP version 1.1 took a lot longer than originally anticipated, and many draft specifications for version 1.1 were published and discussed. Vendors implemented products conforming to these draft specification and claimed HTTP 1.1 compliance, even though no official HTTP 1.1 standard yet existed.

By now, though, the situation is finally starting to stabilize. The standard for HTTP version 1.1 is finally complete; implementations are beginning to converge on a common interpretation of the standard, and the community is starting to create formal compliance tests to ensure interoperability. As the World Wide Web extends beyond personal computers to appliances, personal digital assistants, wireless telephones, and other systems, the importance of HTTP 1.1 as a true, interoperable standard will only increase.

A.2 HTTP Version Differences

When the Internet Engineering Task Force finalized the specification for HTTP version 1.0, they recognized that the protocol had significant performance and scalability problems. The IETF's parent body (the Internet Engineering Steering Group, or IESG) insisted that version 1.0 be published as an "Informational" document only, and they went so far as to insert the following comment in the standard itself:

> The IESG has concerns about this protocol, and expects this document to be replaced relatively soon by a standards track document.

The replacement for HTTP version 1.0, of course, is HTTP version 1.1. Version 1.1 offers several significant improvements over version 1.0. These improvements enhance the extensibility, scalability, performance, and security of the protocol and its systems. The most significant changes HTTP 1.1 introduces are persistent connections, the Host header, and improved authentication procedures.

Table A.1 lists the HTTP methods each version defines. Note that HTTP version 1.0 includes two methods—LINK and UNLINK—that do not exist in version 1.1. Those methods, which were not widely supported by Web browsers or servers, allow an HTTP client to modify information about an existing resource without changing the resource itself.

Table A.1 Methods Available in HTTP Versions

Method	HTTP/0.9	HTTP/1.0	HTTP/1.1
CONNECT			●
DELETE		●	●
GET	●	●	●
HEAD		●	●
LINK		●	
POST		●	●
PUT		●	●
OPTIONS			●
TRACE			●
UNLINK		●	

Table A.2 summarizes the HTTP headers available in each of the versions. Just to be complete, the table includes a column for HTTP version 0.9, but, as we've noted, version 0.9 doesn't actually use any headers. Three headers, Link, Title, and URL, exist in version 1.0 but not 1.1. Those methods are mainly associated with the LINK and UNLINK methods. Like the methods themselves, they have not seen support by popular Web browsers and clients.

Table A.2 Headers Available in HTTP Versions

Header	HTTP/0.9	HTTP/1.0	HTTP/1.1
Accept		●	●
Accept-Charset		●	●
Accept-Encoding		●	●
Accept-Language		●	●
Accept-Ranges			●
Age			●
Allow		●	●
Authorization		●	●
Cache-Control			●
Connection		●	●
Content-Encoding		●	●
Content-Language		●	●
Content-Length		●	●
Content-Location			●
Content-MD5			●
Content-Range			●
Content-Type		●	●
Date		●	●
ETag			●
Expect			●
Expires		●	●
From		●	●
Host			●
If-Match			●
If-Modified-Since		●	●
If-None-Match			●
If-Range			●
If-Unmodified-Since			●

continues...

Table A.2 Headers Available in HTTP Versions (continued)

Header	HTTP/0.9	HTTP/1.0	HTTP/1.1
Last-Modified		●	●
Link		●	
Location		●	●
Max-Forwards			●
MIME-version		●	●
Pragma		●	●
Proxy-Authenticate			●
Proxy-Authorization			●
Range			●
Referer		●	●
Retry-After		●	●
Server		●	●
TE			●
Title		●	
Trailer			●
Transfer-Encoding			●
Upgrade			●
URL		●	
User-Agent		●	●
Vary			●
Via			●
Warning			●
WWW-Authenticate		●	●

A.3 HTTP 1.1 Support

One way to assess the level of HTTP 1.1 support relies on reports from implementers themselves. The World Wide Web Consortium allows developers to report the status of their implementations and to indicate which HTTP 1.1 features they support and which they do not. It appears that the reporting mechanism has been little used since 1998, but tables A.3, A.4, and A.5 summarize the results of those reports.

Some caution is definitely in order when interpreting these results for at least four reasons. First, the information is not particularly recent, and it certainly does not represent the newest releases of popular HTTP clients and servers. It is quite possible (even likely) that vendors have changed their support for HTTP 1.1 since 1998. Second, the data set is rather small. It represents the reports of only 14 client implementations, 18 server implementations, and 8 proxy implementations; in all cases that's far fewer than the number of implementations that exist today on the Web. Third, the information was reported by the implementers themselves and was not verified or audited by an outside party. Finally, in a lot of cases the total number of implementations supporting a feature may be much less important than knowing which ones support that feature. If, for example, a particular feature is available only in two Web browsers but those two represent 95 percent of the Web browser market, the lack of support by other implementations may not matter to some applications.

Table A.3 Methods Supported by HTTP 1.1 Systems in 1998

Method	Clients	Servers	Proxies
CONNECT	64%	39%	75%
DELETE	50%	50%	38%
GET	100%	100%	100%
HEAD	93%	100%	100%
OPTIONS	43%	56%	50%
POST	93%	100%	100%
PUT	64%	67%	50%
TRACE	50%	67%	50%

Table A.4 Headers Supported by HTTP 1.1 Systems in 1998

Header	Clients	Servers	Proxies
Accept	86%	83%	100%
Accept-Charset	64%	67%	63%
Accept-Encoding	71%	67%	63%
Accept-Language	64%	72%	63%
Accept-Ranges	57%	67%	50%
Age	57%	39%	63%
Allow	43%	83%	63%
Authorization	86%	94%	88%
Cache-Control	86%	94%	100%
Connection	100%	94%	100%
Content-Encoding	93%	89%	88%
Content-Language	57%	72%	63%
Content-Length	93%	94%	100%
Content-Location	64%	56%	63%
Content-MD5	29%	50%	38%
Content-Range	64%	72%	63%
Content-Type	86%	100%	100%
Date	86%	100%	100%
ETag	64%	78%	63%
Expect	36%	50%	38%
Expires	57%	78%	63%
From	64%	44%	63%
Host	100%	100%	100%
If-Match	57%	72%	63%
If-Modified-Since	86%	100%	100%
If-None-Match	43%	67%	50%
If-Range	43%	50%	38%
If-Unmodified-Since	50%	78%	63%
Last-Modified	64%	83%	63%
Location	79%	78%	63%

Table A.4 continued

Header	Clients	Servers	Proxies
Max-Forwards	43%	28%	63%
Pragma	86%	83%	100%
Proxy-Authenticate	93%	44%	88%
Proxy-Authorization	93%	44%	88%
Range	64%	67%	63%
Referer	64%	61%	50%
Retry-After	43%	39%	50%
Server	57%	83%	63%
TE	43%	22%	25%
Trailer	36%	17%	25%
Transfer-Encoding	86%	89%	88%
Upgrade	29%	22%	38%
User-Agent	93%	67%	100%
Vary	43%	61%	63%
Via	64%	44%	88%
Warning	50%	28%	63%
WWW-Authenticate	86%	94%	100%
Basic Authentication	93%	94%	100%
WWW-Authenticate Digest	14%	50%	13%
qop-options auth	7%	17%	0%
qop-options auth-int	7%	6%	0%
Authorization Digest	14%	50%	13%
request qop auth	7%	17%	0%
request qop auth-int	7%	6%	0%
Authentication-Info Digest	14%	28%	13%
response qop auth	7%	17%	0%
response qop auth-int	7%	6%	0%
Proxy-Authenticate Basic	79%	39%	75%
Proxy-Authenticate Digest	14%	11%	13%

continues…

Table A.4 Headers Supported by HTTP 1.1 Systems (continued)

Header	Clients	Servers	Proxies
Proxy qop-options auth	7%	0%	0%
Proxy Authorization Digest	14%	11%	13%
Proxy request qop auth	7%	0%	0%
Proxy request qop auth-int	7%	0%	0%
Proxy Authentication-Info Digest	14%	6%	13%
Proxy response qop auth	7%	0%	0%
Proxy response qop auth-int	7%	0%	0%

Table A.5 Status Codes Support in HTTP 1.1 Systems in 1998

Status	Clients	Servers	Proxies
100 Continue	71%	72%	63%
101 Switching Protocols	29%	28%	38%
200 OK	100%	100%	100%
201 Created	50%	50%	38%
202 Accepted	36%	33%	25%
203 Non-Authoritative Information	29%	28%	25%
204 No Content	64%	50%	50%
205 Reset Content	29%	22%	25%
206 Partial Content	57%	61%	50%
300 Multiple Choices	43%	39%	38%
301 Moved Permanently	93%	83%	88%
302 Found	64%	72%	50%
303 See Other	64%	39%	50%
304 Not Modified	86%	94%	100%
305 Use Proxy	57%	28%	50%
307 Temporary Redirect	86%	44%	75%
400 Bad Request	86%	94%	88%
401 Unauthorized	100%	100%	100%
402 Payment Required	64%	44%	88%

Table A.5 continued

Status	Clients	Servers	Proxies
403 Forbidden	86%	94%	100%
404 Not Found	86%	100%	100%
405 Method Not Allowed	64%	72%	63%
406 Not Acceptable	64%	50%	63%
407 Proxy Authentication Required	93%	44%	88%
408 Request Timeout	50%	39%	25%
409 Conflict	50%	39%	38%
410 Gone	43%	22%	25%
411 Length Required	64%	50%	50%
412 Precondition Failed	57%	61%	50%
413 Request Entity Too Large	50%	33%	38%
414 Request-URI Too Long	50%	28%	38%
415 Unsupported Media Type	50%	33%	38%
416 Requested Range Not Satisfiable	57%	44%	50%
417 Expectation Failed	43%	39%	38%
500 Internal Server Error	57%	78%	63%
501 Not Implemented	57%	83%	63%
502 Bad Gateway	43%	28%	38%
503 Service Unavailable	64%	44%	63%
504 Gateway Timeout	57%	44%	63%
505 HTTP Version Not Supported	43%	56%	38%

HTTP in Practice — Building Bullet-Proof Web Sites

Although HTTP—as a network protocol—is certainly an interesting and critical topic, ultimately we use protocols to build systems and services. In the case of HTTP, those systems and services are most commonly Web-based. In this appendix, we step back a little from the protocol itself and explore Web sites from an overall system perspective. Clearly, this approach is specific to a single HTTP-based application; however, it provides important context for HTTP as a protocol, as well as the many supporting protocols we've seen in previous chapters. Lessons learned in building Web site architectures are valuable in other applications of HTTP as well.

The subject of this appendix is building bullet-proof Web sites. For our purposes "bullet-proof" Web sites possess three critical attributes: They are *secure*, they are *reliable*, and they are *scalable*. Security protects Web sites and their users from malicious parties. It prevents malicious parties from disrupting the operation of a site or from accessing users' confidential information. Reliability (which, in technical jargon, is more properly called *availability*, see the sidebar) protects

Reliability and Availability

In the engineering of complex systems, the terms *reliability* and *availability* have precise meanings. A reliable system provides the correct response; an available system is always able to provide some response. Ultimately, of course, users want both reliability and availability. When a banking customer wants to check her balance online, she expects her bank's Web site to be up and running (available), and she expects the balance it advertises to be accurate (reliable). Of the two qualities, however, Web site architecture can really influence only availability. For that reason, this appendix considers the requirements for highly available Web sites, even though, in common usage, that quality is often called reliability. Availability is often expressed as a percentage of the time that a system can be accessed by its users. The standard for the U.S. telephone network is 99.999 percent availability, which represents about 5 minutes of downtime in a year. Even the much less ambitious goal of 99.9 percent availability barely permits one business day of downtime each year.

Web sites from failure, failure of a site's own systems or of the infrastructure on which it relies. Scalability protects a site against success. A scalable Web site can gracefully accommodate a rapid and substantial growth in the number of its users.

Not surprisingly, the qualities that make up a bullet-proof site are related to each other. In many cases the tools and techniques that address reliability also solve scalability problems, and in some cases an approach that improves scalability sacrifices security. This appendix, therefore, doesn't consider each of the key bullet-proof qualities in isolation. Rather, we'll look at a Web site from the outside-in, considering all of the tools and techniques together as we look deeper into the site's architecture. We begin with something critical to any Web site: its connection to the Internet. Then we look at the systems and infrastructure that make up a Web site. The third section examines architectures that protect actual Web applications themselves. In the fourth section we discuss management and monitoring processes needed to keep a Web site up. Finally, the appendix concludes by putting all the elements together in a comprehensive, example site.

B.1 The Internet Connection

As tempting as it is to worry about application software, database management systems, and operating systems, the most vulnerable part of any Internet-based architecture is its Internet connection. An Internet connection, after all, is a site's very lifeline to the Web. That role makes the connection critical for reliability and scalability, and, as the entry point for malicious parties, it can be the focus of many security attacks.

B.1.1 Redundant Links

One of the more challenging aspects of engineering a Web site's Internet connection is protecting that connection from failure. In all approaches the key is redundancy—have the site support more than one Internet connection. It's not normally sufficient, however, just to have two physical connections; equally important is to ensure that the Internet connections are supplied by different Internet Service Providers. In many cases a connection failure is due to operational or systems problems at an ISP, and such problems can affect all of that ISP's connections.

The most straightforward way to provide redundancy is to use mirrored Web sites. In other words, create two (or more) separate sites, each with its own connection to the Internet. Figure B.1 illustrates the configuration.

With this approach, the contents of the different physical sites must be kept identical. Typically this is practical only for static Web sites. If users can dynamically change the state of the site (by, for example, updating their account information), it is difficult to instantly reflect such changes in the backup site.

In addition to creating primary and backup sites, mirroring requires special configuration of the site's Domain Name System (DNS) server. DNS translates between human-readable host names and numerical IP addresses. For example, when users enter the Web address www.microsoft.com in their Web browser, DNS servers may identify the true destination as 207.46.130.45.

With mirroring, the DNS server must provide IP addresses of both sites to client queries. Web browsers that fail to connect with the primary Web server can then automatically attempt a connection with the backup. Unfortunately, the switchover from primary to backup is completely under the control of the client, and typical client behavior may be counter to a site's availability requirements.

Clients generally decide on an IP address only when they attempt to initiate a connection to a Web site. Web browsers will not automatically switch to a backup IP address after a

Provider Diversity

Whether you're designing your own Web site or relying on a Web hosting provider, making sure that your different Internet connections truly come from different ISPs can be surprisingly difficult. The telecommunications industry relies heavily on resellers—providers that resell the facilities of others. That means that the company from which you purchase one of your Internet connections may not be the same company that's actually providing it. If you're not careful you may end up paying two different ISPs that are, in fact, using the same infrastructure, which defeats one of the main reasons for using multiple ISPs in the first place. Also pay attention to the details of your Internet connections. The leased line connections to your building (frequently provisioned by the local telephone company) may rely on the same physical infrastructure even for multiple ISPs. This problem is not just theoretical; companies that were convinced they had multiple Internet connections have been surprised when an errant backhoe eliminated both connections at once because the phone company had used the same physical conduit to bring both leased lines into the building.

Figure B.1 ▶
Mirroring Web sites to multiple servers, each connected to the Internet through a different service provider, significantly improves the reliability of the overall Web site.

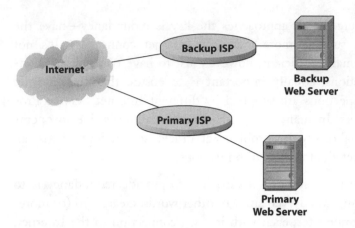

connection has been established. Once a page has begun downloading, the connection is established and switchover is not possible. (With HTTP persistence, this statement is true even if the page contains multiple objects.) If the primary Web server fails during page downloads, users are forced to wait until the download times out, at which point they can click "Refresh" on their browsers to initiate a new connection. With common Web browsers, the timeout period is about one minute. Even this brief period is significant, as research suggests that consumers will wait no longer than about eight seconds before taking their business elsewhere.

Global load balancing addresses some of those concerns by giving the site itself more control over the mirroring. As figures B.2 and B.3 show (and section 5.1 discusses) a global load balancing appliance acts as either a DNS server or an HTTP redirect server for the Web site. When the client requests the IP address for a Web site (figure B.2) or initiates an HTTP session (figure B.3), the global load balancer determines which Web server offers the best performance to the client and directs the client to that server. The client then communicates directly with the designated Web site.

To ensure that clients are not directed to Web servers that have failed, the global load balancer may continuously monitor the health of each server. When it detects a failure,

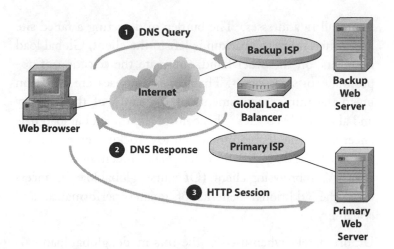

◀**Figure B.2**
A global load balancer can use DNS responses to route clients to one Web server or another. The load balancer acts as the DNS server for the site.

it responds to all queries with IP addresses of only the surviving sites.

The main benefit of global load balancing over simple DNS-based mirroring is responsiveness to problems. DNS maintenance is typically a manual process. Practically, that means it's not possible for a simple DNS-based approach to automatically stop returning IP addresses of failed servers. (Changing the response of a DNS server requires manual reconfiguration.) That's why it is essential for DNS servers to

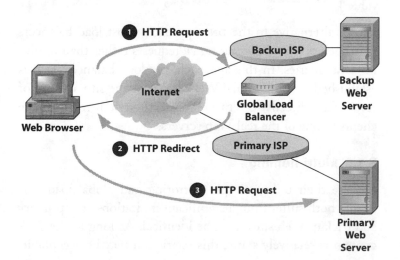

◀**Figure B.3**
HTTP redirection is another technique that allows global load balancers to route clients to different Web servers. In this example the load balancer acts as the site's primary Web server, but, instead of serving the site's content, it merely redirects clients to the real Web servers.

return all IP addresses. The burden of detecting a failed site and switching to the backup is left to the client. Global load balancers, on the other hand, automate the selection of appropriate DNS responses. Their DNS responses are based on up-to-the-minute assessments of the status of the primary and alternate Web sites. This control lets the global load balancer make the decision to switch to a backup server, a decision that the load balancer can make much more quickly than a Web browsing client. (Of course, global load balancers offer the additional benefits of greater performance and scalability.)

Unfortunately, when used in the DNS mode, global load balancers don't provide much help after the DNS query has been resolved. If a Web server fails after a client has been given its IP address, only the client can decide to retry using an alternate IP address. In fact, even when a client might be expected to issue a new DNS query (and thus receive the latest information from a load balancer), the load balancer doesn't have the opportunity. Intermediate DNS servers and client systems often cache the results of DNS queries, ostensibly to improve performance. (In theory, DNS entries include a "Time To Live" value that should prevent such caching. In practice, however, many intermediate servers and clients ignore this value.)

As an alternative to the DNS approach, most load balancers may operate by redirecting HTTP requests rather than resolving DNS queries. In this approach, the load balancer itself is established as the nominal Web server for the site. Instead of responding directly to HTTP requests, though, it redirects the clients to one of the real Web servers.

B.1.2 Multi-homing

Despite their utility, simple mirroring and global load balancing both suffer from a significant limitation—the primary and backup Web sites must be identical. As long as the site's content is relatively static, this restriction may be acceptable.

Dynamic, data-driven Web sites, however, cannot support multiple, isolated Web servers. If a user checks account status after making a Web purchase, the status should reflect the purchase, even if a failover occurs between the two commands and they are sent to different physical Web servers.

Network protection for dynamic Web sites requires multiple, physical connections to the same physical site, as figure B.4 illustrates. Again, to protect against the failure of an entire provider, each network connection must be from a different ISP. This factor makes the configuration considerably more complex than it may at first appear.

The issue with redundant connections is IP addressing. Normally, when an ISP provides Internet access to an enterprise, the ISP assigns IP addresses for that enterprise's systems. In this case, however, more than one ISP provides access. What IP address should the Web server use?

The simplest answer is to use IP addresses from both service providers. Nearly all Web server platforms (certainly including UNIX and Windows) have the capability of assigning multiple IP addresses to a given network interface. In such a configuration, clients could reach such a system using either IP address. If the Domain Name System is configured to provide both IP addresses to any query, clients would automatically fall back to the backup address if the primary were inaccessible. Of course, this approach suffers from the same responsiveness issues as DNS mirroring. It's up to Web browsing clients to detect and respond to network failures, and clients can choose from the IP addresses only when they first

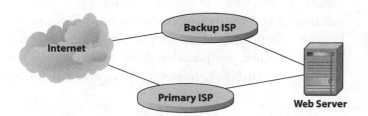

◄ **Figure B.4**
With multi-homing, a Web server connects to the Internet through multiple service providers simultaneously.

Getting IP Addresses

To get IP addresses for your enterprise that are independent of any service provider, you have to follow much the same procedure as ISPs do themselves. That generally means contacting the appropriate authority and justifying your request. Today, IP addresses are the responsibility of the Internet Assigned Numbers Authority, or IANA (www.iana.org). IANA delegates the actual assignment to different regional bodies. In North America, that's the American Registry for Internet Numbers (www.arin.net). In Europe, the IP addressing authority is the Réseaux IP Européens (www.ripe.net); for Asia-Pacific, it's the Asia-Pacific Network Information Center (www.apnic.net). Eventually, authority over IP addresses will belong to the Internet Corporation for Assigned Names and Numbers, or ICANN (www.icann.org).

try to establish a connection. If the IP address becomes inaccessible after the connection is established, then the clients have to wait for the connection to time out.

Web sites with redundant network connections can improve their availability significantly if they acquire their own IP addresses instead of relying on addresses assigned by an Internet Service Provider. Enterprises with their own IP addresses are reachable through any ISP connection and, should a primary connection fail, the Internet will automatically reroute traffic through a backup ISP. This rerouting takes only a second or two, and it is not normally noticeable to users.

Provider-independent IP addresses, combined with redundant Internet connections, may seem like an ideal approach for high-availability Web site architectures. There are, however, drawbacks. In this case the most significant obstacle is complexity. Administering your own IP addresses, and making sure that everyone else on the Internet can reach them, are not trivial tasks. In effect, you're becoming your own Internet Service Provider.

Operating such a configuration requires support for appropriate Internet routing protocols, in this case the Border Gateway Protocol (BGP). Major Internet service providers use BGP to tell each other how to route to various IP addresses. Because you're acting as your own ISP, you'll need to operate your own BGP router or server.

You will also need the cooperation of your ISPs, as they must configure their BGP systems to communicate with your system. The entire process is not for the faint of heart, and it requires a lot of care and attention. A misconfigured or malfunctioning BGP system can, in theory, bring down the entire Internet. (Fortunately, there are protection mechanisms built into the Internet; you probably don't want to be the one to test those mechanisms, however.) It is essential, therefore, that enterprises adopting this technique have sufficient expertise in Internet routing and network connectivity.

B.1.3 Securing the Perimeter

A Web site's Internet connection is not just how legitimate users access the site; it's also the point of entry for malicious parties. Protecting these entry points is imperative, and the tool for doing so is a firewall. Figure B.5 shows a simplified view. Of course, a truly bullet-proof site will use redundant firewalls (and redundant Web servers as well).

As guardians at the gates of a Web site, firewalls have two main tasks. First, they ensure that Internet users can access only appropriate parts of the site. And second, they ensure that users access those parts only in appropriate ways. The two tasks may sound similar, but they actually differ in important ways. The first job, allowing access to only appropriate parts, prevents malicious parties from accessing systems and services within your Web site. Those systems may include other physical systems (such as database servers) or non-Web-related services on your Web servers themselves (such as file sharing). The second task, preventing inappropriate access to appropriate parts of the Web site, protects against denial-of-service attacks. In a denial-of-service attack, a malicious party doesn't try to gain access to inappropriate information; instead, the party simply tries to tie up system resources so thoroughly that legitimate users cannot receive service. Sending a flood of regular HTTP requests, for example, can bog down a Web server. Fortunately, most competent firewalls can recognize and thwart these types of attacks.

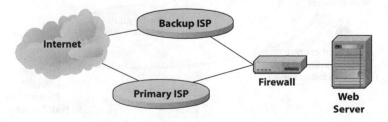

◀ **Figure B.5**
A firewall guards the entrance to a Web site from the Internet. It sees all network traffic destined to systems within the Web site, and it can block messages that are not appropriate.

B.2 Systems and Infrastructure

Once a Web site has ensured that its connection to the Internet is bullet-proof, attention turns to the systems and infrastructure within the site. Here too we find a standard set of tools and techniques that ensure a site's reliability, scalability, and security, all of which we'll examine next. The site mirroring approach, described in the previous section, protects against system and infrastructure failures in addition to Internet connection failures. Local load balancing and server clusters also enhance reliability, and they can be even better tools for scalability. The common architecture for security within a Web site organizes the systems in multiple layers, with a demilitarized zone (DMZ) to act as a buffer between the Internet and sensitive information.

B.2.1 Reliability through Mirrored Web Sites

Although we discussed mirrored Web sites (and global load balancing) in the context of protecting the Internet connection, the same techniques also protect against system failures within a site. If a primary Web server fails, even though its Internet connection remains active, clients can still detect the failure and switch to a mirrored site, as figure B.6 illustrates.

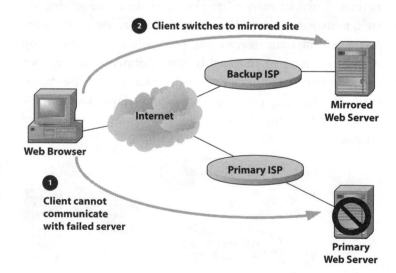

Figure B.6 ▶
Web site mirroring offers protection against server failures, as all clients can be rerouted to a backup system. When, in this example, the Web browser realizes that it cannot communicate with the primary server, it switches to the backup site.

Of course, mirroring suffers from the very same limitations described earlier—the speed at which the architecture responds to failures is under the control of the client rather than the site itself. Also, mirrored architectures are effective only for relatively static sites. As long as the site does not use a lot of dynamic content, though, mirroring may still be an excellent approach for making the site reliable.

The key to evaluating mirroring is to match the technology with the site's availability requirements. As a rule of thumb, it may take as long as three minutes to detect a primary failure and recover by connecting to a backup site. (The actual time depends on many factors, including the specific browser software, the user's attentiveness, and the download time for the page.) Figure B.7 graphs the effect of three-minute failures on overall availability. If, for example, a site requires 99.9 percent availability, it can tolerate as many as 14 failures each month. This level of reliability is easily attainable with current Web servers. Higher availability requirements, however, may be difficult to satisfy solely with site mirroring.

B.2.2 Local Load Balancing and Clustering

Not all Web sites can tolerate the three-minute recovery period that mirroring imposes. Either the cumulative effect of

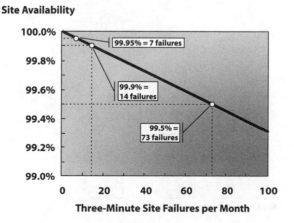

◀ **Figure B.7**
Relying on the browser to recover from a site failure can take as long as three minutes. A site's availability requirements determine the number of such failures it can tolerate.

multiple three-minute outages may exceed the site's availability requirements, or the consequences of a sustained three-minute outage may be too severe. For those situations, local load balancing and clustering offer much quicker recovery times.

Local load balancing and clustering can also significantly enhance the scalability of Web sites. Load balancing, in particular, lets site administrators instantly and transparently increase their site's capacity.

Local load balancing resembles global load balancing, in that a network appliance receives requests from clients and distributes them among multiple Web servers. With local load balancing, however, all systems (appliances and Web servers) share a common local network. Figure B.8 shows a typical configuration.

As with global load balancing, the real benefit of local load balancing is in site scalability and performance; however, by monitoring Web server health and instantly switching away from failed systems, local load balancers offer subsecond recovery from failures. Generally, users are not even aware that a switchover has taken place.

Figure B.8 ▶
Local load balancing is generally confined to one physical location, but it allows for quick recovery from failed systems in a way that is often invisible to browser clients. As this example shows, sites with high availability requirements usually deploy components such as load balancers in redundant pairs. If one load balancer fails, the other takes over.

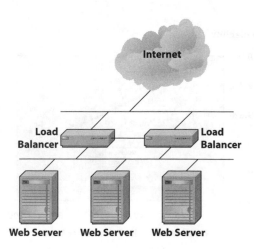

Another difference between local and global load balancers is their normal method of operation. Most local load balancers can respond to DNS requests and perform HTTP redirection. For maximum responsiveness, however, local load balancers interpose themselves directly between the Internet and the Web servers. As HTTP traffic flows through a load balancer, the balancer distributes that traffic to appropriate servers, as figure B.9 illustrates.

As the figures indicate, high availability architectures deploy local load balancers in pairs, with one serving as a backup to the other. This configuration is essential in preventing the load balancer itself from becoming a single point of failure. Evaluate load balancers not just on how fast they detect and recover from a Web server failure, but also on how fast they recover from the failure of one physical balancer. High-quality load balancers can recover quickly enough that users do not notice.

Server clusters are an alternative to local load balancing. Clustering combines many physical systems into a single,

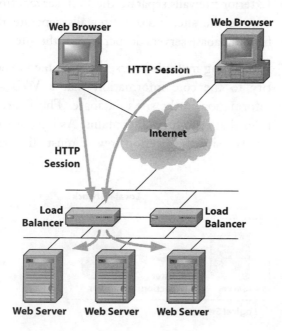

◀ **Figure B.9**
Local load balancers distribute requests among multiple Web servers. They can automatically detect faults and route requests around failed systems. Local load balancers act transparently to Web clients, so they can switch a client to a new server almost immediately, well before the client even notices a problem.

logical system, as figure B.10 illustrates. Should one physical server fail, the cluster continues to operate with the remaining systems.

For static Web sites, server clusters are generally not as desirable as local load balancing. Clusters are much more complex to administer and maintain, and they are usually more expensive to deploy. For full effectiveness, clustering also requires special support from applications, in this case the Web server software. On the other hand, clusters can play an important role in protecting dynamic Web applications, as the next section discusses.

B.2.3 Multi-Layer Security Architectures

The previous section introduces firewalls as the primary technology for securing the perimeter of a Web site. Firewalls are also important for providing security within a site. Figure B.11 shows a typical security architecture for bullet-proof Web sites. As the figure shows, firewalls create a multi-layer architecture by bracketing the site's Web servers. Exterior firewalls separate the Web servers from the Internet outside the site; interior firewalls separate the Web server from database servers deeper within the site.

By creating multiple layers, this architecture adds more security to the core information that a Web site manages—information in the site's database. The figure highlights the rules that each firewall contains. As long as the site is a public Web site, the exterior firewall must allow anyone access to

Figure B.10 ▶
Clustering bonds multiple physical systems together to act as one logical system. In most implementations the logical system can automatically recover from the failure of a physical system.

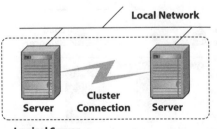

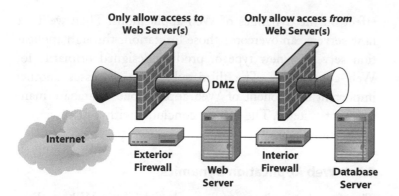

Only allow access *to* Web Server(s)

Only allow access *from* Web Server(s)

DMZ

Internet

Exterior Firewall

Web Server

Interior Firewall

Database Server

◀ **Figure B.11**
Web sites often employ a multi-tier firewall configuration, dividing the site into a public (the Internet), a private (protected databases), and a "demilitarized" zone in between.

the Web servers. Instead of limiting who can access the site's systems, the exterior firewall's main job is to limit which systems can be accessed. In particular, the exterior firewall allows outside parties to communicate only with the Web servers; it must prevent outside parties from accessing any other system within the site. The interior firewall, on the other hand, focuses its protection on who can access the database servers, not what systems can be accessed. Specifically, the interior firewall makes sure that the Web server is the only system that can access the database server.

This architecture adds an extra layer of protection for the site's critical data. An attacker can compromise either of the two firewalls and still not gain access to the protected information. A successful attack requires breaching both firewall systems.

B.3 Applications

So far we've looked at bullet-proofing the infrastructure of a Web site architecture by protecting both its network connectivity and its systems and servers. In this section we turn our focus to the Web application itself. Bullet-proofing Web applications is actually more complex than it may appear, primarily because of the characteristics of the HTTP protocol. The first subsection explores those characteristics and their effect on the dynamics of Web applications. Then we'll see how servers can overcome those limitations through application servers, a new type of product designed primarily for Web applications. The third subsection discusses another important component of Web applications—database management systems. The section concludes with a discussion of application security.

B.3.1 Web Application Dynamics

The fact that we're even discussing dynamic Web applications is a testament to the flexibility of the Web's architecture and the ingenuity of Web developers. The World Wide Web, after all, was originally conceived as a way of organizing relatively static information. In 1989, it would have been hard to imagine how dynamic and interactive the Web would become. In fact, the communication protocols and information architecture of the Web don't support dynamic applications naturally and easily.

The fundamental challenge for dynamic Web applications is overcoming the stateless nature of the Hypertext Transfer Protocol. As we've seen, HTTP is a simple request-and-response protocol. Clients send a request (such as a URL) and receive a response (a Web page). Basic HTTP has no mechanism that ties one request to another. So, when a Web server receives a request for the URL corresponding to "account status," HTTP can't tell the server which user is making the request. That's because the user identified herself by logging in using a different URL request.

A critical part of dynamic Web development is overcoming the stateless nature of HTTP and tracking a coherent user session across many requests and responses. Protecting this session information is also the key to providing high-availability Web applications. Systems and networks may fail, but, as long as the session state is preserved, the application can recover.

Tracking Sessions

Although there are several esoteric approaches available, most Web sites rely on one of two ways to track Web sessions across multiple HTTP requests. One approach is URL mangling. This technique modifies the URLs within each Web page so that they include session information. When the user clicks on a link, the mangled URL is sent to the Web server, which then extracts the session information from the request. A second approach uses cookies, which explicitly store state information in the user's Web browser. The server gets cookie information from the browser before it responds to any request.

There are two different levels of protection for Web session information: persistence and sharing. With persistence, session information is preserved on disk rather than in memory. If a Web server fails, it can recover the session information when it restarts. Of course, this recovery is effective only if the server is capable of restarting. Also, the site is not available during the restart period.

A more thorough method of protecting state information is sharing it among multiple systems. If one system fails, a backup system can immediately take over. This recovery protects the session while the failed system restarts, and it can preserve the session even if the failed system cannot be restarted.

B.3.2 Application Servers

The difficulty of tracking session state (much less protecting it from failure) is one of the significant factors that has led to the creation of a new type of product: application servers. Although each vendor has its own unique definition, application servers exist to run Web-based services that require coordination of many computer systems. (The term "application," in this sense, refers to a particular business service, not a single-purpose software program such as an Excel or Photoshop.) Figure B.12 highlights the application server's role as the central coordinator for a business.

Even though application servers were not designed specifically to make Web applications highly available, their central role in a business architecture makes availability and reliability critical. As a consequence, some application server products have extensive support for high-availability applications. Even if a particular Web site architecture does not require the coordination of disparate systems like application server products advertise, the Web site may still take advantage of application server technology just to improve its availability.

Figure B.12 ▶
Application servers can become the
focal point of a dynamic Web site,
coordinating among Web servers,
databases, and legacy systems. As the
master coordinator of a site's
responses, application servers can
naturally assume some responsibility
for site availability.

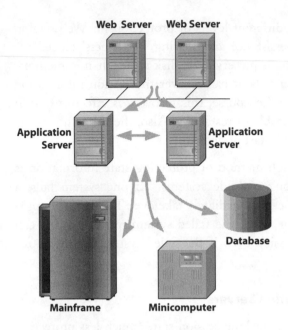

Application servers tend to support high availability using
either of two general approaches. The first approach deploys
the application server software on server clusters. We first
discussed server clusters in the context of Web servers, but,
as we noted then, software that runs on server clusters must
be specifically designed to take advantage of clusters. In general, Web server software is not designed in that way; however, some key application servers are. With this
configuration, illustrated by figure B.13, the application server
software appears as a single entity to the Web servers it supports. The clustering technology handles failover using its
normal recovery mechanisms.

Some application servers choose to support high availability
with their own mechanisms rather than relying on server
clusters. This approach gives the application server more
control over failover and recovery, and it keeps the software
from becoming dependent on a particular operating system's
cluster support. Because most application servers can run on

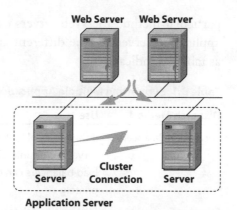

◄ Figure B.13
Some application servers run on clustered systems, taking advantage of the cluster's fault tolerance and recovery services. In such configurations, the application server software doesn't have to worry about failure and recovery itself.

multiple operating systems, this independence may be an important factor in their approach to high availability.

Although the specifics vary by vendor, using an application server's own fault tolerance generally results in a configuration similar to figure B.14. One factor that the figure highlights is the need to distribute the Web servers' requests among multiple application servers, and to automatically switch those requests away from any failed systems. The exact mechanism that's most appropriate here depends on the

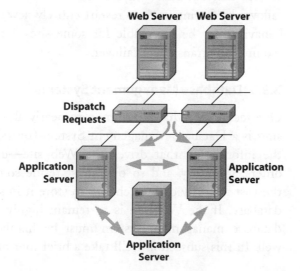

◄ Figure B.14
Other application servers have their own mechanisms for redundancy and availability. Application servers that take on this responsibility must coordinate among themselves so that one server can cover for another.

particular method the Web servers use to communicate with application servers. Three different approaches are common, as table B.1 indicates.

Table B.1 Supporting Multiple Application Servers

Dispatch Method	Use
Local Load Balancers	If the protocol for Web server to application server communication is HTTP, standard local load balancers can distribute requests appropriately.
Ethernet Switches	Ethernet switches with layer 4 (or layer 7) switching capabilities can usually distribute multiple protocols, not just HTTP.
Multi-Use Systems	The simplest approach may be to run both Web server and application server software on the same physical systems. The site's protection mechanism for Web server failures also protects against application server failures.

When evaluating application servers for high-availability Web sites, it is important to look closely at the server's session-level failover support. Automating failover for individual sessions is a technical challenge, and some application servers that advertise "high availability" support automated failover by forcing users to restart entirely new sessions. This behavior may be acceptable for some sites, but others may require truly transparent failover.

B.3.3 Database Management Systems

One technology that is common to nearly all dynamic Web sites is a Database Management System (DBMS). Ultimately, the information that drives the Web site—user accounts, orders, inventory, and so on—must reside somewhere, and the vast majority of sites choose to store it in some form of database. If the Web site is to remain highly available, the database management system must be highly available as well. In this subsection we'll take a brief tour of some of the approaches that protect databases from failures. Two of the approaches rely on hardware or operating system software, while three are strictly features of the DBMS applications themselves.

The hardware clustering technology we've already discussed is a common technique for protecting database systems. As we've seen before, hardware clustering does require that the application software include special features to take advantage of its failover technology. In the case of database management systems, however, that support is widespread and quite mature.

One technology that is completely independent of the database application is remote disk mirroring. Remote disk mirroring uses special hardware and ultra-fast network connections (typically via fiber optic links) to keep disk arrays at different locations synchronized with each other. This technology, which is common in the telecommunications and financial services industries, is not really optimized for high availability. It is, instead, intended mainly to protect the information in a database from catastrophic site failures (a fire, for example). Still, if there is an effective recovery plan that brings the backup disks online quickly enough, remote disk mirrors can be an effective component of a high-availability architecture.

In addition to these two techniques that are primarily outside the scope of the DBMS itself, most database systems support high-availability operation strictly within the DBMS. The approaches generally fall into one of three techniques: parallel servers, replication, or standby databases.

The highest performing option is parallel servers, which essentially duplicate the functionality of a hardware cluster using only DBMS software. Figure B.15 shows a typical configuration. Multiple physical servers act as a single database server. When one server fails, the remaining servers automatically pick up and recover the operation. Recovery is gen-

DBMS Vendor Specifics

For our discussion of database technology, we've tried to present the issues and solutions in a way that is independent of specific database management systems. Fortunately, most of the major database vendors—IBM, Informix, Microsoft, Oracle, and Sybase—have similar features and options. There are certainly differences between the products, but, to cite a specific example, for our purposes Informix Enterprise Replication, Oracle Advanced Replication, and Sybase Replication Server are roughly equivalent. In addition to implementation differences, however, not all of the techniques we describe are available from all vendors. Microsoft, for example, does not have a separate database clustering product. Instead, SQL Server relies strictly on the clustering support of the Windows operating system.

Figure B.15 ▶
Parallel database configurations are
essentially clusters that have been
optimized for database applications.
As with traditional clustering
technology, the entire system
automatically recovers if one of its
components fails.

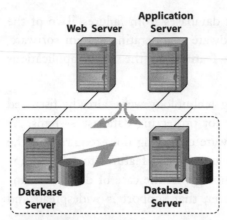

Parallel Database System

erally transparent to the database clients such as Web servers
or application servers, which continue unaware that a failover
has occurred.

Another approach for protecting database systems is replication. Replication uses two (or more) separate database servers, along with database technology that keeps the two
servers synchronized. Replication differs from parallel servers
because it does not present the separate servers as a single
logical database. Instead, clients explicitly connect with one
or the other database, as figure B.16 indicates. (Some database systems require that all clients connect with the same

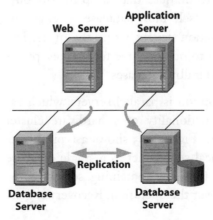

Figure B.16 ▶
Database replication keeps multiple
copies of a database synchronized
with each other. If one database
system fails, clients can continue
accessing the other system.

server, but more advanced implementations can support interaction with the replicated servers as well.)

When a database server fails, the database clients must recognize the failure and reconnect to an alternate database. Although this is not as transparent nor as quick as a parallel server implementation, most database vendors have technology to speed up the detection and reconnection considerably, and it can generally (but not always) proceed transparently to the database user.

The third database technology that can improve availability is standby databases. With standby databases, all clients communicate with a primary database server. As figure B.17 shows, that server keeps an alternate server informed of the changes. The alternate server, however, is not usually synchronized with the primary server in real time. Instead, there is a time delay that can range from a few seconds to several minutes and even longer. Should the primary server fail, the alternate must be quickly brought up to date and all database clients redirected to the alternate server. In this case, recovery

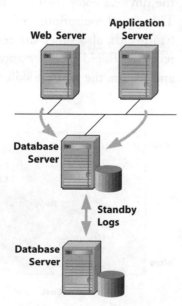

◀ **Figure B.17**
Standby logs allow a database to keep a record of all operations it performs. This log can help recreate the state of the database should the main system fail. Such recovery, however, is rarely fully automatic, so it may take much longer than other methods.

is not normally transparent to the users, and during the recovery process the Web site will be unavailable.

Although the time lag between changes to the primary and alternate databases may seem like a disadvantage, in some situations it may also be a significant advantage. If, for example, an application executes a database query that corrupts the database, a vigilant database analyst may intercept the standby logs and delete the query before it executes on the alternate database, thus preserving the data in the alternate database. Any delays that the Web site introduces for this purpose, however, should occur after the standby log is moved to the alternate server. That provides the greatest protection from catastrophic site failures.

Although we've discussed each of these techniques in general terms, it's important to recognize that different DBMS vendors implement each approach differently. Choosing between the approaches, however, is generally a trade-off between responsiveness and cost. As the chart in figure B.18 highlights, approaches that support rapid recovery are expensive. They require a lot of communications traffic between the physical components to keep them tightly synchronized. This synchronization, in addition to requiring network bandwidth, also slows the response of the server to normal requests. Rapid recovery approaches are also more complex and require the greatest skill to deploy and maintain. On the

Figure B.18 ▶
Database reliability technologies are inevitably a trade-off between cost and recovery speed. The faster the recovery, the more expensive the technology and its implementation.

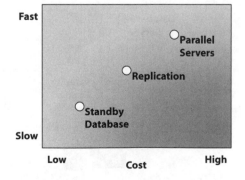

other hand, approaches that minimize the complexity and cost are not able to recover from failure as quickly.

B.3.4 Application Security

If the Web site interacts dynamically with its users, it may wish to provide security for that interaction. Security may be useful even if the interaction is nothing more than allowing users to personalize or customize the pages; it certainly is important if the site manages the users' financial information (e.g., an online bank) or conducts electronic commerce. The first goal of application security is to verify the identity of the end user. A second, optional goal is to ensure the privacy of the information exchanged.

As we've seen in chapter 4, HTTP has several mechanisms to authenticate end users. As we also saw, however, many of HTTP's mechanisms have easily exploited weaknesses. For this reason, Web sites should be extremely careful in their use of HTTP authentication, making sure that the weaker, default modes are not employed. This caution applies even if the site is using authentication to protect information with relatively little value. Human nature makes it hard to resist the temptation to reuse passwords on multiple Web sites. And, although a portal site may not think that its content justifies strong authentication, if the portal site allows attackers to intercept its users' passwords, its users may be extremely unhappy when their intercepted passwords are used to access online brokerage accounts.

B.3.5 Platform Security

Security-conscious Web sites worry about the security of their platforms as much as the security of their applications. Today, nearly all Web sites rely either on Windows or Unix as an underlying operating system for their servers, and neither has been shown to be perfect in protecting against network attacks. Other commercial software, including Web servers and application servers, suffers a similar fate.

Fortunately, the network security community is effective both at discovering vulnerabilities and reporting them to the responsible vendors. The vendors are usually well motivated to respond rapidly with patches and fixes. The main weakness in this process is its reliance on site administrators to proactively monitor their vendors for updates and apply those updates as they become available. It can be difficult for administrators, under the gun for a myriad of other issues, to find the time required to keep all products up to date. Bullet-proof security, however, demands nothing less. Keep in mind that as soon as a patch or fix is made publicly available, the vulnerability the upgrade addresses is also publicly available. And although it may take extremely clever engineers to discover a vulnerability, exploiting a known vulnerability, once it has been made public, can be trivial. Administrators that do not keep their software completely up to date at all times run a high risk of a security breach of their sites.

B.4 Staying Vigilant

So far in this appendix, we've looked at what it takes to design and deploy bullet-proof Web sites. Design and deployment are just the beginning, however. It is equally important to make sure that a site stays available. That calls for network management, monitoring, and intrusion detection, as well as strict procedures for site maintenance and upgrades. This section considers those issues.

B.4.1 External Site Monitoring

One of the most basic steps you can take to ensure that a Web site remains available is to measure its availability. And there is no better way to measure availability than to act as users. Web site monitoring services exist just to make those measurements.

Web site monitoring services generally rely on a network of probes deployed across the Internet. As figure B.19 shows,

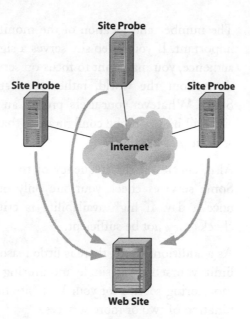

Site Probe

Site Probe

Site Probe

Internet

Web Site

◀ **Figure B.19**
Web site monitoring relies on a network of probes to periodically emulate users and simulate transactions with the site. The probes can measure the site's responsiveness and detect site failures.

these probes periodically access a Web site by emulating actual users. The service collects the results from these access attempts and presents them to an administrator, usually via a secure Web site. Some services also provide immediate notification of site failures via email, pager, or telephone.

When evaluating site monitoring services, there are several factors to consider. First, be sure the service's primary focus fits your requirements. Nearly all services provide information on performance (such as download times) as well as availability. If that's important to you, look at those services with a performance focus. If, on the other hand, availability is your top concern, be careful not to pay for performance measurements that you don't need.

Another factor is the depth the service provides. Some services simply perform quick checks of static URLs. Others are much more sophisticated and can even carry out a complete ecommerce transaction. Monitoring services can also check other applications, such as email and file transfer servers.

The number and location of the monitoring probes are also important. If your Web site serves a significant international audience, you may want to focus on services that have probes throughout the world, rather than strictly in the United States. Whatever your users' profile, an ideal monitoring service will have a probe configuration that matches that profile as closely as possible.

Also, check out the frequency of the probes' measurements. Some services check your site only once an hour, or even once a day. If high availability is critical, such infrequent checks may not be sufficient.

As a additional note, there is little reason (other than cost) to limit yourself to a single monitoring service. The perfect monitoring service for your Web site may, in fact, be a combination of two or more services.

Finally, if your Web site is particularly specialized or, perhaps, is not intended for a general Web audience, an alternative to monitoring services is deploying your own monitoring software. The same issues that are important for a monitoring service—level of monitoring, location of probes, and so on—are important with this approach as well. Deploying your own monitoring application, however, gives you complete control over the implementation decisions.

B.4.2 Internal Network Management

Web site monitoring services provide an important measure of a Web site's health, but by themselves, they won't give you a complete picture of your site. That's because external probes can measure your site only as if they were users; they can't tell you what's going on behind the scenes. That visibility requires a network and systems management application.

To understand the importance of internal network management, consider what happens when one of the systems in a two-node hardware cluster fails. If the cluster is operating correctly, then the other system will take over. The failover should be transparent to users—and to any external monitoring service. Your Web site, however, is now at risk. It has just become vulnerable to a single point of failure. If the remaining cluster node also fails, the site goes down. Obviously, in such a situation you need to know about the failed cluster node quickly so that it can be repaired or replaced. It's the job of an internal network management system to alert you to the problem.

The common denominator for most network management applications is the Simple Network Management Protocol (SNMP). As figure B.20 shows, management applications use SNMP to query the status of network devices, including servers, switches, hubs, routers, and firewalls. Even some uninterruptible power supplies support SNMP. An effective management application collects SNMP-based information and presents a coherent, overall view of a network's health to its users.

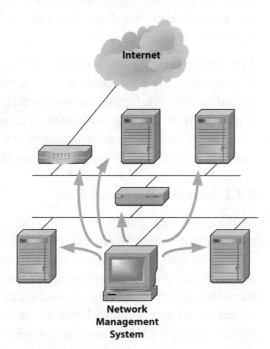

◀ **Figure B.20**
A network management system monitors the health of all network devices that make up a Web site.

The more sophisticated network management applications do much more than simply query device status. They can correlate the status of several devices and even diagnose the root cause of network problems. Sophisticated management frameworks also integrate with other applications such as customer support, trouble ticketing, and inventory control. The larger the overall enterprise (and the more sophisticated its information technology infrastructure), the more likely it will find the capabilities of sophisticated management applications appealing.

Unfortunately, although SNMP support is common in network devices and appliances, it is less popular in high-level software. Database management systems, application servers, and Web server software, for example, may not provide a way for SNMP-based management software to query their status. Quality products in all of those categories will provide some method of management; however, that method may not be SNMP. Management via Web browsers, for example, is a popular alternative. Unfortunately, it's also usually proprietary and, consequently, does not permit an integrated, unified view of the entire Web site.

The bottom line, as always, is to understand your own needs. If interoperability with a network management framework is critical to your site, be sure the commercial software that you deploy in your site supports SNMP management. If, on the other hand, unified network management is less important, multiple management views may be acceptable.

B.4.3 Intrusion Detection

In the same way that bullet-proof Web sites need network management systems to monitor the status of network systems, such Web sites must also monitor their security. Security monitoring is the task of intrusion detection systems. An intrusion detection system, or IDS, continuously looks for unauthorized access, network attacks, and other types of malicious actions. When it detects suspicious activity, the IDS can alert administrators and, in some cases, actively defend against the attack.

There are two different types of intrusion detection: host-based and network-based. Some commercial products combine both approaches, but most systems generally adopt one strategy over the other. Host-based systems add special software agents to the systems being protected—Web servers, DNS servers, application servers, database management systems, etc. These agents carefully monitor various components of the local system, including, for example, the Windows event log, the UNIX /etc/passwd file, and other components critical to system security. If the agent detects suspicious activity, it reports its suspicions to a central management station. As figure B.21 shows, the management station correlates reports from all the IDS agents and presents a comprehensive view to the network administrator. The management station can also take action to alert the administrator should the activity warrant it.

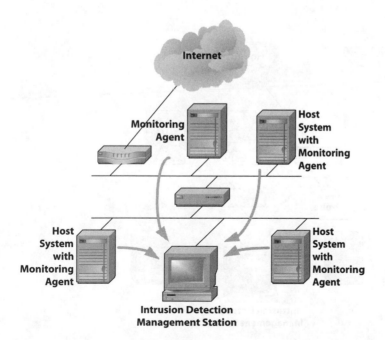

Internet

Monitoring Agent

Host System with Monitoring Agent

Host System with Monitoring Agent

Host System with Monitoring Agent

Intrusion Detection Management Station

◀ **Figure B.21**
Intrusion detection systems may use special software agents installed on host systems to watch the activity on those systems and report anything suspicious.

Network-based intrusion detection relies on a similar architecture; distributed monitoring systems report to a centralized management station. Instead of software agents monitoring events, however, a network-based IDS relies on special-purpose network hardware. These hardware devices, illustrated in figure B.22, are placed on the network where they can monitor all network traffic.

The two approaches, as you might expect, have their own strengths and weaknesses. Host-based agents have a much more comprehensive view of an intruder's actions, but they themselves may be vulnerable to attack. If an attacker can successfully gain access to a host system, that attacker may be able to disable or defeat the monitoring agent. Network-based agents are generally impervious to attacks themselves, but they can only infer what is happening on a host system because they have access only to the network traffic going to or coming from the system. Clever attackers may disguise their actions so as to slip by a network-based monitor, while

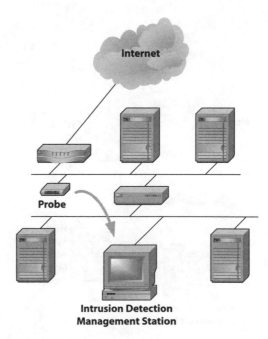

Figure B.22 ▶
Intrusion detection systems may also rely on special network probes to watch for suspicious activity. The probes monitor network traffic directly, independently of the site's host systems.

a host-based monitor, even if it cannot discern the actions, may be able to see the effects.

Both host-based and network-based intrusion detection systems usually employ one of two strategies to detect malicious behavior. The first strategy is often called *profiling*. With profiling, the IDS passively monitors the network for a short period of time to learn. Passive monitoring teaches the IDS the normal activities that take place on the network. The IDS then becomes active, and, in this stage, simply looks for activity that is markedly different from normal. The second intrusion detection strategy relies on *signatures*. An IDS using signatures has a predefined set of activities that represent attacks, and the IDS continuously looks for those activities. Neither profiling nor signatures are perfect, and both approaches often generate a significant number of false positives, indications of a problem when, in fact, none exists. A department reorganization, for example, may change the profile of network traffic significantly enough to trigger a profiling IDS. And otherwise harmless activities such as diagnosing a network failure may trigger a signature-based IDS. Nevertheless, as long as the frequency of false alerts is not great enough to cause the administrator to ignore the system, intrusion detection is a valuable tool in protecting the security of Web sites.

B.4.4 Maintenance and Upgrade Procedures

A reality of the Web is that things change. Rapidly. Just as you put the finishing touches on an optimum high-availability site architecture, the site will require revisions, maintenance, or upgrades. Unfortunately, it is during such changes that Web sites are most vulnerable. Carefully managing changes to an operating Web site is critical to keeping the site up.

Fortunately, some of the same technology that enhances a site's availability also permits non-disruptive maintenance and upgrades. Most hardware clustering products, for example, allow administrators to transparently take one of the physical systems offline, upgrade it, and then bring it back into the cluster, all without disturbing the operation of the rest of the cluster.

The most critical factor for site maintenance, however, is not technology. Rather, it is people and processes. Web sites that expect to achieve high availability must have strong processes and thoroughly documented procedures that govern all aspects of site operation. Some key areas include the following:

- *Change and Configuration Management.* High-availability sites must keep track of all details of their configuration and operation, including software releases, hardware components, and network connectivity. All changes made to the site—in any area—should be immediately reversible should problems arise.

- *Testing and Staging.* Before any change is applied to a live production site, it should be tested on a staging site that mimics the production site as closely as possible. Surprises are inevitable, and much better received when they don't affect real users. Because an ideal staging site completely duplicates the production architecture, it may be expensive to deploy. Staging sites often serve a dual purpose, therefore, acting also as a complete standby site for the production environment.

- *Tracking and Logging.* When it comes time to actually implement a change or upgrade, it is important to log every action involved in the change, no matter how trivial. If a problem occurs, an unambiguous record is invaluable in restoring the site to operation.

B.5 The Big Picture

In this appendix we've looked at many of the elements that make up bullet-proof Web sites. We've seen how to protect the site's Internet connection, its servers, database systems, and applications. We've also looked at essential tools for operating and maintaining the site, and we've considered the importance of strict procedures for site upgrades. Now it's time to put all these elements together.

Figure B.23 illustrates one possible architecture for a high-availability, scaleable, and secure Web site. The figure combines many of the elements discussed in this appendix, and it

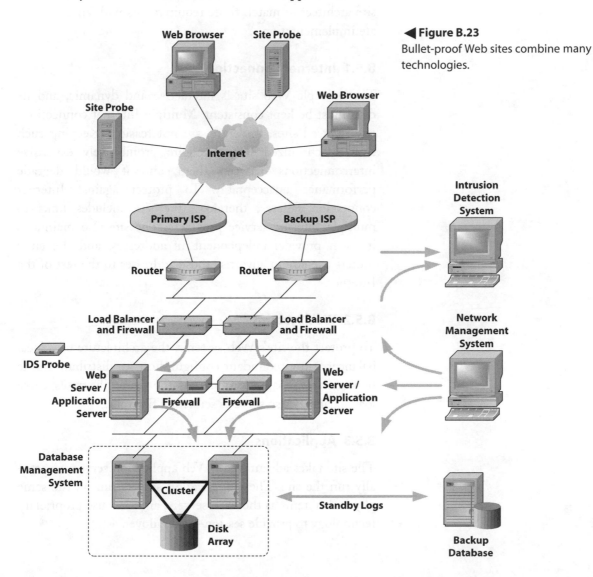

◄ Figure B.23
Bullet-proof Web sites combine many technologies.

introduces a few additional details. Although no vendors are named, the architecture contains only systems that are commercially available today. This architecture is not just theoretical; it can be used to create real Web sites today.

Of course, the architecture in the figure is only one of many possibilities, as we've tried to show throughout this article. Every Web site has unique requirements, and it is up to the site architect to match those requirements with an appropriate implementation.

B.5.1 Internet Connection

The example Web site is interactive and dynamic, and its data must be kept consistent. Multiple Internet connections to dispersed sites, therefore, are not feasible. Keeping such sites synchronized would require prohibitively expensive interconnections between them, and it would degrade performance unacceptably. To protect against Internet connection failures, therefore, the site includes links to multiple Internet service providers. The site also maintains its own provider-independent IP addresses, and the site's routers use BGP to advertise those addresses to the rest of the Internet.

B.5.2 Web Systems

To protect the site's Web systems, the architecture uses local balancers (in a redundant configuration) to distribute traffic between two separate systems. As the figure illustrates, these load balancers also serve as screening firewalls.

B.5.3 Applications

The site takes advantage of Web application servers to actually run the site. These application servers run on the same physical systems as the Web servers, and they use proprietary technology to provide session-level failover.

B.5.4 Database Management System

The site's database management system runs on a hardware cluster and is supported by a Redundant Array of Inexpensive Disks (RAID) system. By relying on hardware clusters rather than database software, the site lets other software in addition to the DBMS take advantage of the cluster's high-availability features.

Notice also that the DBMS and the application servers are separated by a second set of redundant firewalls. The two sets of firewalls define the demilitarized zone (DMZ) common in Web site architectures.

The site also uses standby logs to back up the database to a second site. The backup database protects the site's data, but because the backup site does not include a full Web system, the standby process does not add significantly to the site's availability.

B.5.5 Network Management and Monitoring

The site uses a combination of external monitoring and internal network management to ensure that it continues to operate. A Web site monitoring service provides the external monitoring, while the site uses its own network management system, based primarily on SNMP, for internal management.

B.5.6 Intrusion Detection System

In addition to a traditional network management application, the site operates an intrusion detection system. The IDS system combines host-based monitoring agents and network-based probes, all reporting to a central IDS management station.

REFERENCES

The following sources have more detailed information on many topics in this text. Individual references, with commentary, are grouped by general information, base HTTP specifications, other security protocols, caching protocols, and information on HTTP versions.

General References

Although many books have been written about the architecture of the Internet, the closest things to official standards are two documents published by the Internet Engineering Task Force (IETF). IETF documents may be found from the organization's Web site at http://www.ietf.org.

Robert Braden, ed. *Requirements for Internet Hosts — Communication Layers* [RFC 1122]. The Internet Engineering Task Force. October 1989.

Robert Braden, ed. *Requirements for Internet Hosts — Application and Support* [RFC 1123]. The Internet Engineering Task Force. October 1989.

There is also an IETF document that defines uniform resource identifiers.

Tim Berners-Lee, Roy T. Fielding, and Larry Masinter. *Uniform Resource Identifiers (URI): Generic Syntax* [RFC 2396]. The Internet Engineering Task Force. August 1998.

HTTP Specifications

The specifications for HTTP and contained in a series of documents from the IETF.

Roy T. Fielding, James Gettys, Jeffrey C. Mogul, Henrik Frystyk Nielsen, Larry Masinter, Paul J. Leach, and Tim Berners-Lee. *Hypertext Transfer Protocol — HTTP/1.1* [RFC 2616]. The Internet Engineering Task Force. June 1999.

John Franks, Phillip M. Hallam-Baker, Jeffery L. Hostetler, Scott D. Lawrence, Paul J. Leach, Ari Luotonen, and Lawrence C. Stewart. *HTTP Authentication: Basic and Digest Access Authentication* [RFC 2617]. The Internet Engineering Task Force. June 1999.

David M. Kristol and Lou Montulli. *HTTP State Management Mechanism* [RFC 2965]. The Internet Engineering Task Force. October 2000.

Keith Moore and Ned Freed. *Use of HTTP State Management* [RFC 2964]. The Internet Engineering Task Force. October 2000.

Jeffrey C. Mogul and Paul J. Leach. *Simple Hit-Metering and Usage-Limiting for HTTP* [RFC 2227]. The Internet Engineering Task Force. October 1997.

Separate Security Protocols

The official specification for the Secure Sockets Layer protocol (version 3.0) is available in several formats at http://www.netscape.com/eng/ssl3/.

Alan O. Freier, Philip Karlton, and Paul C. Kocher. *The SSL Protocol Version 3.0*. Netscape Communications Corporation. 4 March 1996.

Please note that some of the formats include errata to the original specification. The errata itself are also available from the same site.

SSL 3.0 Errata. 26 August 1996.

The Transport Layer Security specification is a proposed standard of the IETF.

T. Dierks and C. Allen. *The TLS Protocol Version 1.0* [RFC 2246]. The Internet Engineering Task Force. January 1999.

The Secure HTTP specification is also an IETF document, although it is designated experimental.

Eric Rescorla and Allan M. Schiffman. *The Secure HyperText Transfer Protocol* [RFC 2660]. The Internet Engineering Task Force. August 1999.

Caching Protocols

Some of the caching protocols mentioned in chapter 5 are specified in IETF documents.

Duane Wessels and K. Claffy. *Internet Cache Protocol (ICP), version 2* [RFC 2186]. The Internet Engineering Task Force. September 1997.

Duane Wessels and K. Claffy. *Application of Internet Cache Protocol (ICP), version 2* [RFC 2187]. The Internet Engineering Task Force. September 1997.

Paul Vixie and Duane Wessels. *Hyper Text Caching Protocol (HTCP/0.0)* [RFC 2756]. The Internet Engineering Task Force. January 2000.

Other protocols and technologies were developed by individual vendors. Some documentation is available from the vendors' Web sites.

Cache Array Routing Protocol (CARP) v1.0 Specifications. Microsoft Corporation. Available at http://www.microsoft.com/Proxy/Guide/carpspec.asp

"Chapter 11, Using the Client Autoconfiguration File" from *Netscape Proxy Server Administrator's Guide*. Netscape Communications Corporation. At http://developer.netscape.com/docs/manuals/proxy/adminux/autoconf.htm

Web Cache Communication Protocol. Cisco Systems. Available at http://www.cisco.com/warp/public/732/wccp/index.html

Most of the other protocols discussed in chapter 5 are documented only in vendors' documents and Internet drafts that are not publicly available at the present time.

Previous HTTP Versions

The specification of HTTP version 1.0 is an IETF document, as is the explanation of HTTP version numbers.

Tim Berners-Lee, Roy T. Fielding, and Henrik Frystyk Nielsen. *Hypertext Transfer Protocol — HTTP/1.0* [RFC 1945]. The Internet Engineering Task Force. May 1996.

Jeffrey C. Mogul, Roy T. Fielding, Jim Gettys, and Henrik Frystyk Nielsen. *Use and Interpretation of HTTP Version Numbers* [RFC 2145]. The Internet Engineering Task Force. May 1997.

The original definition for HTTP is still available on the Web site of the World Wide Web Consortium.

Tim Berners-Lee. *The Original HTTP as defined in 1991*. Available at http://www.w3.org/Protocols/HTTP/AsImplemented.html

Both the World Wide Web Consortium and other research organizations have documented HTTP compliance on the Internet.

HTTP/1.1 Feature List Report Summary. World Wide Web Consortium. Available at http://www.w3.org/Protocols/HTTP/Forum/Reports/

Balachander Krishnamurthy and Martin Arlitt. *PRO-COW*: Protocol Compliance on the Web. 1999. [Published as AT&T Labs—Research Technical Memorandum #990803-05-TM and as HP Labs Technical Report HPL-1999-99.]

GLOSSARY

Accept An HTTP request header by which a client indicates the type of content it can accept.

Accept-Charset An HTTP request header by which a client indicates the character sets that it can accept.

Accept-Encoding An HTTP request header by which a client indicates the character encodings that it can accept.

Accept-Language An HTTP request header by which a client indicates the languages that it can accept.

Accept-Ranges An HTTP response header by which a server indicates that it can accept future requests for partial ranges of the object.

ACK A TCP flag that the sender uses to acknowledge a previous TCP segment.

Address A value that uniquely identifies a system on a network. An IP address uniquely identifies a system on the Internet.

Age An HTTP response header by which a server estimates the age, in seconds, of the object.

Algorithm A parameter in the HTTP Authorization and WWW-Authenticate headers by which the sender indicates a particular digest algorithm.

Allow An HTTP entity header that indicates the particular HTTP methods that the object supports.

Application A communications service that relies on underlying communications protocols; Web browsing using HTTP is an application.

Application Server A special system that coordinates Web access to a variety of other systems, including database management systems and mainframe services. Application servers can play a key role in the reliability of Web site architectures.

Asymmetric Cryptography A type of cryptography which uses two different keys—one to encrypt messages and another to decrypt messages. The keys are constructed so that knowledge of the encryption key does not reveal the decryption key. Asymmetric cryptography is also called public key cryptography because the encryption key can be made public without compromising the security of the system.

Authentication A security function which verifies the identity of a communicating party.

Authentication-Info An HTTP response header by which the server provides additional information about an authentication exchange.

Authorization An HTTP request header by which a client authenticates its identity.

Availability The degree to which a system such as a Web site can be accessed by its users.

Bandwidth A measurement of network capacity.

Base64 An encoding method that expresses arbitrary binary data strictly in characters from the ASCII character set.

Border Gateway Protocol (BGP) A routing protocol used by networks on the Internet to exchange topology information that determines how IP datagrams reach their destinations.

Browser A user application that is an HTTP client; common examples include Microsoft's Internet Explorer and AOL's Netscape Navigator.

bytes A parameter of the HTTP Accept-Ranges header that indicates the server can accept future range requests that specify bytes.

Cache A system that remembers retrieved information so that it can return that information in response to subsequent requests.

Cache Array Routing Protocol (CARP) A set of rules that cooperating cache servers can use to distribute cached objects among themselves without overlap.

Cache-Control An HTTP general header that directs the behavior of intermediate caches through which the message passes.

Certificate In general, data that both includes and validates a public key. Also, an SSL message that carries a certificate.

Certificate Authority An organization that issues public key certificates and vouchsafes for the authenticity of the party that possesses the public and private key pairs.

Certificate Request An SSL message that the server uses to ask a client to produce its public key certificate and proof that it possesses the corresponding private key.

Certificate Verify An SSL message that a client uses to prove that it possesses the private key corresponding to a public key (carried in Certificate message).

Certificate-Info An HTTP header used with Secure HTTP to identify a public key certificate.

Change Cipher Spec An SSL message that activates the most recently negotiated set of security services and parameters.

Character Set A specific mapping of characters to a binary representation; ASCII is a common character set.

Chunked A special HTTP transfer encoding that breaks a large object into smaller pieces and transfers the smaller pieces individually.

Cipher Suite A combination of cryptographic algorithms, parameters, and key sizes.

Client The party in a communication that initiates the exchange.

Client error A HTTP status code (in the range 400-499) that indicates an error in the client's request.

Client Hello An SSL message that the client uses to introduce itself and propose a set of cryptographic parameters for a session.

Client Key Exchange   An SSL message that the client uses to transfer an encrypted session key that both parties will use to encrypt the remainder of the session.

close   A parameter in the HTTP Connection header that tells the recipient that the sender will close the connection after the current request.

Clustering   A technique that combines multiple physical systems and allows them to act cooperatively as a single logical system. Clustering can improve both performance and availability.

cnonce   A parameter of the HTTP Authentication-Info and Authorization headers that carries a random value selected by the client. Random values strengthen security because it is difficult for adversaries to guess or predict their values.

Comment   An attribute of an HTTP cookie that provides a brief explanation of the use of the cookie.

CommentURL   An attribute of an HTTP cookie that provides a URL for a detailed explanation of the use of the cookie.

Communication Protocol   Rules that communicating parties follow in a communication exchange. Protocols specify both syntax (the format of exchanged messages) and semantics (how the systems respond to messages).

compress   An HTTP encoding format based on the UNIX "compress" data compression program.

CONNECT   An HTTP method by which a client requests a tunnel to a distant server.

Connection   An HTTP general header that lists other headers in the message that should not be forwarded by an intermediate system. Also, the logical association that TCP establishes between two communicating parties.

Content   Entities carried in the message body of HTTP messages.

Content-Encoding   An HTTP entity header that identifies the encoding of the object.

Content-Language   An HTTP entity header that identifies the human language used by the object.

Content-Length   An HTTP entity header that identifies the size, in bytes, of the object.

Content-Location   An HTTP entity header that identifies the location of the object.

Content-MD5   An HTTP entity header that carries a message digest of the object.

Content-Privacy-Domain   A Secure HTTP header that indicates the format of cryptographic parameters used for the session.

Content-Range   An HTTP entity header that identifies the partial range of the object carried in the current message body.

Content-Type   An HTTP entity header that identifies the type of the object. Also, a Secure HTTP header that identifies the type of information secured by the message.

Cookie   An HTTP request header by which a client returns state management information to a server; the information would have been provided by the server in response to a previous request, and it allows the server to associate different requests with each other. More generally, a cookie is the state management information.

Cookie2   An HTTP request header that a client uses to indicate that it can accept HTTP version 1.1. Set-Cookie2 headers in responses.

count   A parameter to the HTTP Meter header by which intermediate servers indicate the number of times an object has been viewed.

Credentials   Information that provides and verifies an identity; examples of credentials include usernames and passwords and public key certificates (along with proof of the corresponding private key).

Database Management System (DBMS)   A software system that stores and organizes data for easy retrieval.

Datagram   The basic unit of information transmitted across the Internet and other IP-based networks.

Date   An HTTP general header that carries the date and time that the message was created.

deflate   The HTTP encoding format that uses the zlib format defined by RFC 1950.

DELETE   An HTTP method by which a client requests that a server remove an object.

Digest Authentication   An authentication technique in which the sender combines data with a secret password and calculates a cryptographic message digest. The recipient verifies the sender's possession of the password by repeating the calculation and checking for the same result. Note that both sender and recipient must know the password.

Discard   An attribute of an HTTP cookie that asks the client to delete a cookie.

Disk Mirroring   A technology that uses multiple physical disk drives to keep copies of data. Should one disk drive fail, the data may be recovered from other disk drives.

Domain   A parameter of the HTTP WWW-Authenticate header that indicates or hints to the client which username and password to provide. Also, an attribute of an HTTP cookie that defines the domain of servers to which the cookie applies.

Domain Name System (DNS)   The system and protocols used on the Internet to map names, such as www.waterscreek.com, to IP addresses, such as 207.155.248.9.

dont-report   An attribute of the HTTP meter header by which a server indicates that it does not want to receive page view counts for the object.

do-report   An attribute of the HTTP meter header by which a server indicates that it wants to receive page view counts for the object.

Encoding   How an object is formatted, either for storage (content encoding) or transfer (transfer encoding).

Encryption-Identity   An HTTP header used by Secure HTTP to identify the party for whom a message should be encrypted.

Entity   An object transferred by HTTP.

Entity Tag   An arbitrary value that servers assign to an HTTP entity that uniquely identifies that entity.

ETag   An HTTP response header that carries the object's entity tag value.

Expect   An HTTP request header by which a client indicates a behavior that it expects of the server.

Expires   An HTTP entity header that identifies the time and date after which an object should no longer be considered valid.

File   The component of a uniform resource identifier that specifies the object itself; often it is a file name.

FIN   A TCP flag that indicates the party is closing the TCP connection.

Finished   An SSL message that concludes cryptographic negotiations.

Firewall   A special purpose system that monitors all information passing between a site and the Internet looking for security problems.

Fragment   The component of a uniform resource identifier that indicates a specific region within an object.

Frame   The smallest unit of information transferred by some network technologies.

From   An HTTP request header that identifies the human user (typically an email address) making the request.

Gateway   A system that translates between different protocols.

GET   An HTTP method that clients use to request objects.

Global Load Balancing   A technique that distributes multiple physical Web servers in multiple locations on the Internet and directs clients to the closest server.

gzip   An HTTP encoding method that uses the format of the GNU gzip program.

HEAD   An HTTP method with which a client asks a server to return the headers associated with an object without returning the object itself.

Header   Parameters of an HTTP message other than the object being transferred.

Host   An HTTP request header that identifies the host for the object being requested. Also the component of a uniform resource identifier that indicates that host.

Hyper Text Caching Protocol (HTCP)   A communication protocol that cache servers can use to coordinate their operation.

Hypertext   A document that contains active links to other documents.

Hypertext Markup Language (HTML)   A language for hypertext documents.

Hypertext Transfer Protocol (HTTP)   A communications protocol for transferring hypertext documents and other objects.

identity   An HTTP encoding method in which the object is unchanged.

If-Match   An HTTP request header by which a client asks the server to carry out its request only if certain conditions (known as preconditions) are true.

If-Modified-Since   An HTTP request header by which a client asks the server to carry out its request only if the object has been modified since the date and time specified in the header.

If-None-Match   An HTTP request header by which a client asks the server to carry out its request only if certain conditions are not true.

If-Range   An HTTP request header by which a client asks the server to return the requested range of an object only if the precondition is true; otherwise, the server should return the entire object.

If-Unmodified-Since   An HTTP request header by which a client asks the server to carry out its request only it the object has not been modified since the specified time and date.

Informational   An HTTP status code (in the range 100-199) that provides information without indicating the final status of the request.

Integrity Protection   A security service that allows recipients to detect if data has been modified in transit.

Intermediate Server   A system that places itself between the client and server, accepting the client's requests and forwarding them to the server.

International Standards Organization (ISO)   An organization that develops standards for many areas, including communication protocols.

Internet   The worldwide, interconnected collection of networks based on the Internet Protocol.

Internet Assigned Numbers Authority (IANA)   The organization that assigns IP addresses and protocol parameters. Eventually, the Internet Corporation for Assigned Names and Numbers will assume this responsibility.

Internet Cache Protocol (ICP)   A communication protocol that cache servers can use to coordinate their operation.

Internet Content Adaptation Protocol (ICAP)   A communication protocol that can let intermediate servers adjust content, for example, to adapt it for handheld display screens.

Internet Corporation for Assigned Names and Numbers (ICANN)   The organization that assigns authority for registering and administering domain names on the Internet. Eventually, ICANN will also assume responsibility for assigning IP addresses and protocol parameters.

Internet Protocol (IP)   The communication protocol that is responsible for delivering datagrams to their destination on the Internet.

Internet Service Provider (ISP)   A communications service provider that offers connectivity to the Internet.

Intrusion Detection System (IDS)   A system that monitors networks and computer systems looking for activity that indicates a possible security breach.

IP Address   A binary value that uniquely identifies a system on the Internet, usually written as, for example, 172.16.1.18.

ISO 639   An international standard that specifies two-letter abbreviations for human languages; for example, ISO 639 designates "en" to represent English.

ISO 8859-4   An international standard character set that corresponds to the earlier ASCII standard.

JavaScript   A programming language often used within Web pages.

Keep-Alive   A non-standard HTTP header, primarily used with HTTP version 1.0, that indicates a desire to keep the connection active after the current request.

Key-Assign   An HTTP header used by Secure HTTP to assign a convenient identifier to a cryptographic key.

Last-Modified   An HTTP entity header that indicates the time and date the object was last modified.

Layer   A particular set of communication services, typically provided by a single communications protocol. Multiple protocols, operating at distinct layers, provide a complete communications service.

Linefeed   The ASCII character represented by the binary value 0001010 and used in most UNIX systems to indicate the end of a line of text; HTTP uses the combination of a linefeed character and a return character to mark the end of its lines.

LINK   An HTTP 1.0 method (and associated header) that clients could use to add a link to an object.

Load Balancing   The technique of using multiple physical systems to act as a single logical server and distributing request among the physical systems so that no one system is overloaded. When the physical systems are all on the same local network, the technique is known as local load balancing; when the systems are distributed across the Internet, the technique is known as global load balancing.

Local Load Balancing   Load balancing when the systems sharing the load are all located on the same local network.

Location   An HTTP response header that identifies the location of the object.

MAC-Info   A Secure HTTP header that carries a message authentication code (also known as a message digest).

max-age   An HTTP Cache-Control directive that specifies the maximum amount of time an object may remain valid in a cache. Also, an HTTP cookie attribute that specifies the maximum lifetime of the cookie.

Max-Forwards   An HTTP request header that specifies the maximum number of intermediate servers through which the request may pass.

max-reuses   An HTTP Meter directive that limits the number of times an object may be returned to the same user from a cache.

max-stale   An HTTP Cache-Control directive that specifies the maximum time after a cached object becomes invalid that a cache can still return it in response to clients that indicate they will accept stale objects.

max-uses An HTTP Meter directive that limits the number of times an object may be returned to different users from a cache.

Message Body The part of an HTTP message that carries the object being transferred.

Message Digest A cryptographic algorithm that calculates a small binary value for a large object; it has the property that if the original object changes at all, the digest calculation result will change as well. Such algorithms are also known as secure hash algorithms.

Message Digest 5 (MD5) A particular message digest algorithm.

Meter An HTTP header that controls whether an object may be stored in a cache and, if so, gives cache servers a way to report accesses of the object to the origin server.

Method The type of an HTTP request.

min-fresh An HTTP Cache-Control directive that specifies the minimum age that must be remaining on an object for a cache server to return it.

Mirrored Site A Web site with more than one server where each server contains an identical copy of the site's contents.

Mozilla The informal name for the Netscape Navigator Web browser, so called because Netscape built upon, and intended to surpass, the then-dominant Mosaic browser.

Multi-homing The practice of providing a system or a Web site multiple network connections to the Internet.

must-revalidate An HTTP Cache-Control directive that indicates an object should not be returned from an intermediate cache unless that cache server first validates its copy with the origin server.

Mutual Authentication A security service whereby both communicating parties verify each other's identity.

Name An HTTP Cookie attribute that assigns a name to the cookie.

nc Short for nonce count, a parameter of both Authentication-Info and Authorization headers that indicates the number of times a particular nonce value has been used.

Network Element Control Protocol (NECP) A communications protocol by which servers such as cache servers can control the operation of routers, switches, and other network elements.

Network Management The process of provisioning, configuring, and monitoring systems within a network infrastructure.

nextnonce An HTTP Authentication-Info parameter that servers use to provide a new nonce value to clients.

no-cache An HTTP Cache-Control directive that indicates an object should not be stored in a cache.

nonce A parameter in HTTP Authorization and WWW-Authenticate headers that carries a random value; used to strengthen the security of the authentication exchange. Also, an HTTP header used with Secure HTTP.

Nonce Count (nc) Used in its abbreviated form (nc), a parameter of both Authentication-Info and Authorization headers that indicates the number of times a particular nonce value has been used.

Nonce-Echo An HTTP header used by Secure HTTP to return a nonce value.

no-store An HTTP Cache-Control directive that identifies sensitive information (such as a password) that should not be stored with an object in a cache.

no-transform An HTTP Cache-Control directive that indicates an object should not be transformed (e.g. compressed to save space) by a cache server.

only-if-cached An HTTP Cache-Control directive that asks an intermediate server to respond to a request only with a cached copy.

opaque A parameter that carries an arbitrary value provided by a server in an WWW-Authenticate header (and returned by the client in the subsequent Authorization header) that the server uses internally to facilitate processing the request.

OPTIONS An HTTP method by which a client asks a server the options its supports, either in general or in conjunction with a specific resource.

Origin Server The ultimate source of an HTTP resource.

Packet   The smallest unit of information transferred by some network technologies.

Page View   The retrieval of an object by a client.

Parallel Servers   A database technology that operates multiple physical systems as if they were a single logical system.

Password   The component of a uniform resource identifier corresponding to the user's password.

Path   An attribute of an HTTP cookie that defines the areas within the site to which the cookie applies. Also, the component of a uniform resource identifier that defines a region within a site.

Peer   The system with which one system is communicating.

Persistence   A technique that keeps the TCP connection open after an initial HTTP exchange so that the connection may be reused for subsequent exchanges.

Pipelining   A technique by which a client sends one HTTP request immediately after another, without waiting for a response to the earlier request.

Port   The TCP address of a particular application within a system. The IP address identifies the system, while the port number distinguishes multiple applications within that system. HTTP cookies include a port attribute, and uniform resource identifiers may include a port component.

POST   An HTTP method that clients use to provide data to a resource on the server, most commonly used to submit forms.

Pragma   An HTTP general header that provides additional information about a message.

Prearranged-Key-Info   A Secure HTTP header that identifies keys previously established by the communicating parties.

Precondition   A condition that the client wishes the server to confirm before carrying out a request. Preconditions are specified in If-Match and similar headers.

Private Key   One key of a pair used in asymmetric cryptography. The private key is never shared with other parties.

private   An HTTP Cache-Control directive that indicates that a particular object is private and should only be returned by cache servers to the same user.

Profiling   A technique used by intrusion detection systems by which they record a site's normal network and system activity and trigger on any significant deviations from that normal behavior.

Protocol   Rules that communicating parties follow in a communication exchange. Protocols specify both syntax (the format of exchanged messages) and semantics (how the systems respond to messages). Also the component of a uniform resource identifier that indicates the particular protocol to use to access an object.

Proxy Auto Configuration (PAC)   A script that configures HTTP clients with information about which proxies to use and when and how to use them.

Proxy   An intermediate server that receives client requests and forwards them to the actual server.

Proxy Cache   A proxy server that also functions as a cache.

Proxy-Authenticate   An HTTP header that a proxy server uses to request authentication of a client.

Proxy-Authorization   An HTTP header that clients use to authenticate themselves to a proxy server.

proxy-revalidate   An HTTP Cache-Control directive that tells proxy servers not to return a cached copy of the object without validating that copy with the origin server.

public   An HTTP Cache-Control directive that tells cache servers that the object may be returned to other clients, not just the original requestor.

Public Key   One of a pair of keys used in asymmetric cryptography. The public key may be freely shared with other parties without compromising security.

Public Key Certificate   A collection of data that both includes and validates a public key.

Public Key Cryptography   A type of cryptography which uses two different keys—one to encrypt messages and another to decrypt the messages. The keys are constructed so that knowledge of the encryption key does not reveal the decryption key. Also known as asymmetric cryptography.

PUT   An HTTP method that clients use to send objects to servers.

q   A parameter known as quality factor that may be included in Accept, Accept-Charset, Accept-Encoding, Accept-Language, and TE headers. The quality factor allows client to express a relative preference for different options of each of these headers.

qop   A parameter of Authentication-Info, Authorization, and www-Authenticate headers that indicates the type of security services requested or used for an exchange.

Quality Factor (q)   Used in its abbreviated form (q), a parameter in Accept, Accept-Charset, Accept-Encoding, Accept-Language, and TE headers. The quality factor allows client to express a relative preference for different options of each of these headers.

Quality of Protection (qop)   Used in its abbreviated form (qop), a parameter of Authentication-Info, Authorization, and www-Authenticate headers that indicates the type of security services requested or used for an exchange.

Query   A component of a uniform resource identifier that provides additional parameters to the file. The query component is most commonly used with Web forms to convey simple user input, normally with a GET method instead of a POST.

Range   An HTTP request header that a client uses to request part of a resource rather than the entire object.

realm   A parameter in Authorization and www-Authenticate headers that specifies a particular application or service for which the user is being authorized.

Reason-Phrase   A text description of an HTTP status that appears in a Status-Line.

Redirection   The process by which a server tells a client to reissue its request but for a different uniform resource identifier. Redirection status codes are in the range 300-399.

Referer   An HTTP request header in which the client indicates the source of a request; often this header contains the uniform resource identifier of the Web page that contains the link the user followed.

Reliability   The property of a system that measures the degree to which the system operates properly.

Repeat Client Security   A security service introduced in HTTP version 1.1 that allows the client and server to renegotiate keys. Key renegotiation provides additional security for clients that frequent the same server.

Replay Protection   A security service that prevents adversaries from recording valid messages and later replaying those messages and successfully masquerading as an authorized client.

Replication   A database technology that maintains multiple synchronized copies of databases on different physical systems.

Request   The message that initiates a client/server interaction. Clients send requests to servers, and servers reply with responses.

Request for Comments (RFC)   A specification or other document produced by the Internet Engineering Task Force; the HTTP version 1.1 specification is RFC number 2616.

Request-Line   The first line of a client's HTTP message, consisting of an HTTP method, a uniform resource identifier (the Request-URI), and an HTTP version.

Request-URI   The part of an HTTP Request-Line that specified the uniform resource identifier for the request.

Response   The server's answer to a client's request. Also, a parameter of the HTTP Authorization header that carries the result of a client's message digest calculation.

Retry-After   An HTTP response header that gives the client a time after which it should retry its request.

Return   The ASCII character represented by the binary value 0001101 and used in Macintosh systems to indicate the end of a line of text; HTTP uses the combination of a linefeed character and a return character to mark the end of its lines.

Reverse Proxy Cache   A proxy cache server deployed by or operated for Web servers rather than Web clients.

rspauth   A parameter of the Authentication-Info header that carries the result of a server's message digest calculation.

RST   A TCP flag that indicates a connection should be reset.

Scaleability   The quality of a system or design that permits it to easily and gracefully accommodate significant increases in load.

Secure   An attribute of an HTTP cookie that tells the client to return the cookie only on subsequent requests that are secure from eavesdropping.

Secure Hash   A cryptographic algorithm that calculates a small binary value for a large object; it has the property that if the original object changes at all, the secure hash calculation result will change as well. Such algorithms are also known as message digest algorithms.

Secure HTTP (SHTTP)   A communications protocol based on HTTP, as well as several enhancements to HTTP itself, that provides for secure communications. SHTTP is classified as an experimental protocol and is rarely used today.

Secure Sockets Layer (SSL)   A communications protocol developed initially by Netscape Communications that provides a secure communications channel for various applications. SSL is commonly used to secure Web communications today. The Transport Layer Security protocol is a newer version of SSL.

Security   Protecting communications against various adversaries, including those that masquerade, eavesdrop, or alter the message contents.

Segment   A single TCP message.

Server   The passive party in a client/server communications exchange. Clients initiate the communication, and servers respond to clients' requests. Also, an HTTP response header that allows a server to indicate its vendor, version number, etc.

Server error   An HTTP response code in the range 500-599 that indicates an error in the server.

Server Hello   An SSL message in which the server selects security parameters for the session.

Server Hello Done   An SSL message that servers send to indicate that they have concluded their part of the initial SSL negotiation.

Session ID   An arbitrary value that parties use to identify an SSL session. Both parties can resume an earlier session by referencing its session ID during initial negotiations.

Set-Cookie2   An HTTP response header that servers use to send cookies to clients.

SHTTP-Certificate-Types   An HTTP header used by Secure HTTP to identify the format of public key certificates.

SHTTP-Cryptopts   An HTTP header used by Secure HTTP to carry general cryptographic options.

SHTTP-Key-Exchange-Algorithms   An HTTP header used by Secure HTTP to identify cryptographic algorithms used to exchange keys.

SHTTP-Message-Digest-Algorithms   An HTTP header used by Secure HTTP to identity cryptographic algorithms used to calculate the digest of a message.

SHTTP-Privacy-Domain   An HTTP header used by Secure HTTP to identify the format of cryptographic information.

SHTTP-Privacy-Enhancements   An HTTP header used by Secure HTTP to list privacy enhancements desired or used for a message.

SHTTP-Signature-Algorithms   An HTTP header used by Secure HTTP to identify cryptographic algorithms used to digitally sign messages.

SHTTP-Symmetric-Content-Algorithms   An HTTP header used by Secure HTTP to identify cryptographic algorithms used to encrypt message contents.

SHTTP-Symmetric-Header-Algorithms   An HTTP header used by Secure HTTP to identify cryptographic algorithms used to encrypt message headers.

Signatures A technique used by intrusion detection systems that detects attacks by comparing network and system behavior against behavior that is known to indicate attacks.

Simple Network Management Protocol (SNMP) A communications protocol that allows network administrators to remotely monitor, configure, and manage networked systems.

Site The collection of systems that provide service to Web clients, including HTTP servers, load balancers, caches, firewalls, application servers, and database management systems.

Site Monitoring A service that monitors the health and performance of a Web site, usually by simulating the behavior of users.

s-maxage An HTTP Cache-Control directive that limits the amount of time an object may be kept in a cache if that object is accessed by multiple clients.

SSL Acceleration A technique for improving Web site performance by using special purpose hardware to perform SSL's cryptographic calculations. Such hardware is generally faster than software implementations.

stale A parameter of the WWW-Authenticate header by which the server indicates that it has received a request based on parameters that have already expired.

Standby Database A technique of database operation that records the actions in the primary database and replays those actions, generally after some delay, on a backup database.

State Management In HTTP, the process of associating different client requests with each other so as to form a coherent session; HTTP state management relies on cookies.

Stateless The property of normal HTTP communications where any request is independent of all others.

Status Code A three-digit numeric value that indicates the result of an HTTP request.

Status-Code The part of an HTTP Status-Line that carries the numeric status code.

Status-Line   The first line of an HTTP response; it consists of an HTTP version, a Status-Code, and a Reason-Phrase.

Strong   A property of an entity tag that implies objects with the same entity tag value are identical.

Subtype   A minor classification of content types. For example, the content type "text/xml" has a major classification (type) of "text" and a minor classification (subtype) of "xml."

Successful   HTTP status codes in the range 200-299 that indicate that the client's request succeeded.

Symmetric Cryptography   A type of cryptography in which both parties possess identical keys.

SYN   A TCP flag that indicates the start of a connection.

TCP Multiplexing   A technique for improving Web site performance that uses special purpose systems to manage multiple TCP connections to clients, relaying requests and responses on a smaller number of connections to the servers.

TE   An HTTP request header that tells the server which transfer encodings the client can accept in a response.

Timeout   An HTTP meter directive that the origin server uses to specify the maximum time between cache server reports.

Title   An HTTP 1.0 header that carries the title of a object.

TRACE   An HTTP method that allows a client to discover the intermediate systems between it and the origin server. A server responds to a TRACE request by returning the request itself (including any Via headers) in the message body.

Trailer   An HTTP general header that indicates some additional headers follow the message body.

Transfer-Encoding   An HTTP response header that identifies the encoding format applied to the object for its transfer to the client.

Transmission Control Protocol (TCP)   A reliable transport-layer protocol used on the Internet. TCP ensures that data is delivered without error and in the correct order to the recipient system.

Transparent Cache   A cache server that is generally invisible to clients and servers alike. Transparent caches intercept HTTP requests (or have routers or other network elements intercept requests on their behalf) without the knowledge of the client.

Transport Layer Security (TLS)   The successor to the Secure Sockets Layer protocol, defined by the Internet Engineering Task Force. Like SSL, TLS provides a secure communications channel for various applications.

Transport Protocol   A communications protocol that operates at the transport layer of a communications system. Transport protocols generally have the responsibility for providing an appropriate level of reliability to the communications.

Tunnel   An intermediate server that adds some additional service (such a security) to the communications between a client and origin server.

Type   A major classification of content types. For example, the content type "text/xml" has a major classification (type) of "text" and a minor classification (subtype) of "xml."

Unicode   A character set that can represent not just Roman characters (as is the case of ASCII), but also characters from languages such as Chinese.

Uniform Resource Identifier (URI)   A textual description of an object on the Internet; most commonly a uniform resource locator (URL). Also, when used in its abbreviated form (uri), a parameter of the Authorization header that repeats the URI of the request.

Uniform Resource Locator (URL)   A uniform resource identifier that describes an object by giving its location on the Internet, including the server storing the object, the application protocol needed to retrieve it, and the name of the object on that server. Also, an HTTP 1.0 header that carries the URL of an object.

UNLINK   An HTTP 1.0 method that clients could use to remove a link from an object.

Upgrade   An HTTP general header that asks the other party to upgrade the communications to a different protocol.

User-Agent   An HTTP general header that identifies the client's vendor, version number, etc.

username   A parameter of an HTTP Authorization header that contains the username for the request. Also, the component of a uniform resource identifier that contains a username.

Vary   An HTTP response header that lists HTTP headers other than the Request-URI that determined the server's response. Cache servers can use this information to determine if it is appropriate to return the same object on subsequent requests.

Version   An attribute of HTTP cookies that identifies the version of HTTP state management that the parties are using; the current version is 1.

Virtual Host   A single physical Web server acting as several different Web sites. Internet service providers that offer Web hosting often share their systems among multiple customers in this manner.

Warning   An HTTP general header that carries additional information about a message, usually intended to warn of potential cache problems.

Weak   A property of an entity tag that implies objects with the same entity tag value are equivalent, but not necessarily identical.

Web   Short for the World Wide Web, the collection of HTTP servers and applications accessible on the Internet.

Web Cache Communication Protocol (WCCP)   A communications protocol developed by Cisco Systems that allows cache servers to coordinate their operation with access routers.

Web Proxy Auto Discovery (WPAD)   A set of rules that clients may use to automatically locate a proxy auto configuration script.

will-report-and-limit   An HTTP meter directive by which a proxy server indicates it can support metering.

wont-ask   An HTTP meter directive by which an origin server indicates that it will not ask for metering of an object.

wont-limit   An HTTP meter directive by which a proxy server indicates that it will support metering (namely, by reporting usage), but it will not limit page views.

wont-report   An HTTP meter directive by which a proxy server indicates that it will support metering (namely, by limiting page views), but it will not report usage.

World Wide Web (WWW)   The collection of HTTP servers and applications accessible on the Internet.

WWW-Authenticate   An HTTP response header that asks a client to reissue its request with user authentication credentials.

Your-Key-Pattern   An HTTP header used by Secure HTTP to identify a cryptographic key.

INDEX

X

Electronic Edition License Agreement

1. License. John Wiley & Sons, Inc. ("Wiley") hereby grants you, and you accept, a non-exclusive and non-transferable license, to use the accompanying CD-ROM, referred to as the "Software".

2. Term. This License Agreement is effective until terminated. You may terminate it at any time by destroying the Software and all copies made (with or without authorization).

3. Authorized Use of Software. You shall have the right to load the [Software] on a single computer and at single location designated by you. You may not use the Software on a network or multi-user basis. Upon termination of this License, you agree to destroy all copies in any form. IF YOU TRANSFER POSSESSION OF ANY COPY OF THE SOFTWARE TO ANOTHER PARTY, YOUR LICENSE IS AUTOMATICALLY TERMINATED.

4. Use Restrictions. You may not (a) copy the Software, except to load it into a computer in accordance with instructions set forth in the User's Manual; (b) distribute copies of the Software to any other person; (c) modify, adapt, translate, reverse, engineer, decompile, disassemble, or create derivative works based on the Software (d) copy, download, store in a retrieval Software, publish, transmit, or otherwise reproduce, transfer, store, disseminate, or use, in any form or by any means, any part of the data contained within the Software except as expressly provided for in this License; (e) transfer, resell, sublicense, lease, or grant any other rights of any kind to any individual copy of the Software to any other persons; (f) remove any proprietary notices, labels, or marks on the Software. You shall take reasonable measures to maintain the security of the Software.

5. Proprietary Rights. You acknowledge and agree that the Software is the sole and exclusive property of Wiley, and the Software is licensed to you only for the term of this License and strictly under the terms hereof. Wiley owns all right, title, and interest in and to the content of the Software. Except for the limited rights given to you herein, all rights are reserved by Wiley.

6. Warranties, Indemnities, and Limitation of Liability. THE SOFTWARE IS PROVIDED "AS IS," WITHOUT WARRANTY OF ANY KIND, EXPRESS OR IMPLIED, INCLUDING BUT NOT LIMITED TO THE IMPLIED WARRANTIES OF MERCHANTABILITY OR FITNESS FOR A PARTICULAR PURPOSE. WILEY NEITHER GIVES NOR MAKES ANY OTHER WARRANTIES OR REPRESENTATIONS UNDER OR PURSUANT TO THIS LICENSE. Wiley does not warrant, guarantee or make any representations that the functions contained in the Software will meet your particular requirements or that the operation of the Software will be uninterrupted or error free. The entire risk as to the results and performance of the Software is assumed by you. If the Software disc is defective in workmanship or materials and Wiley is given timely notice thereof, Wiley's sole and exclusive liability and your sole and exclusive remedy, shall be to replace the defective disc. In the event of a defect in a disc covered by this warranty, Wiley will replace the disc provided that you return the defective disc to Wiley together with a copy of your receipt. If Wiley is unable to provide a disc that is free from such defects, you may terminate this License by returning the disc and all associated documentation to Wiley for a full refund. The foregoing states your sole remedy and Wiley's sole obligation in the event of the occurrence of a defect coming within the scope of the limited warranty.

IN NO EVENT SHALL WILEY, ITS SUPPLIERS, OR ANYONE ELSE WHO HAS BEEN INVOLVED IN THE CREATION, PRODUCTION OR DELIVERY OF THE SOFTWARE OR DOCUMENTATION BE LIABLE FOR ANY LOSS OR INACCURACY OF DATA OF ANY KIND OR FOR LOST PROFITS, LOST SAVINGS, OR ANY DIRECT, INDIRECT, SPECIAL, CONSEQUENTIAL OR INCIDENTAL DAMAGES ARISING OUT OR RELATED IN ANY WAY TO THE USE OR INABILITY TO USE THE SOFTWARE OR DATA, EVEN IF WILEY OR ITS SUPPLIERS HAVE BEEN ADVISED OF THE POSSIBILITY OF SUCH DAMAGES. THIS LIMITATION OF LIABILITY SHALL APPLY TO ANY CLAIM OR CAUSE WHATSOEVER WHETHER SUCH CLAIM OR CAUSE IS IN CONTRACT, TORT OR OTHERWISE.

The limited warranty set forth above is in lieu of all other express warranties, whether oral or written.

(Some states do not allow exclusions or limitations of implied warranties or liability in certain cases, so the above exclusions and limitations may not apply to you.)

7. General.

(a) This License may not be assigned by the Licensee except upon the written consent of Wiley.

(b) The License shall be governed by the laws of the State of New York.

(c) The above warranties and indemnities shall survive the termination of this License.

(d) If the Licensee is located in Canada, the parties agree that it is their wish that this License, as well as all other documents relating hereto, including notices, have been and shall be drawn up in the English language only.